Routledge Revivals

Modernism and the Christian Faith

First published in 1921, this title addresses the difficulties faced by the modern Christian Church in terms of policy, administration, and the development of liberal theology, in light of the changes taking place within society at the start of the twentieth century. John Alfred Faulkner deals with such subjects as the nature of authority within Christian theology and its relationship to liberalism, Christianity and the supernatural, and the shift in emphasis from the metaphysical Christ to the moral or practical Christ and his historical reality. An interesting reissue, this title will be of particular value to theology students researching the role of Christianity in modern society, and the impact of liberal theology on its core doctrines.

Modernism and the Christian Faith

John Alfred Faulkner

First published in 1921
by George Allen & Unwin Ltd

This edition first published in 2015 by Routledge
2 Park Square, Milton Park, Abingdon, Oxon, OX14 4RN
and by Routledge
711 Third Avenue, New York, NY 10017

Routledge is an imprint of the Taylor & Francis Group, an informa business

© 1921 George Allen & Unwin Ltd

The right of John Alfred Faulkner to be identified as author of this work has been asserted by him in accordance with sections 77 and 78 of the Copyright, Designs and Patents Act 1988.

All rights reserved. No part of this book may be reprinted or reproduced or utilised in any form or by any electronic, mechanical, or other means, now known or hereafter invented, including photocopying and recording, or in any information storage or retrieval system, without permission in writing from the publishers.

Publisher's Note
The publisher has gone to great lengths to ensure the quality of this reprint but points out that some imperfections in the original copies may be apparent.

Disclaimer
The publisher has made every effort to trace copyright holders and welcomes correspondence from those they have been unable to contact.

ISBN 13: 978-1-138-81282-6 (hbk)
ISBN 13: 978-1-315-74854-2 (ebk)

Modernism and the Christian Faith

BY
JOHN ALFRED FAULKNER

> Reason teaches us that those who are truly pious and philosophical honor and love the truth alone, refusing to follow the opinions of the ancients if they are worthless.—Justin Martyr, 1 *Apol.* 1.
>
> According to the word it is much more desirable to give assent to doctrines by reason and wisdom than by mere faith.—Origen, *Contra Celsum*, 1. 13.

Copyright, 1921, by
JOHN ALFRED FAULKNER

Printed in the United States of America

First Edition Printed April, 1921
Reprinted July, 1922

The Bible Text used in this volume is taken from the American Standard Edition of the Revised Bible, copyright, 1901, by Thomas Nelson & Sons, and is used by permission.

CONTENTS

CHAPTER	PAGE
PREFACE	7
I. AUTHORITY	9
II. INSPIRATION	28
III. MIRACLE	56
IV. JESUS–I	79
V. JESUS–II	99
VI. JESUS: QUESTIONS AND ASPECTS	117
VII. ATONEMENT	137
VIII. PAUL AS THE AFTER-CHRIST	167
IX. TRINITY	184
X. RITSCHL OR WESLEY?	208
XI. HELL	237
APPENDIX	264
Note A. Walter Pater on "Come unto Me"	264
Note B. Dr. G. A. Gordon on the *a priori* Ruling Out of the Divinity of Christ, and on Christ as the Eternal Prototype of Humanity in the Life of God, and the Resulting Kinship of Humanity with God	265
Note C. Prof. G. B. Foster and Dr. Gordon on Jesus	269
Note D. Prof. Alfred Seeberg on the Primitive Conception of Jesus	270
Note E. Prof. Erich Schaeder on Christ Praying to the Father	271
Note F. Bishop McConnell on Christ and the Creeds	272

CONTENTS

Note G. Dr. Horton on the Church's Loss of the Cross 273

Note H. Dr. David Smith on Atonement in the Light of the Modern Spirit 274

Note I. "Original Sin." "Total Depravity." 279

Note K. Drs. Gordon, Lidgett, Kahnis, Schultz, and White on the Trinity, and Church on the Incarnation 280

Note L. Prof. Schaeder on the Spring of the Trinity 284

Note M. Until He Come 286

Note N. The Alleged Early Martyrdom of John .. 292

Note O. Miracle and Sadhu Sundar Singh 300

Note P. The So-called Virgin Birth 301

INDEX 303

PREFACE

It was once the privilege of this writer to address the New York Preachers' Meeting on a subject connected with church polity and administration. One of the ablest of the younger clergy who took part in the discussion expressed the ardent wish that we might have a treatment of our doctrines in the same spirit of love of truth alone and frank facing of difficulties which he said was illustrated in the address of the morning. This book is an attempt to meet that wish.

Again, in talking with graduates of our Seminary it has come to me that many of them are dissatisfied with the teachings which they received even as late as the recent years that cover my own connection with the faculty. This question pressed: How can I repay my debt to these noble fellows—and they are only a small section of thousands of clergy and laymen touched by the same spirit—unless I do my humble part to carry out our Lord's words to Peter (Luke 22. 32)? Is there anything in historic Christianity which in substance the modern man cannot only receive but joyfully fight for with the calm assurance and high elation of Wordsworth's "Happy Warrior"? Is there anything in the spirit or results of science which makes it impossible for modern men to carry out the exhortation of that vigorous and downright spirit who urged his readers "to contend earnestly for the faith which was once for all

MODERNISM AND THE CHRISTIAN FAITH

delivered unto the saints" (Jude 3)? This book is an answer to that question.

Once more, I have been thrown into the company of a small band of intellectuals, all ministers except one who was formerly in the pulpit but is now a teacher, all representing the very left wing of evangelical churches, and three of them Unitarians. Some of the following essays were read to this group to get their reaction, to find out their criticism of Christianity as I understand it. Can they prove that anything herewith submitted is irrational or unscriptural or unchristian? Has Christianity when rationally understood anything to apologize for in the face of reason and the modern mind? May not a book thus providentially evoked meet the needs of wider circles?

Of course the words "modern" and "liberal" are used in their technical or artificial significance, for convenience, without blame or praise.

I have confined myself to those matters which are supposed to be most difficult to faith and most offensive to present-day thought. So far as I know I have treated them with absolute candor.

Foreign theologians have been occasionally quoted, first, because they are not so well known to English-speaking readers, and second, because many of them have devoted to these questions lifelong meditation and labor in a spirit of single-hearted devotion to truth and with an intellectual equipment never surpassed. Remember also that when I bring in words of other writers to buttress or illustrate any statement, they are usually those of the liberal school.

Chapters III, VIII, and X appeared in their original form in the Methodist Review, New York, and are used by kind permission of editor and publisher.

CHAPTER I

AUTHORITY

It is one of the maxims of liberal theology that no external authority is binding on the soul, that neither church nor Bible, neither pope nor apostle, has authority over the conscience: this over against the Greek Church that the ecumenical councils have authority with the Bible, the Roman Church that the pope as infallible has authority as interpreter of the Bible and tradition, and the Protestant Church that the Bible is the rule of faith and practice and therefore has authority. The idea of authority is, therefore, not at all new, going back to the question which Christ did not repel, though he did not directly answer: "By what authority doest thou these things? or who gave thee this authority?" (Mark 11. 28.) But among English-speaking people, the special form of this question was raised first, I think, by the Rev. Dr. James Martineau, the eminent Unitarian, in his *The Seat of Authority in Religion*, 1890, third edition, 1891. In a note at the end of this chapter you will find reference to other books.

The title of one of these books, that by the elder brother of the celebrated Saint Francis expert Sabatier, contains an antithesis as false as misleading. If a religion is of the Spirit of God, it is by that fact a religion of authority; and a religion so external as Catholicism, or even Mohammedanism, may have something of the Spirit, and if so, it is by that measure

MODERNISM AND THE CHRISTIAN FAITH

a religion of authority. A juster antithesis would have been, "The Religions Mainly of External and Those of Internal Authority." As a matter of fact, there are in Sabatier's sense no religions of authority in Christianity. Even the Roman Catholic appeals to reason, to conscience, to the inner man, as corroborating his other evidences for being a Catholic. The mistake which is found in the title is found here and there throughout all of Sabatier's discussion. I could take up this whole paper in giving instances, but one or two must suffice. He says (p. 176) that to distinguish between the human and divine parts of Scripture is to destroy the Protestant principle, whereas that is true only of a small part of the post-Reformation theology. It is fundamental to the Protestant view that the Spirit in the Scripture appeals to the Spirit in the Christian, and the Spirit in the Christian not being irrational distinguishes between the religious value of Paul's request for his cloak and his praise of love. He says, again: "The Catholic agrees in advance to accept all that the church teaches or may teach, whether or not it is in conformity to his moral or religious convictions. There have been —perhaps there still are—Protestants who take this attitude with regard to the Bible, and so far, in method at least, they are still Catholics" (p. 161). Whereas, no Catholic agrees to accept in advance anything that a future pope might teach. This is a misrepresentation so gross that it amounts to a slander. If a pope should announce a doctrine notoriously at variance with Catholicism, he would by that very announcement abdicate his position, and the cardinals would elect his successor. Nor have Protestants ever accepted the Bible in the sense stated by Sabatier.

AUTHORITY

If they had, they might just as well have accepted the Koran. It has always been because in the last analysis the Bible was not only not irrational or unworthy of belief, but because its religious and moral contents met their highest ideas and mastered them, and presented them with a Saviour who gave them peace.

Let us now take up this matter of authority and see what the facts are.

The child is born into a world the arrangements of which he finds pretty well fixed by authorities quite exterior to himself. But as he grows he does not rebel against that fact as irrational. He soon finds himself also under the authority of parents. His liberties are restricted, many inconvenient and even distressing things he has to submit to, because of this external regimen. When he becomes old enough to reason, however, he soon sees that this external authority was not only the most rational thing for him, but that it was the only thing that saved him from destruction. He finds that to have submitted to it was both his highest duty and highest pleasure, for it was the only way of realizing his destiny. In fact, he never submitted to it except in the sense that he submitted to the air that he breathed and the food that he ate. In other words, he found that parental authority was part of the beneficent order of the universe of which he is himself a part.

"The air that he breathed." He soon finds that there is another external authority which binds him. Let us call it the authority of science. If he touches fire he is burned; if he drinks poison, he becomes sick. He is not consulted about this; it makes no

MODERNISM AND THE CHRISTIAN FAITH

appeal to his reason; he simply finds that this outside authority holds. As he grows older it enlarges mightily until he finds the whole universe a series of laws or facts which have nothing whatever to do with his point of view, for which his conscience was never consulted, but which are eternally true whether he wants them to be true or not. He finds no pragmatism in the universe, but simply external fact, external authority, whether it "works" or not. But, beautiful to tell, he finds that his mind is attuned to this universe of law, that though his teachers and textbooks speak as external authorities he has the power of testing their statements, tracing these laws for himself, and finally extending the boundaries of knowledge by discovering new laws or new facts for himself. His soul, therefore, does not rebel against this scientific world of authority but becomes a part of it, and thus discovers its fruition and joy. His soul is made for science and science is made for his soul, and his service to it is not that of a slave but that of husband and wife to each other where authority is transformed into love.

But authority is not through with the child yet. An invisible hand is thrust out which interferes with his pleasures and desires. It is the hand of civil law. But here again the other forms of authority prepare him for this, and he soon feels that this also is a part of a divine plan as necessary as it is loving. He must live in a community, and that can only be when the members of it realize that no man lives for himself, but each for all. It is only on the surface that this interferes with his liberty. He mounts up to his higher liberty when he becomes so far a part of the civil order that he obeys it as unconsciously

AUTHORITY

as he breathes. Closer still is the moral grip. We are in a world where compelling voices outside of us cry out, "Thou shalt not steal, thou shalt not lie." We are not left to find this out by the inner monitor. Of course later the inner authority, as in the other spheres, says "Amen" to the voice from without. The two voices blend and become one. But if they do not, if the inner authority prompts us to take our own way, we are brought up with a sharp turn by the external authority. But in the long run we feel that this is wise, that morals cannot be entirely a matter of individual choice, that the public conscience has rights as well as the private conscience.

Now, here are five kinds of external authority which we all take for granted, which we all believe necessary, and which are, in fact, indispensable for the well-being of the world, or even for any kind of a tolerable world. If the objector cries out against this system, "I am beset behind and before, I cannot stand these limitations," we reply: "You have yet much freedom left. But if you want more, go to the desert, or go to some savage land and build up your own state." Now, would it not be singular if religion, of all the interests of humanity, were the only one outside the realm of authority, the only one in which there were no forecasting voices, no predetermining laws of the universe, nothing fixed from of old, no truth hoary with age and sacred with the assent, love, of noble spirits who walked with God in the prime of the world? Would it not be strange if here alone the tender spirit, uncradled by a motherless lack of prevision, were left naked to the raucous voices of contrary winds, of a thousand fighting sects? Is here alone caprice, here alone arbitrariness,

MODERNISM AND THE CHRISTIAN FAITH

here alone the unpointed way, the uncharted sea, the starless heaven, here alone a sky without the pole star?

That cannot be. What have we then? You say, "God." Right. We do not argue that. Let God be the authority. We do not ask now whether truth and right are such because God declares them, or God declares them because they are truth and right. It is all one, anyway. If there is any God at all, he is eternal, and he is eternally truth and righteousness and love. Now, how will God direct? how will he show us the way, how will he be authority? how will he reveal himself? And so, passing by the ethnic religions,[1] let us confine ourselves to Christianity. How is God an authority in Christianity? There have been three or four answers.

1. It is said that his guidance as to truth is shown in his direction of the councils of the representatives of his whole church when gathered together to decide on disputed questions. When they meet in this capacity they are guided by God. This is the answer of the Greek Church, of the Roman Church, and of the High Episcopal Church, and some in Protestant Churches have been inclined in the same direction. This does not mean that the conciliar delegates are guided independently of their own search for truth, their own canvass of all available light, their debates, etc., because the gathering in a council presupposes all this. It means only that in that inquiry and discussion, and as a result of it, the representatives are finally guided to a true result, so that the whole church will not in the end believe falsely.

---

[1] As to Buddhism see my article, "Shall We Become Buddhists?" in *Methodist Review*, New York, May, 1915, pp. 455-469.

AUTHORITY

It is not hard to show objections to this answer. (1) The councils have not been unanimous. How do we know the minority have not been sometimes right? (2) The atmosphere of the councils and the means taken to secure unanimity have been sometimes more worldly (not to say sinful) than Christian, and, therefore, if not Christian, was the result Christian? (3) The character of some of the champions of the conquering faith in some of these councils in their fierce intolerance and fearful passions (say Cyril of Alexandria) was not such as to warrant a divine guidance. In fact, we might suspect the gentle spirit of Jesus would have kept as far as possible away from these conclaves, on the twofold ground that "the wrath of man worketh not the righteousness of God," and "where the Spirit of God is, there is liberty." (4) Worldly power and imperial intrigue were sometimes at work, and that raises the question whether the declarations of faith thus induced were more Christian than the declaration of war of the first of August, 1914, from the same source? We cannot therefore have any certain guarantee that the decisions in any one ecumenical council, from the mere fact that it was such a council, were God-given.

On the other hand, that does not mean that those decisions were necessarily false. History shows that God works with the instruments he has at hand, even if they are far from perfect. We know that the decisions of the first ecumenical councils have been received by practically all Christians as the best that then were historically possible. The first (Nicæa, 325) rejected Arianism in the only decisive way, and ever since the Rev. Dr. Frederick H. Hedge lectured on church history at the Harvard Divinity School

MODERNISM AND THE CHRISTIAN FAITH

in 1857ff., it has been the opinion of Unitarians that as between Arius and Athanasius the latter was by far to be preferred—indeed, that the confirmation of Arius would have been an irreparable calamity. The second (Constantinople, 381) simply confirmed the first. The third (Ephesus, 431) was really in the interest of Christ's genuine manhood. The fourth (Chalcedon, 451) intended to guard the two sides of Christ's nature as each having its rights, the divine and human. The fifth (Constantinople, 553) said that no one need stumble at Christ's divinity because he was crucified. The sixth (Constantinople, 680) sought again to guard Christ's human nature, this time by emphasizing the reality of his human will. It must be remembered that anything like the modern liberal Jesus was never a point at issue in ancient Christianity. The most advanced bishop in any general council never dreamed of anything like that. The man who came nearest to it in all church history from Paul to Luther was the famous courtier and wealthy friend of Queen Zenobia of Palmyra, Paul of Samosata, and though his view would not be caviare to the general among liberals to-day, it was instantly rejected by the whole church so far as she took notice of it. Yes, as to actual alternatives which were before the men of the ecumenical councils, they reached the only conclusions possible according to their best light. The contrary conclusion in any one case would have been a calamity.

But there is a deeper aspect of this view which is more attractive. It is not important that at some time in the past this or that doctrine was promulgated, but it is important whether that doctrinal evolution which went on from Christ to Phillips Brooks,

AUTHORITY

which took in Ignatius, Irenæus, Athanasius, Augustine, Thomas Aquinas, Luther, Calvin, Wesley, Channing, was in any sense divinely ordered, whether the Spirit of God was brooding over the waters of that long stream, and was fructifying them by seeds of truth. If he was, then history becomes an authority; then there is this kernel of truth in the Catholic thought of a teaching tradition, namely, that in essentials the church has not gone fundamentally astray. If in the heart of her confession the church had been allowed for two thousand years to believe a lie, if the substance of her belief as to Christ, atonement, salvation, immortality, has been false since Christ left till to-day, then the gates of hades have prevailed against her with a vengeance. Because it is the truth, and the truth alone, which makes Christianity what it is: not buildings, wealth, members, but the truth alone. Our liberal friends are apt to be so offended at some exaggerated or false aspect of a doctrine that they have not the patience to ask, "What is the essence of that doctrine which has kept its vitality for nineteen centuries, which has fed innumerable saints and thinkers, and has been the solace of troubled hearts in all the Christian ages?" They forget the authority of history, the appeal of that democracy of truth, namely, the confession of myriads of Christians of all ranks, in all ages, that majestic unanimity, that impressive harmony of devotion and prayer and faith of countless multitudes, at the heart of which was the substance of the historic creeds, and which without that substance would have failed long long ago. In fact, it is doubtful whether, historically speaking, Christianity would have survived during the irruption of the barbarians

MODERNISM AND THE CHRISTIAN FAITH

and the long eclipse of the early Middle Ages without not simply the substance but the historic creeds themselves. They were the bones which kept the body together, the vertebræ, without which the church would have collapsed in helpless incohesion. And can we not say even now that it is doubtful whether the church will subsist through the coming centuries when that bulwark of fact and truth which it confesses in its ancient and modern creeds is dissolved by the subjective fancies of its preachers and teachers.

Martineau speaks of the "divine claims upon us in our historical inheritance of religion" (p. 125). Yes, the past makes a claim, and it makes a divine claim, and a divine claim is authority. Nor should the preacher unduly slight the help which this authority gives to him. Extending far beyond him and above him, covering him with their authority, are thousands of saints, martyrs, confessors, theologians, for whom he stands, and it is they and the truth they lived and died for rather than himself which bring the people to his church. "Nothing but the history that lies behind the message can give it force, when spoken by common men" (Leckie, p. 53). His church is founded not on himself but on the prophets and apostles, Jesus Christ himself being the chief corner stone.

2. It is said that God speaks to us through one special voice, namely, the bishop of Rome. This is the answer of the Roman Catholic Church. What he delivers *ex cathedra* on matters of faith and morals is infallibly guided by God. This claim is refuted by history, but I cannot stop to give that history here. For us who are not Roman Catholics a better question is, What is the truth of which this is a perversion?

AUTHORITY

Is it not this, that God does speak to us not simply in documents and assemblies but in living men and women? It is the doctrine of the superman—the prophet who becomes an organ of the voice of the Eternal and brings in a new time. It is the Isaiah of the Exile. It is Paul opening up the gospel for the world and the world for the gospel. It is Athanasius driving out the demigods. It is Francis of Assisi proclaiming, "The greatest of these is love." It is Luther, John Robinson, Wesley, Channing (who made living once more the truth of the divine humanity). These and a thousand others are infallible, because and wherein they touched the world to higher issues and turned the stream of time into more lifegiving channels. Their infallibility is not in their religious teachings taken in detail, but in both their teachings and life taken as a voice of God which re-created the world. But so far as their theology was a part of this dynamic, either in substance or expression, either in part or in general drive, it cannot be entirely withdrawn from the glory of their deed. This is the truth in the theory of Rome that God speaks to us through a pope.

> "Ever their phantoms rise before us,
> Our loftier brothers, but one in blood.
> At bed and table they lord it o'er us
> With looks of beauty and works of good."

"He is a monarch who gives a constitution to his people," says Emerson; "a pontiff who preaches the equality of souls and releases his servants from barbarous homages, an emperor who can spare his empire."[2] I spoke of authority mediated to us through

[2] *Uses of Great Men*, quoted by Leckie, *Authority in Religion*, p. 112.

the democracy of true souls in the past. Here it is mediated by an aristocracy; God's supermen, men in religion like Shakespeare in literature, of whom there will never be another. These are the stars that dwell apart, shining with undimmed splendor, and simply because they shine, authority. Nothing is so infallible as light. These men and women are that because they saw the light, they were light, and thus gave it forth. This revelation could only be described. Their message was "as the coming forth of light," says Frederick Denison Maurice. "It was not the light of an outward sun, it must be the light of which that which is gathered up in outward suns is the image. It was not a bodily eye which received this light; but it *was* an eye; you could give it no other name. God himself must have opened it, that it might behold him. In his light it saw light."[3]

3. It is said that the authority of God comes to us through the Scriptures. This is the answer of all churches, including the older Unitarian.

The only difference between the Protestant and Catholic is that the latter says that tradition and church are of coordinate authority, especially in interpretation of Scripture, whereas the former says that as a *rule* of faith Scripture is supreme. In getting at truth some standard must be authoritative, and if there is a conflict of standards, that must be considered decisive of whose claims there is no doubt. Such is the Protestant position. Recent Unitarians have forsaken the position of their elder brethren on this matter.

This idea of the Bible as authority is founded on its inspiration by God. Just as Shakespeare has the

---

[3] *Prophets and Kings of the Old Testament*, Boston, 1853, p. 425.

AUTHORITY

inspiration of genius which sets him apart from all other writers, so it is claimed the Bible has the inspiration of religion so pure, so high, so mighty, that it is set apart from all other bibles. This inspiration is from God, either mediately or immediately, and therefore the Book is specially divine. This does not mean that all parts of it are equally divine, that all parts are not also human, that the human and divine do not vary and interplay, that there are not mixtures and errors in its vast evolution; it only means that *as a whole* it is a revelation from God, progressively unfolding his truth in various ways in the process of history, according to a loving purpose of redemption in Christ, who is its unity, its crown, its Lord, whose Spirit gave it and therefore is greater than it. The inspiration of the Bible does not mean that other bibles are not also from God so far as they contain goodness and truth; it means only that this is specially from God because it reveals his life in a way different from all other bibles, and in that difference not relatively, but essentially, superior.

Now, the reason we believe this is not because the church says so, though the church always has said so, and that the church should be deceived on so important a matter would be another triumph of hades; nor is it because millions of thinkers, saints, scholars, and men of lowlier estate, have found the Bible so, though they have. The reason why we believe the Bible is religious authority is because the Spirit there meets the Spirit here, and they recognize each other. In its light we see light. It finds us; it shames us; it searches us through and through; its light is so compelling that sometimes we shrink from it abashed and at other times it makes us to sit in the heavenly places. The Bible's inspiration or authority is simply its inner religious and moral light.

Let me say what I have to say on this in some comments on a recent book by an eminent scholar and liberal who gives a sketch of the history of modern religious ideas and who represents the radical "modern" view. This book must have been written in haste, as many of its statements are so ill considered as to be quite surprising. He says that the Protestant view of the Bible is a departure from Luther's earlier emphasis on the gospel as the proclamation of the grace of God in Christ. But Luther did no more than every evangelist has done and does. And he held this gospel not as over against the Bible as the rule of faith, nor independent of it (for he *always* held high views of the inspiration and authority of Scripture),[4] but as a convenient summing up of what he knew from Scripture and experience to be the heart of the gospel.

It is quite beside the point to be ringing the changes on "external authority," both uncharitable and inaccurate. How is the Bible an authority? Because the light and glory of God, of truth and love, dwell in it and shine forth from it into our hearts and so become a part of us, and thus the Scripture becomes an inner authority in us and therefore in a sense an external authority to us. It is never simply an "external authority." Nor is it fair to compare this with the old conception of the authority of the church, which was general council or pope deciding questions. The oft-repeated liberal and Roman Catholic state-

---

[4] See my quotations from him in *The Encyclopædia of Sunday Schools*, ii, pp. 645–649 (1915), and Scheel, *Luthers Stellung zur heiligen Schrift*, 1902, pp. 66ff.

AUTHORITY

ment that Protestantism simply substituted the infallibility of the Bible for that of the pope or church is simply not true in the form intended.

It is said that Protestants have "reread the Bible from age to age so as to make it a new book." Like the fresh glory of every new day, the Bible is always a new book, but only in that recreative spiritual sense. With the birth of Protestantism came the birth of scientific exegesis, and there has been no rereading of the Bible in the sense stated. For instance, the Reformation creeds still express substantially the faith of all evangelical churches, so far as that faith is biblical. In fact, outside of Catholic beliefs, there has been little change from the early church till to-day. The Apostles' Creed arose A. D. 100–150, and it is still read in the churches of all confessions. When the author says that the Protestant idea of "an infallible self-interpreting Bible is bound to disappear," it may be replied: Not for Christians, because the Bible is always verifying itself in its religious and moral truth (any truth so far as it is truth is infallible) to the conscience of the believer, just as the sun ever anew assures the eye that sees that it is shining.

Nor is it true that evangelicals believed that only those who accepted the Bible would be saved. Wesley was one of them, and he believed that heathens may be saved and that Unitarians may be pious and so on the road to salvation.

It is invidious and unfair to say that the church has always believed that the Bible was an "authoritative creed intended to bind men's minds and consciences." Of course so far as a man thinks the Bible is true he allows it to hold him, but the church has,

MODERNISM AND THE CHRISTIAN FAITH

rather, thought of the Bible as a spiritual sun to illuminate minds and consciences ("The entrance of thy words giveth light"). In that illumination they find the truth, or, rather, the truth finds them, and that truth does "bind" mind and conscience in a happy servitude that is glorious freedom and is the only true freedom.

"To a man who has a consciousness of his own oneness with the Divine, prophecy and miracle are unimportant." That is like saying, "To a man who enjoys liberty in America, Magna Charta and Washington are unimportant," or, "To a Methodist who is happy in a Saviour's love Luther and Wesley are unimportant." The internal fact does not make the external fact unimportant. It is wiser to ask, "What were the truth and help in prophecy and miracle, what their historical function, and what their message for to-day?"

Nor are the religious truths of the Bible affected by evolution, by the assertion that "everything is in the making," by pragmatism, by the relativity of truth. Christ is complete, he is not in the making, Christianity, justification, conversion. Our knowledge of these facts grows, but that ever-growing knowledge makes us all the more sure of their truth. Besides, some of these truths have been a part of the experience of countless souls in all churches, Catholic and Protestant, and have been from the beginning till now, and thus have a double seal.

"God still reveals himself to man as truly as he ever did"—as "truly," but not in the same way. There never has been another Paul (not to speak of another Christ), and never can be, because the historical situations and historical revelation which pro-

AUTHORITY

duced him can never be repeated. For that reason the truth received from Christ and Paul need never be revealed again, and is never revealed again, but is illuminated and enlarged by deeper knowledge of it.

It is said that authority is not needed because we are devoted to the kingdom of God. Devotion to a glorious ideal outside of us is a noble thing, but where did we learn about the kingdom of God? Who told us about it? The Person who was the King and the Kingdom, and the Book without which, historically speaking, we should never have known about him or it, have some "authority," have they not? Besides, one man devoted to the Kingdom thinks it is his duty to go into a monastery, another to do something worse still. Subjectivism needs to be corrected by the despised "authority" of Bible and Christianity which is both "external" and internal.

In spite, therefore, of our very liberal friends, the modern world has not transcended the Bible in its essential message, nor will it transcend it. Its doctrines show their vitality by lending themselves to reinterpretation and enlargement by ever-growing knowledge of the Bible and of all science.

4. It is said that the authority of God voices itself in the individual conscience and soul. This is the liberal answer, and it is true. Every revelation and every truth in the other fountains of authority once had their seat in the soul of some man. They were not piped from heaven, they were not the hollow echo of a voice, they were not handed over, but they were lived through in the secret places of the spirit where God meets man. Therefore they were not given forth to be received by mechanical authority, as an engineer's textbook, but they were addressed to the

MODERNISM AND THE CHRISTIAN FAITH

intelligence and conscience, before which they waited with respect to be received. "Come now, and let us reason together, saith Jehovah." A message that cannot vindicate itself in that forum is doomed. Because the spirit of man is the lamp of Jehovah (Prov. 20. 27), and what comes from God without meets the God within, and they know each other. There is truth, then, in the liberal contention that the final authority is the soul of man. Otherwise, why should not the Koran displace the Bible? But that is no liberal discovery. Augustine and Scotus Erigena held there were two sources of knowledge, *recta ratio* and *vera auctoritas*. Both had their rights, and each reacted on the other. Abelard too placed *ratio* beside *fides*, and repudiated *mere* authority-faith. "Not because God said anything is it to be believed, but because it has been proved to be so."[5]

Therefore faith is to be made clear and probable to reason. Anselm made faith supreme, but he made a large use of reason. His *Cur Deus Homo* is simply a huge essay in rationalism—the attempt to prove the necessity of the incarnation by reason, yes, by "reason alone," says Anselm (2. 23). The very *raison d'être* of Protestantism is its right of appeal to the soul, of course illuminated by every divine light, from absurd or corrupt or even unworthy doctrines. And we differ from the liberal only in this: we enlarge his conception of authority. Not to the individual in his naked independence, cutting himself from the moderating influences of universal intelligence; but to the individual molded, informed, uplifted by the Higher Pantheism, namely, the Ever-Living God who in history, science, art, has spoken mediately; in seer,

[5] *Introductio ad theologiam*, 2, 3.

AUTHORITY

prophet and apostle has spoken immediately; in church and charity has spoken institutionally; in sacrament symbolically; in saints, theologians, thinkers, and the mighty host of the pure in heart has come near in leading and in light, in comfort and consolation; and especially in Jesus Christ has himself looked out of our eyes. For on this question of authority we need to universalize the excessive individualism of the liberal, who needs to remember that simple yet profound pedagogical principle of Jesus about becoming little children; and to consider a wider application of a famous passage: "The Lord knoweth the reasonings of the wise, that they are vain. Wherefore let no one glory in men. For all things are yours; whether Paul, or Apollos, or Cephas [Peter], or the world, or life, or death, or things present, or things to come; all are yours; and ye are Christ's, and Christ is God's."[6]

[6] 1 Cor. 3. 20-23.

NOTE.—The book by Martineau, mentioned at the beginning of this chapter, was followed immediately by the Ely Professor of Divinity in Cambridge, Dr. V. H. Stanton, *The Place of Authority in Matters of Religious Belief*, 1891. Since then you can read the very dry but able discussion by Professor Julius Kaftan in *The American Journal of Theology*, October, 1900; the article by the candid Roman Catholic layman, Dr. Wilfred Ward, in the first volume of *The Hibbert Journal*; the suggestive and sometimes sparkling chapters of the Rev. John Oman, *Vision and Authority*, 1902; the article by Professor Bernard, of Dublin, in *The Expositor*, 1905; the fundamental treatment by Principal and Professor Iverach in the second volume of the *Encyclopædia of Religion and Ethics*, 1910; and those two admirable books which show the vigorous thinking and good scholarship of Scotch pastors, Dr. D. W. Forrest, *The Authority of Christ*, 1906, and the Rev. J. H. Leckie, *Authority in Religion*, 1909. I must not forget to mention the slashing Unitarian manifesto of the late Professor Auguste Sabatier, of Paris, *Religions of Authority and the Religion of the Spirit*, 1904; admirably translated by Mrs. Louise Seymour Houghton. In 1911 Av. C. P. Huizinga came out with an able book, *Authority: its Function in Life, Ethics, and Religion;* and in 1912 P. T. Forsyth with *The Principle of Authority*—both strong meat for thoughtful readers.

CHAPTER II

INSPIRATION

MANY of my readers will recall that seething decade 1883–93, when all the doctrines of Christianity were put in the crucible. Not to go beyond our own land, it was the time when the Andover professors were turning Christianity up from the bottom in their search for the eternally true in it and their effort to state that truth in modern terms, and though nothing could be less exciting than the moderate and scholarly way they went about this task, they made a sensation that was world-wide. It was the time—largely as a result of this Andover movement—when one of the most famous and useful missionary societies in the world, the American Board of Commissioners for Foreign Missions, was thrown into the throes of bitter controversy over the question whether the churches which supported the Board should have the deciding voice as to the theology of the candidates offering for service, or whether the officers of the Board could decline applicants because of alleged liberal views. It was the time when the Union Theological Seminary professors in New York were feeling the Presbyterian symbols and traditions too galling, were seeking relief and found it; when one of their number, the stormy petrel of that time, Dr. Charles A. Briggs, though always conservative in essentials, was causing any amount of trouble to his less forward fellow Presbyterians, more by reason in

INSPIRATION

part of his angry way of irritating them by his characterization of their views, and was finally suspended for heresy, but found refuge in the wide-open arms of the Protestant Episcopal sister. It was the time when Lane Theological Seminary in Cincinnati was having the same trouble over the too progressive advance of their two biblical professors, Llewelyn J. Evans and Henry Preserved Smith. It was the time when the warrior-like new editor (1888–92) of the *Methodist Review*, New York, felt a nervous fear that the ark of God was going to smash, and came to the rescue with slashing attacks in speech and writing on the "rationalists" who were doing the devil's work, and which brought out an article by a humble pastor in *The Christian Advocate* (May 23, 1889), which vindicated for biblical scholars the rights of investigation and opened an era the fruits of which we enjoy to-day. It was the time when on our shores also were felt the waves of that storm precipitated in Scotland by Professor W. Robertson Smith's Bible articles in the ninth edition of the *Encyclopædia Britannica*, and the ecclesiastical proceedings in the Free Church which were the result of them. It was the decade which began with the publication (1883) of the new Congregational Creed, which broke up the Calvinism of the New England fathers without at the same time breaking up historic Christianity, and it closed with the Declaratory Statements or other revisions of the Westminster Confession by some of the Presbyterian churches of Scotland. What theological searchings of heart in that great time! Yes, it was one of the most decisive decades in modern Christian history. When it opened it was a question whether the modern critical views of men who stood on the

MODERNISM AND THE CHRISTIAN FAITH

fundamentals of historic Christianity would win toleration, when it closed that was no longer a question.

Among the questions threshed out anew in those years, when it was a joy to live, was that of the inspiration of Scripture. As the early church had to vindicate its freedom from Jewish bondage, the ancient church its doctrine of Christ, the mediæval church itself from barbarism, the Reformation church its doctrine of salvation, the eighteenth-century church its spiritual life, the nineteenth-century church its world-wide mission, so the end of that century brought up for consideration two doctrines never altogether satisfactorily handled—that of the Bible and that of atonement, and one doctrine of which it might almost be said that it had never been handled at all, that of the future life. I remember in that closing decade or two of the nineteenth century the number of books which came out on those three topics, and how busy I was kept in reading them to try to find out for myself what was the exact truth on those three vital doctrines on which my four years in theological seminaries had left me at sea. For the doctrine of inspiration that literature was opened by what remains to this day the greatest work ever written on the subject in any language, the two thick octavos of Professor George T. Ladd, of Yale College (as it was called then), *The Doctrine of Sacred Scripture* (Charles Scribner's Sons, 1883)—a book written in the true spirit of German learning in its thoroughness, scholarship, and impartiality.

Perhaps the historical is as good a method of approach as any. What was the feeling of the Jews of Christ's time about their sacred writings? One does not have to read the New Testament far to find

INSPIRATION

that that feeling was one of extreme reverence. Though the scribes were charged with "making void the word of God by their traditions" in one matter,[1] yet their very tradition was founded on a superstitious and perverted reverence for the Scripture. "Halacha and Haggada support themselves upon the word of Scripture, or lean upon the same. Even before the rehearsing of the law and reference to the tradition stands the searching into the Scripture (compare 2 Chron. 24. 27; John 5. 39; Acts 17. 11)."[2] In the Sermon on the Mount Christ does away with certain things in the law, and elsewhere claims that for the hardness of the people's hearts a concession was made in the matter of divorce, but his general attitude corresponds with that of his people, namely, of utter reverence. Therefore the smallest letter of the law shall not pass away till all be fulfilled.[3] He and the apostles appeal to Moses and find divine truth in the words of the law.[4] Everywhere in the true spirit of the Jews is it understood that God speaks in Scripture.[5]

The first Christians took over this view as a matter of course. Law and prophets are the word of God. The Spirit of God has really spoken through their mouths. "Their method of using the Scripture was determined by their view that everywhere in the

---

[1] Matt. 15. 6; Mark 7. 13.

[2] O. Holtzmann, *Neutestamentliche Zeitgeschichte*, 2 Aufl., 1906, p. 192. The halacha was Jewish traditional law, precepts not found in written law, but which explained and applied it. Haggada was interpretation, application, or instruction.

[3] Matt. 5. 18.

[4] Luke 20. 37; Gal. 3. 16.

[5] Matt. 1. 22; 2. 15; Acts 4. 25; 13. 34; Rom. 16. 26; Heb. 3. 7; 9. 8; 10. 15; 1 Pet. 1. 11; 2 Pet. 1. 26.

MODERNISM AND THE CHRISTIAN FAITH

Old Testament it is God who speaks. Everything individual, human, steps in the background, whether it is simple narrative, lyric expression of feeling, popular opinion, or whatever. And therein the apostolic church formally and manifoldly agreed with the synagogue in the way of interpretation and use of the Old Testament. For the time was not yet ripe to place the Old Testament in such objective distance to distinguish sharply the simple sense from the use."[6] This does not mean that the Christians did not recognize transient elements in the Old Testament. Christ was the end of the law for righteousness.[7] The ritual laws were only a shadow of good things to come.[8] John was the greatest of the prophets because he stood nearest to Christ, but the least in the new kingdom is greater than he.[9] This did not mean a lessening of the divine authority of the ancient covenant, which so far as the written word of God went was the only authority the first Christians knew. Christ refers the Emmaus pilgrims to the prophets, and beginning from Moses and the prophets he expounds all the Scriptures concerning himself.[10] He says that David in the Spirit calls him Lord.[11] It is by the "Scriptures of the prophets" that the mystery of Christ is now made known according to the commandment of the eternal God.[12] Whoever wrote Second Peter, it springs from the heart of primitive Christianity which testifies that "no prophecy of scripture is of private [or special] interpretation. For no prophecy ever came by the

---
[6] Diestel, *Geschichte des alten Testamentes in der Christlichen Kirche*, 1869, p. 11.
[7] Rom. 10. 4.
[8] Heb. 10. 1.
[9] Matt. 11. 11.
[10] Luke 24. 25ff.
[11] Matt. 22. 43.
[12] Rom. 16. 26.

INSPIRATION

will of man, but men spake from God, being moved by the Holy Spirit." [13] Paul almost personifies the Scripture in his vivid thought of its power: it foresees,[14] it concludes,[15] entirely in the spirit of his Master, who says that what is written cannot be broken.[16] The whole New Testament takes for granted the divine word of the Old, written once for all and written for us.[17] And the classic passage 2 Tim. 3. 16 only says with fine precision what went without saying to every Christian of the first century. (Later there came in a reaction not so much against the Old Testament as against the Jews, with the view that the Christians were the only covenant people, that the Jews were not and never had been such a people, that the Old Testament has really no just historical connection with the Jews but belongs to the Christians entirely, that circumcision and the sacrificial and ceremonial law are invented by the devil, who is also behind the whole Jewish understanding of the Old Testament, which however is a divine book: so the Epistle of Barnabas.) The attitude of the New Testament toward the Old is that also of the so-called apostolic fathers. They do not, as a rule, mention the author in quoting, but content themselves with, "God saith," "the Scripture saith," "the Holy Writing saith," "it is written," "the Holy Spirit saith," "the Holy Word saith," etc. The Old Testament was a living word of God, loved and honored to the early Christians.

What was their view as to what we call the New Testament? Of course the writers had no idea that

[13] 2 Pet. 1. 20, 21.
[14] Gal. 4. 8.
[15] Gal. 4. 22.
[16] John 10. 35.
[17] Rom. 15. 4; 1 Cor. 9. 10.

MODERNISM AND THE CHRISTIAN FAITH

they were producing Scripture. All their pieces were simply *Gelegenheitsschriften*, manuscripts put forth on occasion to meet an emergency or special situation. The historical writers do not confess any special assistance of the Spirit. On the contrary, the one best endowed among them from the literary side, Luke, goes to his task with the workmanlike sense and apparently apparatus too of a modern historian, having accurately traced the gospel history from the start and now resolves to write it down in order.[18] A slight study of New Testament writers shows an independence, a diversity of aim, of style, of method, of teaching, of achievement, utterly at variance with the old idea of inspiration whether verbal or plenary in the ordinary sense. They were certainly not the "hollow passage for a voice, which mocks the voices of many men," but were as human as Robert Browning or Carlyle, each speaking with his own voice in his own words the truth that he had to speak.

Only it was truth, and God was behind it as he is behind all truth, but here in special measure. This the writers themselves felt and confessed. That special characteristic was that it was the truth of Christ and the truth for faith. These lofty deeds and words that are written as a selection from many are written "that ye may believe that Jesus is the Christ, the Son of God; and that believing ye may have life in his name."[19] It is this religious passion, this religious or Christian destination and afflatus, which breathes through, dominates, and covers the New Testament from end to end. Paul recognized that for this purpose he needed divine illumination or impartation. It is as though Paul said: "God

[18] Luke 1. 3.   [19] John 20. 30, 31.

INSPIRATION

revealed the deep things of himself to us through the Spirit, for it is only the Spirit who searcheth those depths. In fact, even less than the depths, the things of God none knoweth save the Spirit. But it was that very Spirit which we received, not the spirit of the cosmos, but the Spirit which is from God for the very purpose that we might know the things freely given to us by God. And those things thus revealed we speak, here also not without help, not in words which man's wisdom teacheth, not in the phraseology of the Stoics or other philosophers, which some of you Corinthians were expecting, or in other high-flown language, but in words which the Spirit teacheth (not dictates, but teacheth), combining spiritual things with spiritual (words), or interpreting spiritual things to spiritual (men). For we have the mind of Christ." [20] This refers specifically to words spoken, not to words written, but as Paul spoke and could speak not otherwise than he wrote, this passage covers his epistles as well as his addresses. Besides, a comparison of his speeches with his epistles shows that he wrote as he spoke. It is therefore fair to say that Paul makes the claim that the religious and moral content of his work is revealed by God, and that in communicating the same he has been helped by God. In other words, what he received is revelation and what he wrote and spoke is inspiration—of course not absolutely as mantic, but relatively. This does not mean that Paul said when he wrote, "This is revealed to me by God, and therefore it is Scripture," but it does mean that he might have said, and did on the right occasion say, "This gospel which I give forth I have received from God, and

---
[20] See 1 Cor. 2. 10–13, 16.

even the words in which I set it out are not the conventional garb of Greek wisdom but the divine simplicity of truth."

How far in the consciousness of the New Testament writers their religious message was felt as from God we do not know. That they considered the central things for which they stood and for which they died as the gift of God is absolutely certain. But Paul distinguishes from these as well as from the Old Testament revelation the advices which he gives here and there.[21] Nor would assistance of the Spirit take the place of common sense, meditation, study, inquiry, and general equipment. There is an immediateness, a spiritual power and illumination, a sense of a divine authority and compulsion, and of firsthand dealing with the Spirit and his truth—there is all this in the New Testament writings in such a degree that they justify themselves as from God; they verify their message as inspired. More inspired than the Old Testament? Yes and No. Less inspired but more revealed. For it is as Kahnis says: "Since Origen until to-day the conclusion has been drawn, if the Old Testament is inspired, then the New must be more inspired. But this conclusion is incorrect. The New Testament has, of course, a higher revelation, and the spirit of the apostles was a higher one than that which animated the prophets. But the Old Testament spirit was more bound to the letter [more mantic, more compelled to give forth exactly what was said], and thus favored more the inspiration than the New Testament, which, a spirit of freedom, allows the word to be free."[22] Where

---

[21] Compare 1 Cor. 7. 6; 10. 25, 26 "I think," 40 "after my judgment."
[22] *Die lutherische Dogmatik*, 2 Aufl., 1874, vol. i, p. 291.

INSPIRATION

the Spirit of the Lord is—and he was poured out abundantly on apostles and their companions—there is truth, there is inner illumination, there is the citizenship in heaven, but there is also freedom.[23] In fact, that was a kind of password in the early church. It was a liberty never known before, and known now only by those whom Christ emancipates, the liberty of the glory of the children of God.[24]

If the other writers of the New Testament are not so insistent on their claim to have the divine truth as Paul, that is because they did not have his fight to make, and not because they write with less immediateness of authority. John speaks for the rest as well as for himself.

"That which was from the beginning, that which we have heard, that which we have seen with our eyes, that which we beheld, and our hands handled, concerning the Word of life (and the life was manifested, and we have seen and bear witness, and declare unto you the life, the eternal *life*, which was with the Father, and was manifested unto us); that which we have seen and heard declare we unto you also, that ye also may have fellowship with us: yea, and our fellowship is with the Father and with his Son Jesus Christ. And these things we write that our joy may be made full. And this is the message which we have heard from him and announce unto you, that God is light, and in him is no darkness at all." [25]

What was the estimate of what we call the New Testament by the Apostolic Fathers? Did they quote it as on a par with the Old or simply for embellish-

---

[23] 2 Cor. 3. 17.
[24] Rom. 8. 21.
[25] 1 John 1. 1–5.

MODERNISM AND THE CHRISTIAN FAITH

ment or illustration? The words of the Gospel are sometimes introduced, The Lord said, or, The Lord said in the Gospel, and once a quotation from the Old and one from the New are placed on a level and referred to the Scriptures.[26] Barnabas quotes Matthew 20. 16 as Scripture ("as it is written").[27] Generally quotations or echoes of both are liberally sprinkled over a writing without any word of introduction. Both stood practically on the same plane, and it is evident that apostolic writings sprang immediately to a place of prominence as guiding lights. But it was too early for critical appreciation, as apocryphal Gospels are quoted as well as four of the apocryphal writings of the Old Testament, and it was too early for a definite placing of our New Testament as a Rule of Faith on a par with the Old.

The Apostolic Fathers distinguished between themselves and the apostles. Westcott puts the matter with studied moderation. "Already they began to separate the apostles from the teachers of their own time as possessed of an originative power. Without any exact perception of the completeness of the Christian Scriptures, they began to draw a line between them and their own writings. As if by some providential instinct, each one of those Fathers who stood nearest to the apostolic writers plainly contrasted his writings with theirs, and placed himself upon a lower level. The fact is most significant for it shows in what way the formation of a New Testament was an intuitive act of The Christian Body, derived from no reasoning, but realized in the course

---

[26] Polycarp, *Ad Philippianos* 12. The Greek text is lacking here, and this is Latin.
[27] Barnabas 4.

INSPIRATION

of its natural growth, as one of the first results of its self-consciousness."[28] Every Christian of the middle of the second century would have felt his views entirely voiced by the Muratorian Fragment of about 175. "Though various chief ideas are taught in the different books of the Gospels, it makes no difference to the faith of believers, since in all of them all things are declared by one principal Spirit concerning the nativity, passion, resurrection, manner of life (of the Lord) with his disciples, and his double advent, first in lowliness and humiliation which has taken place, and afterward in glory and royal power which is to come."

"We have learned from none others (says Irenæus), the plan of our salvation than from those [the apostles] through whom the gospel has come down to us, which they did at one time proclaim in public, and later by the will of God handed down to us in the Scriptures to be the ground and pillar of our faith. For it is unlawful to assert [as is done by Gnostics] that they preached before they possessed 'perfect knowledge,' as some venture to say, boasting themselves improvers of the apostles. For after our Lord rose from the dead, [the apostles] were invested with power from on high when the Holy Spirit came down, were filled from all and had perfect knowledge."[29] He then refers to the writing of the four Gospels. All through Irenæus the inspiration of the New Testament is assumed, and we may leave the development with him (about 180), as since his time until to-day that assumption has been a living conviction.

So much for the feeling of the primitive Christians,

---
[28] *The Bible in the Church*, 1864, issue 1887, p. 87. See p. 88.
[29] Irenæus, *Against Heresies*, 3. 1; compare chap. 3.

MODERNISM AND THE CHRISTIAN FAITH

so much for the historical approach. But what is the inspiration of the Scripture? What is the glory of the Bible? It is a commonplace to-day to say that it is not its historical accuracy in nonessentials, the moral perfection of all its allowances in its early stages, nor the religious perfection of its preparatory steps. It is not its equal inspiration in all parts, nor its positive inspiration in any part where not needed. It is not the "control" of mantic or medium, it is not a seance nor satisfaction of curiosity, it does not take the place of research, observation, judgment on the part of the writers, and it allows full play to their style, their individuality, even their religious point of view (1 and 2 Kings–Chronicles, Paul–James) within the general sweep of its onward revelation. It did not transport its writers to modern times, rob them of their Oriental atmosphere or their limitations as dwellers in that eld of time, make them write history as a college professor or religion from the platform of the modern prejudice to the supernatural. What, then, was it? What did it accomplish?

1. On a lower plane one might say that as to history the inspiration of Scripture keeps the writers to the general purpose of God as giving the essential facts in the progress of redemption. It is not history for history's sake, but history for salvation's sake. But it is history, and this separates it from all other Oriental religious literature, which is entirely devoid of the feeling for history, for the external fact. It is history from the prophetic point of view, as a part of the message of religion, and so while it uses or may use any source it cares to use—Babylonian creation accounts, old traditions handed down with marvelous accuracy according to Eastern custom from father to

INSPIRATION

son, stories and legends and snatches of folk song (for the Oriental like our Indian naturally spoke in poetry) as well as written accounts—it makes the light of divine revelation shine through them, and organizes them from the point of view of moral and religious impressiveness. That is one reason for its splendid frankness, recording without a gloss the sins of its own heroes. It cleanses its sources and makes them available for the everlasting instruction of mankind.

2. The inspiration of Scripture is its fullness of the life of God, not absolute fullness at any one time, but relative fullness according to circumstances, preparation, civilization, and pedagogical tact and necessity. Carlyle said that to find a man to teach religion you must get a man who has religion. Well, the writers of the Bible had religion, or, rather, it had them. So God moves in its pages as nowhere else—an immediacy and sense of first-hand touch with him such as no other literature affords. We surmise, the Bible writers know; we reason, they see. "These men see the works of the Lord, and his wonders in the deep."

"Sorrow is hard to bear, and doubt is slow to clear.
Each sufferer has his say, his scheme of weal and woe.
But God has a few of us whom he whispers in the ear;
The rest may reason and welcome."

God whispered in their ear, and what they heard they told. No other book gives that sense of the presence of God in the soul. Even such a man as Heine felt it. "Neither vision nor ecstasy, neither voice from heaven nor bodeful dream, has pointed the way of salvation to me. I owe my enlightenment quite simply to the reading of a book.... The Book, the Bible.... He who has lost his God may find him again in this volume, and he who has never known him will there be met by the breath of the divine word." [30] This has given the Book of Psalms its wonderful preeminence as the book of the soul. Through it flows the life of God as water around the body of a swimmer. Therefore it has touched human lives as no other pagan book of religion has even approached, touched them on their general level of daily routine and in all kinds of crises. Witness the remarkable book of Prothero, *The Psalms in Human Life* (1903). "They express in exquisite words the kinship which every thoughtful human heart craves to find with a supreme unchanging loving God, who will be to him a protector, guardian, and friend. They utter the ordinary experiences, the familiar thoughts of men, but they give to these a width of range, an intensity, a depth, and an elevation, which transcend the capacity of the most gifted. They translate into speech the spiritual passion of the loftiest genius; they also utter with the beauty born of truth and simplicity, and with exact agreement between the feeling and expression, the inarticulate and humble longings of the unlettered peasant. So it is that in every country the language of the Psalms has become part of the daily life of nations, passing into their proverbs, mingling with their conversation, and used at every critical stage of existence" (pp. 2, 3). "As the hart panteth after the water brooks, so panteth my soul after thee, O God." That is the eternal charm of the Psalms, their impelling power over souls. For that reason "for every recorded incident there are millions of cases unknown beyond the secret cham-

---

[30] Quoted by Brook, *The Bible*, in *Foundations*, 1912, p. 29.

INSPIRATION

bers of the heart, in which the Psalms have restored the faith, lifted the despair, revived the hopes, steeled the courage, bound up the wounds of the struggling, suffering hosts of humanity." The inspiration of the Bible is its God-light and God-passion, its answer to the cry of humanity, Who will show us God?

3. The inspiration of the Bible is its moral light, its answer to the conscience. Infidels have made much of the imperfect doings in the early history of Israel, but it is only the full Bible's light that has placed them in a position to criticize. What we consider the cruelties of antiquity were taken as a matter of course at that time, just as slavery was by our forefathers. In dealing with hordes of semi-savages God had to permit deeds which shock us because trained by the evolution which he started then, but which were as historically necessary in his education of the race as the Witanagemot was in the development of popular government. "The times of this ignorance God winked at." But take the Bible through, its moral beauty and power are irresistible, and separate it by a deep gulf from every other sacred book. Even the Old Testament stage sounds a lofty moral note and an urgent demand for righteousness which make its prophets and psalms still the despair of the world. There are indeed the imprecatory psalms for which we apologize and exclude from the range of inspiration. But that is due to morbid sentimentality rather than to healthy goodness. The men who override the world in murder and lust, for whom no penitence is morally possible, should be stricken down before they ruin still more. To pray for God's speedy vengeance upon them is only another version of "Thy kingdom come." Israel's

MODERNISM AND THE CHRISTIAN FAITH

enemies were exactly that kind of men, and there are times in history when prayer for their overthrow is like Milton's 19th Sonnet, William Watson's poem on "Abdul the Damned," born out of the horrors of the Armenian massacres of 1895, which pale away before the purple demonic deeds of wholesale annihilation of the same nation in 1916–17, or like Julia Ward Howe's "The Battle Hymn of the Republic," which came out of the same ethical indignation as the imprecatory psalms. The occasional overdrawn rhetoric of a poetic line in those psalms need not blind us to the justice of which they are the sound expression. There are times when they have an indispensable message to the world.

The moral vigor of the Bible, the high-water mark which it reaches in this field, and to which it constantly calls mankind, calls from an advance position ever ahead even of its believers and lovers,—this is an influence most stimulating and salutary. It is one of the divinest notes of the Bible, and it is interesting that it was this aspect of its divinity (of course not excluding others) which sometimes overslaughs the rationalism of the radical in his moments of finer insight, as in the case of Auguste Sabatier:

> It is this persistently creative stimulating action (he says) upon the moral life which gives the Bible authority, an authority which is wholly spiritual and is one with the experiences and aspirations of piety. It has no more need of official verification than the light which enlightens the eye, or the duty which commands the conscience, or the beauty which ravished the imagination. The efficacy of the divine word is at once the inward sign, the measure, and the foundation of its authority.... The Bible continues and perpetually maintains the revelation of God in the souls of men, keeping fresh and strong by its primitive

INSPIRATION

simplicity. Drawing its authority from its own efficacy, it has in itself the means of making itself immediately recognized by the soul that is athirst for righteousness and truth.... The experiences of Christians are moral facts, bearing eloquent witness to the power of the Bible. What other book can awaken dumb or sleeping consciences, reveal the secret needs of the soul, sharpen the thorn of sin and press its cruel point upon us, tear away our delusions, humiliate our pride, and disturb our false serenity? What sudden lightnings it shoots into the abyss of our hearts! What searchings of conscience are like those which we make by this light? And when we have gained a right apprehension of our shortcomings and spiritual poverty, when the need of pardon, the hunger for righteousness, and the thirst for life torture the soul to desperation, what other voice than that of the Son of man has power to allay our pain, convince us of the love of the Father, the love which passeth knowledge, in which all shame and remorse are swallowed up and the flame of a holy life is kindled in the soul? The word which pierced us like a sharp sword now sheds itself like a balm over all our wounds, like consolation over all our sorrows. It becomes a source of inward joy, a strength for life, and a hope which shines beyond death itself. These experiences are facts. This light shining into the darkness of the inner life is a fact. This repentance and confession, this spiritual new birth, these aspirations toward goodness and God, this shame of hidden sin, this thirst for eternal life, are facts. The power which produces such effects is also a fact. The word which draws us irresistibly to God and so invincibly attaches us to him can come from none but him.... Such is the inspiration which piety feels and finds in Holy Scripture.... This experience of the Christian is expanded and confirmed by the agelong experience of the church.... Wherever the Bible is in honor it remains the safeguard of Christian liberty; an ever-living agent of reformation, a power for progress and for life. [31]

Sabatier did not see that this gives his whole case away. If the Bible is thus the spiritual life and light of men, it is God-inspired and therefore in so far infallible as to the religious elements which accomplish this.

---

[31] *The Religions of Authority and the Religion of the Spirit*, 1904, pp. 241–244.

MODERNISM AND THE CHRISTIAN FAITH

4. The inspiration of the Bible is its humanity, its human adaptability. A book that so perfectly fits the human soul, masters and guides it, that ministers to its deepest need, satisfies its longing, must come from the Maker of that soul. Its humanity is its divinity. "And need I say," remarks Coleridge, "that I have met everywhere [in the Bible] more or less copious sources of truth and power and purifying influences; that I have found words for my inmost thoughts, songs for my joy, utterances for my hidden griefs, and pleadings for my shame and my feebleness. In short, whatever *finds* me bears witness for itself that it has proceeded from a Holy Spirit, even from the same Spirit 'which remaining in itself, yet regenerateth all our powers, and in all ages entering into holy souls maketh them friends of God and prophets.' [32] ... In every generation and wherever the light of revelation has shone, men of all ranks, conditions and states of mind have found in this volume a correspondent for every movement toward the better felt in their own hearts, the feeble a help, the sorrowful a comfort. You in one place, I in another, all men somewhere and at some time meet with an assurance that the hopes and fears, the thoughts and yearnings which proceed from and tend toward a right spirit within us, are no dreams or fleeting singularities, no voices heard in sleep, no specters which the eye suffers but does not perceive."[33] This perfect adaptability of the Bible to the soul and of the soul to the Bible, its simple unambitious humanness uniting with its lofty divinity, "the guide of all

---

[32] *Confessions of an Inquiring Spirit*, letter 1, Morley's ed., p. 15. Quotation is from Wisdom, 7.

[33] This part of Coleridge quoted by Brook, in *Foundations*, pp. 28, 29.

INSPIRATION

the arts and acts of the world which have been noble, fortunate and happy"—this is its inspiration.

5. The consolatory power of the Bible is its inspiration. All the ancient religions, all the heathen faiths to-day, are destitute of solace for the afflicted and bereaved. The sacred books of the world have a message for the strong and the thoughtful, men who are trained to judge and sift their ideas, but they have no message for the sorrowful. There is more help for the soul in the twenty-third psalm, more relief for the anxious heart in the fourteenth chapter of John, than in all the dreary spaces of the Koran and the interminable rolls of Hinduism. While the sterner aspects are not lacking, God is revealed as the God of all comfort, the succorer of the needy and distressed. Not only so, certain parts of the Bible have always been the inspiration of the moral and social reformer, and no program of social and national advance has ever gone beyond the principles laid down in Scripture. Individual philanthropists and socialists have for various causes reacted against the Bible and Christianity, but their passion for the amelioration of the ills and injustices of mankind has been the fine flower which has grown on the soil which Christianity has prepared and on that soil alone.

6. The inspiration of the Bible is its Christ. What makes the Bible the Word of God? Not because all parts of it are dictated by the Holy Spirit, nor because the same fullness of revelation pervades all parts, nor because the peculiarities of the writers were flattened down to a dead level, nor because the variety and charm of its literature were checked, nor its human beauties nor human infirmities forestalled. But the Bible is the Word of God because in the

MODERNISM AND THE CHRISTIAN FAITH

center of its organism One is living to whom alone in its supreme sense the phrase, "the Word of God," is to be applied, who is the source of spiritual life, and who is the Lord of the Scriptures. Read John 1. 1, 2, 4, 16. The true Word of God is Jesus, and the Bible is the Word of God because it testifies of him. He is greater than the Scriptures, as the sun is greater than the moon. They shine by his light, he unites in living unity their literature, he blends in harmony their many-toned voices. The history of the Bible starts from him and leads to him, its poetry sings of him, and its prophecies speak for the principles of righteousness of which he is the ground, and foretell the glories of his person and his kingdom. Christ is the soul of the Scriptures. Where does the world present another spectacle of a literature, produced in the changing fortunes of a thousand years, the human qualities of which were left unfettered, bound together as a living organism—because that vast literature from Genesis to Revelation is an organic whole and it is the only literature in the world that is—by the spirit of One who used the master passion of a nation as the vehicle of his life and truth? This is the uniqueness of Scripture. This is its inspiration. The testimony of Jesus is the spirit of prophecy.[34] He, and he alone, is the Daystar which arises in the hearts of his disciples, compared with which the word of prophecy is only a lamp shining in a dark place.[35] He therefore is the test of the value of the different parts of Scripture.

A few questions remain. What is the relation of revelation to inspiration? For practical purposes of

---
[34] Rev. 19. 10.
[35] 2 Pet. 1. 10.

INSPIRATION

the Bible reader they may be looked upon as identical. In theory, revelation refers to the religious truths directly communicated by God to his servants, for which their natural powers unaided were incompetent, inspiration to those truths as embodied in Scripture. We must remember that there is an economy in God's dealings with man ("Gather up the fragments, that nothing be lost," John 6. 12), and his supernatural assistance is given only when necessary.[36]

What is the relation of inspiration to the church? The inspiration of Scripture is not a detached phenomenon, but is vitally connected with the believing community, by whom it is to be judged and its genuine and false forms to be discriminated. "I speak as unto wise men, judge ye what I say."[37] There was a body of truth lying back in the society of the elect, and inspiration came out from that and rested upon it and appealed to it. There was no esoteric clique of holy hierophants, as in heathenism, who had the monopoly of the divine light and to whom the mass must go for wisdom from above as for water to a town pump. There were inspired men, but they were only first among equals. "The impulse (of inspiration in the Epistles) came from the body of truth which lay behind, of which the spoken and written word were only alternating modes of expression. The inspiration of the New Testament was more that of an indwelling abiding spirit than that of the Old. It was one form of that great outpouring which flooded not an individual here and there but the

---

[36] Perhaps the best brief treatment of revelation and inspiration from one side is Ladd, *Doctrine of Sacred Scripture*, vol. ii, pp. 452-494, and from another articles under those titles by Warfield in *International Standard Bible Encyclopædia*, vols. iii and iv (both very able).

[37] 1 Cor. 10. 15.

MODERNISM AND THE CHRISTIAN FAITH

whole society."[38] But the individual was inspired, and because his inspiration was on the background of a common illumination he was known and acknowledged to be inspired. For that reason no important biblical book ever had any struggle to be acknowledged as divine. Does the inspiration of the church, however, mean, as Garvie hints,[39] that if she were to-day cleansed and had a like receptivity for truth as in the apostles' time a similar revelation of the Spirit might be given? The form changes according to historical conditions and necessities; the substance abides. The first age needed the facts and truths of the Christian religion; therefore Christ and the apostles gave them. That foundation having been laid, it not only need never be laid again—it can never be laid again. All progress in Christian truth since then is an evolution, not an accretion. There is not a single true doctrine in the long history since apostolic times but that is implicit, if not explicit, in apostolic sources. God is an economist. It was his work to lay foundations then; having done that, he will not do it again. See Heb. 6. 1–3.

What is the relation of inspiration to the canon? If the Bible books had lacked that immediacy and self-witnessing authenticity of the voice of God, which is one of their marks, they would never have won their place in the canon. But the canon itself was an historical evolution, with the marks of the ups and downs of that process. The inspiration of

---

[38] Sanday, *Inspiration: Bampton Lectures*, 1893, 4th ed., 1901, p. 353. So Ladd: "Revelation and inspiration themselves belong to the entire religious community: in specific kind, though by no means in degree or result, they are the same for all members of the community." *Lib. cit.*, ii, p. 492.

[39] *Handbook of Christian Apologetics*, 1913, p. 66.

INSPIRATION

1 Cor. 13 does not cover the holy Fathers of the fourth century. But because the church herself had the Spirit she recognized that Spirit in her books, and a cursory examination of the books she did not take up in the canon shows she had both common sense and spiritual discernment. Leaving aside two or three unimportant books, no committee of experts to whom such a question might now be submitted would reach any other conclus on as to the New Testament, and mainly as to the Old, than that reached by the ancient Christians. My own judgment is that the least attested book—say Second Peter or Jude—in spiritual vigor and purity of apostolic fire so far surpasses the strongest book in the second century that you might say the difference is in kind as well as in degree. In the Old Testament the situation is different, and few would object to taking Esther out and putting Wisdom in. Charles finds in certain parts of Jewish Apocrypha (for example, on immortality) a genuine inspiration and an ethical advance on the Old Testament.[40] At the bottom the canon is an open question, but it is one that was not disturbed by Christ and the apostles. As Loisy says: "The Saviour and the apostles have cited a body of divine writings, and it does not appear that in their instruction they desired to innovate as to the compass and authority of that collection. Neither the apostolic writings nor the tradition of the Christian church ever carried the trace of an express decision rendered by Jesus Christ and the apostles touching the canon of the

---

[40] R. H. Charles, *Eschatology*, 2nd ed., 1913, pp. 179, 226ff. The boundaries of the canon are not a hard-and-fast barrier, says Sanday, *lib. cit.*, 258. See Strachan, *Inspiration* (Protestant), in *Encyclopædia of Religion and Ethics*, vol. vii, p. 239, col. 1 (1915)—fine discussion.

MODERNISM AND THE CHRISTIAN FAITH

Old Testament, much less still a decision which would formally rectify the opinions received in the Jewish world." [41] They took the canon as they found it.

What is the relation of inspiration to the Rule of Faith? In the early church there grew up brief statements of faith and of the chief Christian facts, such as, for instance, came to be crystallized in our Apostles' Creed. These were called the Rule of Faith, and were prompted by the needs of instruction, by the vogue of heresy, etc. In the Greek and Roman Churches of the Middle Ages this Rule, the Creeds, tradition, and the Scriptures, were the Rule of Faith as norms of teaching. As the Roman Church appealed to tradition as in part a justification of her beliefs and ways, the reformers of the sixteenth century went back to the Scriptures alone as the rule in cases of doctrines necessary to salvation. It was really a cry of freedom. "You can't fasten on us a yoke of ceremonies, dogmas, practices as obligatory on peril of our souls which you and we know are not commanded in Scripture as obligatory, or perhaps not even mentioned, for you yourselves allow the Scripture is a rule. It is not only a rule, it is henceforth the only rule for these essential things. Out, therefore, with your thousand additions!" This was one of the most beneficent achievements of the Reformation. But to-day the "modern" man finds even this minimum a yoke. Why? Because of the abuse of proof-texts, because of the variant or contradictory doctrines which were supposed to be found, because there is a progress of doctrine in the Scripture, because of alleged differences of doctrinal conception, and because of the "assured results" of biblical criticism.

[41] *Canon de l'Ancien Testament*, 1890, p. 97.

INSPIRATION

On the other hand, it is fair to say that those who feel this objection themselves appeal to the Scripture to corroborate their ideas whenever they think best, even to parts which their school generally thinks unauthentic, like the fourth Gospel and the Pastoral Epistles, an involuntary testimony to the compelling value of the Bible as a test of religious truth, and to the fact that it is impossible to cut out the Bible as a source of his ideas to a man who stands on any Christian ground. What he denies at one time he follows at another. Nor is he to be blamed for this inconsistent tribute to Christianity. For the Bible as a rule of faith rests solely on its inspiration, that is, on the volume, purity, strength, rationality, and self-convincing light and power as from God of its religious message. If that inspiration is a fact, it is a rule of faith; if it is not a fact, it is not a rule of faith, and the statements of Christ and the apostles on God, sin, salvation, justification, Christ, the Spirit, the future life, etc., are of no more account to me as guiding my faith than the imaginings of my neighbor who gets his religious views from Buddha, Christian Science, the swami, Kant, his own reason, or any of a thousand sources.

What is the relation of inspiration to infallibility? By infallibility I simply mean truth and not error, truth without error. As I see it, all truth is infallible truth. For a thing to be true and not infallibly true is a contradiction in terms. If you are reading this book now, it is infallibly true that you are reading it. What is meant by the infallibility of the Scripture, then, is that when discovered by scientific exegesis its teachings on faith and morals in its general drift and spiritual implications and essence, are truth and

MODERNISM AND THE CHRISTIAN FAITH

not error. Those teachings can be depended upon. You can base your salvation upon them here and hereafter. You can appeal to them as your rule, you can live in them and live on them, you can especially find Christ in them, and, finding him, you have God, you have eternal life. That is what I mean by the Bible being infallible as a religious guide. And its infallibility depends on its inspiration by the Spirit and is its inspiration.

What is the difference between the inspiration of Scripture and that of the other sacred books of world religions? In Hinduism, which contains by far the larger part of those books, a distinction is made between the *sruti* ("that which is heard") and *smirti* ("that which is stored up in the mind") books. In the former (the Vedas, etc., a vast tract), the inspiration is full, direct, overwhelming, verbal, breathed out from Brahman alone. In the latter, intelligence, study, diligence, literary activity pertain. In Buddhism I do not find any doctrine of inspiration laid down, but in the famous rock inscription of King Asoka, B. C. 249, it is said that "all that our Lord Buddha has spoken, my Lords, is well spoken: wherefore, sirs, it must be regarded as having indisputable authority, so the true faith shall last long." [42] This makes this literature sruti. But for three or four centuries after the death of Buddha (the date of which is very uncertain, Max Müller, B. C. 477, Rhys Davids, 420–400) there were no written records of his words, at least none that were looked upon as canonical, and therefore with

---

[42] See this edict translated by Kern in the admirable and scholarly book of T. S. Berry, *Christianity and Buddhism* (Non-Christian Religious Systems series, S. P. C. K.) London (1891), p. 131-132, note.

INSPIRATION

all the almost miraculous tenaciousness of the Oriental memory the question of inspiration or even of the genuineness of Buddhist Scriptures hardly comes up. As to Islam it is well known that the Koran is also *sruti*, it is *wahi zahir*, external inspiration, words and thoughts being communicated by God to Mohammed in the fullest and directest sense. The inspiration of the Bible, however, is part of an historic process which takes up the elements which make the process. The contributions of men are many, varied, and fascinating, and give the Book its very human appeal, human in its weakness and its greatness, its imperfections and its genius; but the contribution of God is his presiding over that evolution, guiding it to the supreme goal of redemption by the Christ to the end of salvation for all mankind who will receive it, and in his own time and manner revealing himself and his truth for that salvation with a beauty, cogency, fullness, variety, breadth, depth, and self-evidencing brightness—the brightness sometimes of congenial warmth and kindly light, at others with an all-consuming flame—which make the Bible as a whole the Book of God which shines in its own glory. And it is a glory that asks nothing from priest or pope or council or theologian, but only that the humble and contrite heart may rejoice in it, and give back light for light.

CHAPTER III

MIRACLE

In 1909 Dr. George A. Gordon, minister of the Old South Church, Boston, published a book, *Religion and Miracle*,[1] which made a sensation. It was the first time, I think, in which an orthodox Congregational minister in America had in effect repudiated miracles, and so was received with acclaim by all rationalists and with surprise by all who held to supernatural Christianity. There were two fine things about this book. The first was the dedication. "I dedicate this Book to the inspiring memory of my Father, George Gordon, of Insch, Scotland—born and bred to the vocation of farmer: a brilliant mind, one of the bravest of men, to whom the order of summer and winter, seedtime and harvest, was a token of the infinite Good Will, and who toiled in the fields of time in the sense of the Eternal." The other was the fine vindication of spiritual personal religion as obedient and loving trust in a personal God, as over against materialistic philosophy. But when you come to look into this book more closely as to its special thesis, two or three things force themselves upon you. (1) It starts out with a long-since obsolete definition of miracle, a definition which pervades the entire book and vitiates it. Miracle is the "suspension or violation of natural law" (p. 72). Such a

---
[1] Published by Houghton, Mifflin Company. Quotations used by permission.

MIRACLE

definition was held by some fifty years ago, I think by no Christian theist to-day. Not only so, the author makes miracle as in effect equivalent to a "wonder or portent" and compares it to the "vulgar appeal to sense, the tricks and feats of the wizard" (p. 89) —certainly a singular misrepresentation in so large minded a writer of the Christian conception of miracle. (2) Even so, the author holds miracles possible. "Dogmatic denial of miracle on the ground of natural law cannot be justified by logic. No man knows enough to be warranted in the statement that miracle has never occurred in the history of man and the cosmos. The dogmatic negative is excluded on this subject" (p. 29). (3) He greatly exaggerates the uniformity of nature. "So far as science goes it finds nature uniform in its behavior" (p. 30). Just the contrary. It is uniform till a new force strikes it. The very fact of its responsiveness to intelligence, breaking up its uniformity into a thousand hitherto unknown forms, is the pledge of the advance of science. (4) The book is much better than its thesis, and ever and anon contradicts it. "The natural order cannot prohibit or in any way limit or mar the wisdom of Jesus; the vision of Jesus is unconditioned; his freedom is not in the keeping of any force other than in his own mind" (p. 88). If that is true, Jesus himself is miraculous. He is *the* miracle. His works then follow as a matter of course. "Nature at her best, miracle at its highest, is at an infinite depth below the elevation on which the soul of God and the soul of Jesus stand in a communion ineffable." But the soul of Jesus is itself a miracle, that is, something not explained by natural law; the soul of God is a miracle, and the more ineffable it is the more miraculous (if one might so say) it is. In fact, about one third or one half of Gordon's book might be written by one who strongly believes in miracle. However its negative parts treat miracle, its religious affirmations constantly imply it.

In 1911 Dr. Gordon met a worthy second in an Anglican minister and a Fellow in Oxford, the Rev. J. M. Thompson, of Saint Mary Magdalen College: *Miracles in the New Testament.* This author tried to do for the New Testament by criticism what by discussion Gordon did for Christianity in general. He eviscerates the Testament of its miraculous contents by a criticism partly subjective, partly objective, and when objective so arbitrary that it not only leaves that Book not worth the paper it is written on, but the same methods would destroy the value of every historical book in existence and the evidence of every historical event. But here, again, we find a delightful inconsistency preserving with one hand what it casts away with the other. (1) It grants the works of healing. This gives its whole case away, as I shall show later. (2) It allows that the "divinity of Christ is demonstrated by a historical fact—the resurrection" (p. 14). There it is again: Christ is himself *the* miracle, his life is rounded by the most stupendous miracle. "The Gospel of the early Christians is the Gospel of the Passion and Resurrection" —miracle once more. "St. Paul entirely agreed with Acts as to the dependence of church life upon the various gifts of the Holy Spirit" (p. 15). What is the raising of a dead body to the descent of the Spirit upon living people? (3) Not only so, Thompson holds the "Incarnation of our Lord and Saviour Jesus Christ" (p. viii). Now, as a miracle, the Incarnation

MIRACLE

overtops all other events as Mount Everest overtops the plains of Calcutta. Why swallow a camel and then strain out a gnat?

It goes without saying that the progress of natural science has made many minds unfavorable to miracle. But it has had the same effect toward all supernatural religion, and even toward theism—and logically. Once deny miracle, once affirm that everything is under the control of a fixed, unalterable law of so-called nature, then materialism is possible, fatalism, agnosticism, positivism are possible, but no form of Christianity is possible. Religion is the response of a free spirit to a free personal Creator and Lover. That response means the overflowing tides of divine life which are not held within the boundaries of nature. A free God means a free man, and a free man means a rupture of boundaries, a rising from one order to another, and every such ascent is a miracle. If, then, one holds to religion at all, and especially to the faintest type of Christianity, he must hold to miracle.

What, then, is a miracle? A miracle is any deed in an order which is impossible to the forces ordinarily working in that order. Crystallization—at least perfect crystallization—is not a miracle in quartz; but it is a miracle in sandstone. Vegetable life is a miracle in minerals, but not in its own order, except in the sense in which all life is miracle. Animal life is a miracle to the vegetable, but not to itself, and soul life is a miracle to both. There are no forces in the lower realm which can produce the higher, therefore these events are to that lower order miracles. In that higher order the miracle may be mediate or immediate, direct or indirect, using natural forces

MODERNISM AND THE CHRISTIAN FAITH

or supernatural, physical or intellectual or spiritual. So long as the result is divine in the sense that it is beyond the power of the lower grade of agencies, it is a miracle to that grade. When we get to soul, it is a question whether genius is not another name for miracle. The last two thousand years have produced only one *Hamlet*. There is not one chance in millions that the next two thousand years will produce another. In other words the special literary and intellectual powers behind *Hamlet* were such as God has never embodied and will never embody in another soul. That is, to ordinary mortals Shakespeare was a miracle. Take the religious realm. The fourth Gospel is the loftiest religious writing that has ever been penned. It not only surpasses every other religious composition, especially outside of the New Testament, but it surpasses them so greatly that every other seems tame and commonplace beside it. If this has been true for two thousand years, what chance is there that any combination of powers will ever unite in producing another book like it? In other words, in religion the fourth Gospel is a miracle. Of course neither solitariness nor multiplicity in itself makes a miracle. There are millions of cases of crystallization, but every one of them is a miracle to an adjoining realm.

The soul has its own complement of miracle. The capacity to see visions, clairvoyant power such as Swedenborg had when, three hundred miles away, he saw Stockholm burn; the power of seeing absent friends and dying or dead friends, the presentiment of future events—all these and other psychical powers are miracles to less keenly endowed natures. Then there are people whose religious responsiveness is so

MIRACLE

acute, whose temperament is so *en rapport* with eternal things, whose faith is so childlike in its unconquerable trust, that the very heavens seem to bend toward them, the invisible world discloses its secrets, and the Higher Powers actually commune with them in interchange of thought and feeling. The Christian Church has had many such, and I would not deny that even pagan religions have produced rare spirits who enjoyed something akin to this. I remember reading in college Xenophon's *Memorabilia* of Socrates where he says that it was a common subject of talk that Socrates used to say that the Divinity instructed him,[2] and compare the remarkable passage near the end of Plato's Apology of Socrates.[3] Now all these experiences are miracles to the ordinary run of Christians. They have to do with a range of powers as far beyond this ordinary run as a tree is beyond the moss, the lion beyond the snail.

Then, again, in this same realm of soul another series of miracles are constantly taking place, namely, conversion from sin to holiness. Now notice, I do not say that in this and in other instances I have mentioned, no so-called natural forces are used. What I say is that there is and must be something added to those forces, and that that extra power is a miracle to the lower. Those lower powers have proved themselves competent in some cases to lead men to give up bad habits, to swear off this or that indulgence, to start in decent ways of living, but they have never been competent to change the man inside so that every evil thing he hates and every godlike thing he loves. And they have especially

---
[2] *Memorabilia*, book 1, chap. 1, sec. 2.
[3] *Apology*, 40 A, some editions, sec. 31.

MODERNISM AND THE CHRISTIAN FAITH

never been competent to do this for the lost man and woman, the outcast. Every real conversion, therefore, is a miracle—the inrushing of divine life that cleanses the fountains of being, something incompetent to natural law. They are not only miracles, but—if one miracle could be greater than another—they are stupendous miracles. The giving sight to blind Bartimæus as to difficulty is child's play to giving light and life to Jerry McAuley. Perhaps even greater than these are those conversions where strict moralists are flooded with the glory of God. When a cold self-righteous moral man, who has led say for fifty years a perfect moral life, gives that life to the Saviour, and finds a change which in spiritual values and profound experience of divine grace is like going out of a dungeon into God's sunlight—that is even more miraculous than the conversion of Samuel H. Hadley.

In regard to the Bible, the word miracle is generally used of those extraordinary acts of God or his servants which fall in with his work as Redeemer, Saviour, etc. (1) They are comparatively few in number, and even then occur only in turning points or eras of importance. (2) They are not of curiosity or magic, but generally are the outcome of philanthropic or religious need. They are also associated with the message or the preaching, and thus have ethical and spiritual significance. (3) Dissociated from a suitable spiritual atmosphere and response, Christ not only would not do them but could not. That is, he would not imperil the spiritual miracle of repentant souls for the external miracle of healed bodies. (4) Response and need being taken for granted, Christ did not minimize these works in the tone of the lofty

MIRACLE

critic of to-day, but repeatedly appealed to them for his credentials, or made them the starting point of profound spiritual teaching—teaching which in these cases would hang in the air without historical connection or basis if the miracle be denied. Sometimes they seem to be his almost involuntary response to the fearful needs of the time, sufferings that lay waste his heart. (5) So far from denying that he wrought them, like the Oxford Episcopal minister, his bitterest enemies affirmed that he wrought them, though by help that came from below. (6) Nor can we say with the Rev. J. M. Thompson and many others that Christ did some works of healing, but that these were not miracles. It is a familiar topic of modern psychology that mind has tremendous power over matter, and under circumstances can suddenly cure. But there was nothing of the physiological psychologist about Christ, much less of the fakir who calls secret psychical forces to help him exploit his dupes. Nor was there anything dramatic about Christ's cures, where those forces might be suddenly released to reenforce disused nerves and muscles. Besides, the cures themselves were of so radical a kind that they are beyond the power of these secondary agencies. You cannot suddenly give sight to a blind man by sleight-of-hand, and if you try your psychical recipes on Oriental lepers, you will prefer to do it from a safe distance. Nor did the people discriminate in their demands, bringing only a few nervous girls or hysteric women, but they threw down the sickest and deadliest diseased before the Master, who on his part did not wait the "psychologic moment," but without preparation waded into that awful sea of misery. I wish those who are so generous as to

MODERNISM AND THE CHRISTIAN FAITH

leave Christ just a little power as a masterly exploiter of credulous weak-brained neurotics would read the article of R. J. Ryle, M.D., in *The Hibbert Journal*, v, pp. 572–586 (July, 1907). If there were any differences at all in the strain Christ's miracles cost him, if we can imagine one deed more difficult than another, it could not have been the control of inanimate nature, but wrestling with the souls and bodies of men in those terrible diseases of the East, the very sight of which chills to the marrow the sympathetic onlooker. Besides all this, even if we acknowledge that a very few of Christ's miracles might be accounted for by his manipulation of hidden psychical powers, and thus save a remnant from the wreck, the number still remaining is so large that the new theory does not save the veracity of the Gospels. It does not only not save the veracity of the Gospels, but it leaves a pile of Munchausen stories around that sacred Personality—his whole record shot through and through with lies, by men who wrote his life within the memory of thousands of people who knew him and who would have immediately cried out, "We knew Christ, and he never did any of these works."

We must remember also that the apologetic value of these external miracles was vastly greater in the earlier centuries than to-day. The intellectual atmosphere has changed so much that the hasty critic cries out: "Away with your miracles! It is only internal evidence that we want. It is only spiritual truth." Well, if that is all you want, we have enough of it, God knows! But not so quick, high-flown critic! Although Christ was as chary of miracles as he could be, and refused them on demand of super-

MIRACLE

cilious observers, yet as a matter of fact they were historically essential to his work. If he had never performed them, neither he nor his religion would have been heard of. The thing which the modern liberal preacher looks down upon with disdain is the very platform on which he stands, without which both himself and his church would never have existed. All through the Acts and epistles the appeal to the mighty deeds of Christ, especially, of course, to his resurrection, is the undertone. After the resurrection and ascension all the other deeds of Christ fell in their proper place of themselves—and they, and they alone, saved Christianity. If Christ had been only a sayer of the word and not also a doer, if he had said fine things but had done no mighty things, he would have been forgotten in a year. Or, if not entirely forgotten, he would have been mentioned in the Talmud as the Nazarene rabbi Jeshua, who taught so and so and was crucified as a blasphemer. Of course the poets compliment "Lord Christ's heart and Plato's brain," and we say nice things about his gentleness, goodness, and wonderful teaching; but it was not these which made him conquer the Roman. Mark, who wrote his Gospel for that Roman, plunges at once into his deeds—the Man who was greater than his words. In his very first chapter he tells of six distinct miracles, besides summing up others in the words: "He healed many that were sick with divers diseases, and cast out many demons." Luke wanted to show people One who did something as well as teach something,[4] and Peter appealed to those who knew Christ to remember him not simply by his words but by the mighty deeds

---
[4] Acts 1. 1.

MODERNISM AND THE CHRISTIAN FAITH

"and wonders and signs which God did by him in the midst of you."[5] We don't want the scaffolding of a house always, nor do we care if the foundation does not show as long as there is a foundation. But the scaffolding was essential once, and the unseen foundations are essential now. Just so with the miracles of Christ and apostles. At a certain stage of civilization the external signs are essential. You say that making an iron swim or any other striking deed would not predispose you to receive the message of the one who did it. Very likely. But you must not judge the needs of semibarbarians two thousand years ago by your own to-day. Henry M. Stanley went through Africa on the strength of a series of startling works which were miraculous to the natives. We cannot consider so thoughtful a man as Nicodemus lacking in discrimination, and yet he made the confession that the mighty works of Jesus had convinced him of his divine mission. The parent and teacher who refuses to appeal to the sense of wonder would be accused of folly by every psychologist and expert in pedagogy.

> "We live by Admiration, Hope and Love;
> And, even as these are well and wisely fixed;
> In dignity of being we ascend."[6]

"Admiration is a highly philosophical affection," says Sir William Hamilton, "indeed there is no other principle of philosophy but this."[7] To that miracle appeals. "He who would create admiration for goodness must exhibit a good being performing a

---

[5] Acts 2. 22.
[6] Wordsworth, *The Excursion*, book 4.
[7] *Metaphysics*, Lecture 4, p. 55 (Boston, 1859).

MIRACLE

good action,"[8] the very rationale of the miracles of Jesus. Carlyle was fearful that our Dirt Philosophy would destroy the sense of wonder, and with that soul vision. "Wonder is the basis of worship," he says. "The necessity and high worth of universal wonder." "The man who cannot wonder, who does not habitually wonder (and worship), were he President of innumerable Royal Societies, and carried the whole *Mécanique Céleste* and *Hegel's Philosophy*, and the epitome of all Laboratories and Observatories with their results, in his single head—is but a Pair of Spectacles behind which is no Eye."[9]

> I say that miracle was duly wrought
> When, save for it, no faith was possible.
> Whether a change were wrought i' the shows o' the world,
> Whether the change came from our minds which see
> Of the shows o' the world so much as and no more
> Than God wills for his purpose—(what do I
> See now, suppose you, there where you see rock
> Round us?)—I know not; such was the effect,
> So faith grew, making void more miracles
> Because too much; they would compel, not help.[10]

When the need no longer exists, the form changes, the substance endures. Our ministers who are to-day waving aside the early Christian miracles may or may not be good liberals, but are they not lacking somewhat in intellectual humility and historical insight?

But, you say, what about foreign mission fields? Do they not have the same needs as the men of Christ's time? Yes and no. Many of these fields know about Christian civilization, and stand on a far higher plane

---
[8] McCosh, *The Emotions*, p. 50 (New York, 1880).
[9] "*Sartor Resartus*," book 1, chap. XI.
[10] Browning, "*A Death in the Desert*."

MODERNISM AND THE CHRISTIAN FAITH

in knowledge than the lands of the first century. Then in lands less favored our missionaries enter with minds predisposed to the spiritual miracle but not to the external. They have faith for one, not for the other. But, after all, the miracles happen—thousands every year. Where Christ healed one, the medical missionary heals a hundred, and by processes which to the ordinary heathen seem as miraculous as Christ's. "Greater *works* than these shall he do; because I go unto the Father." Not only so, actual instances of demon possession occur as real and virulent as those in Christ's day, and these demons are cast out, as in the early church.

Still the great crux is natural law. Nature is inexorable. As McKane said about injunctions at Gravesend, so she says: "Miracles don't go here. There is a chain of law which holds everything in its place, and you can disturb nothing. The slightest variation by a miracle would tumble the cosmos into chaos." I was much interested in reading the late Professor Bowne's answer to this objection. You know he was a "liberal" theologian, and I was anxious to find out whether he still held the possibility of miracle. He so shifts the emphasis that the objection from natural law vanishes into thin air. He says:

> Nature is no longer a rival of God, but simply the form under which the divine will proceeds in its cosmic outgo. With this result we have almost all that religion really aims at in its insistence upon miracle. Religion seeks after God. It longs to find the Father and to know that he is near. But proceeding on naturalistic and deistic assumptions, we build up a phantom of nature which petrifies man's higher life, and then we look anxiously for breaks in the natural order and pin our faith on miracles, mainly physical, as the sole indication of God's presence, if not

MIRACLE

of God's existence. But with the conception of a supernatural natural we can breathe freely even in the face of the natural order, and are much less concerned about miracle in the sense of a departure from natural law. The distinction between the natural and the supernatural in that case would not lie in the causality, but in the phenomenal relations. The causality would be equally supernatural in both. The natural and the miraculous would be equally products of the divine will, but in the case of miracle there would be a departure of the familiar order so as to indicate to believers a divine presence and meaning. Miracles in themselves would be no more divinely wrought than any other routine event. The only place or function we could find for them would be as signs of a divine power and purpose which men immersed in sense could not find in the ordinary course of the natural.[11]

Bowne says that nature may be looked upon as a space world and time world, but also as a power world. In the two former there is uniformity, but only as long as the latter does not impinge. Whenever it does, there is change. Nature is not a closed *nexus*. It is open all the time to intellect, and the "continuity of natural law" is a fiction. Even Tyndall had to acknowledge this. He admitted that man can work through the system and produce multitudinous effects without breaking any general laws; and if man can, then God might do the same. Bushnell is right in thinking that so far as natural law is concerned all human action is miraculous. Freedom breaks in on the lower order, and that is really a miracle. It is either that or universal determinism, and that overturns reason itself. As having a supernatural root, all things are miracles. All alike root in the ever-living, ever-working will of God. They are miracles also in the sense that they cannot be deduced from antecedent conditions, but

---

[11] Bowne, in *Harvard Theological Review*, vol. iii, pp. 148–149 (April, 1910). Used by permission.

MODERNISM AND THE CHRISTIAN FAITH

continually proceed from the activity of the divine. Considered as a speculative proposition, the difficulty is less to establish the possibility of miracle than to prove the necessary uniformity and universality of law. God as the absolute source of all infinite being is bound by nothing but his own wisdom and goodness. What they dictate, that he does. If they call for uniformity, there is uniformity. If they call for change, there is change. God never acts against nature, because for him there is no nature to act against. There are no "interventions," "interruptions," because nature as a barrier with which God must reckon is a fiction. Thus Bowne. You see how his idealistic philosophy gives short shrift to the natural-law argument against miracle, the law on which nearly all objections are now based.

I then turned with interest to see how this objection struck an eminent German scholar of the "liberal positive" school, Professor Seeberg, of the systematic theology chair of the University of Berlin. He says that natural laws are only formulæ for the regularity of the working of the powers of nature. If we bring God in, then we can say that these laws are established by God and become an expression of his will.[12] Man now comes in not to change the laws but to use them for new structures for which, without him, nature is incompetent. So also in regard to God. His teleological use of nature is on the same principle. There is no doing away of natural law, but instead simply a use of it for higher ends just exactly as man uses that law for his new creations. A miracle is only a special combination of natural powers for the bringing forth of a new effect. Wine or bread

[12] Psa. 148. 5, 6.

MIRACLE

is not made from nothing, but is the result of combination of chemical substances. Chemists have even prophesied the time when starch-flour will not be made from plants, but immediately by chemical processes (just as Christ made wine). In fact, one can think with Leibnitz that in the last analysis miracle was placed from eternity in the plan of the universe, and according to that plan was provided for in the course of nature. Of course, this is an hypothesis, but it cuts short objections from the course of nature. It is in the highest degree noteworthy that a philosopher so expert in nature as Lotze roundly acknowledged the possibility of miracle.[13] There is nothing irrational in miracle; it is only the free act of God in nature, analogous to all creative acts of man in the same territory.[14]

Sir Oliver Lodge has an idea similar to Leibnitz's. We must not think of ourselves as outside the cosmos, trying to modify it by petitions, but we ourselves are an "intimate part of the whole scheme, that our wishes and desires are a part of the controlling and guiding will." The cosmos is so arranged that it takes our desires and prayers as part of its system, so that communion with a higher power is as natural as communion with friends. Lodge seems to reach by a general loose discussion the same conclusion as reached by Bowne by a close philosophical discussion. "Miracles," says Sir Oliver, "lie all around us, only they are not miraculous. Special providences envelop us, only they are not special. Prayer is a means of communication as natural and simple as speech."[15] I

---
[13] *Mikrokosmus*, II, 3 Aufl., p. 53f.
[14] Seeberg, article, *"Wunder,"* in *Realencyk. für Protestantische Theologie und Kirche*, 3 Aufl., vol. xxi, pp. 565, 566.
[15] *Contemporary Review*, vol. lxxxvi, pp. 804–806 (1904).

MODERNISM AND THE CHRISTIAN FAITH

understand him to mean that the cosmos was made from the start as involving prayer, Providence, miracle. Miracle is not less miracle; it simply has its divine place in the order of the universe.

An eminent novelist somewhere says of one of his characters that he looked upon everything as a miracle, and knowing that he knew something. There was nothing great and nothing little, and so he could think his way into the heart of things. It is as Paul says: "In him we live, and move, and have our being." God is all and in all. This is the true pantheism, which while it takes up miracle, flings over all events and all things the glory of God, and makes "every bush aflame with God." You remember Frederick W. Robertson's point about the striking event being necessary for the lower intelligence, whereas the higher mind sees the lightning in the dew: "There is a fearful glory in the lightning because he sees it, but there is no startling glory and nothing fearful in the drop of dew, because he does not know what the thinker knows, that the flash is there in all its terrors. So in the same way, to the half-believer a miracle is the one solitary evidence of God. Without it he could have no certainty of God's existence." So with us, the miracle and the ordinary event are parts of one universe held in the hollow of God's hand.

Taking a large view of history I must feel that miracle is analogous to God's general method, and so is not to be too summarily dismissed by a wave of the hand of "modern science" and the college professor. Take Abraham, Moses, David, Elijah, Isaiah: all came forth like a root out of dry ground, unheralded, unprepared for, whose personality and

MIRACLE

message are not of the earth earthy—every man a miracle. You cannot get Socrates from his predecessors, and Plato still stands in lonely preeminence among thinkers. God sometimes foreshortens the historic process, and turns water into wine without such long brooding. Von Ranke says that the "essential thing in Christianity was not prepared for by any previous imperfect stages; on the contrary, Christianity is an abrupt divine fact—as, indeed, all great productions of genius bear upon them the marks of immediate inspiration."[16] We cannot get Luther and his work out of the Catholicism of 1517; he sprang full armed out of the brain, or, rather, the heart of Germany. The more scholars study him the more they are puzzled, and the more penetrating and sympathetic their insight the more of a miracle he appears, though no man was ever franker. Calvin is simple to understand, and yet can we get him out of the sixteenth century? Nay, verily. John Bunyan —who made him? Most miracles are the small dust of the balance beside his marvelous personality and his literary and spiritual genius. Is it the analogy of history—Christ's way to crown our dull faith with wonders, the pensive boy fisherman to write his deepest Life, the poacher and theater hanger-on to write of the quality of his mercy which is not strained, the blind scribe to indite *Paradise Lost,* and the poor persecuted tinker—hounded by the Episcopalians—to create Greatheart from behind the bars? Who would have guessed Methodism from either Anglicanism or Nonconformity in the eighteenth century? It cannot be accounted for by its historical antecedents; in that degree it is a miracle. And so the Salvation Army,

[16] *Weltgeschichte* ix, H. 2, p. 11.

MODERNISM AND THE CHRISTIAN FAITH

with its thousands of converts rescued from earth's hells in all parts of the world, sitting clothed and in their right minds—it sprang in the arena like a giant full grown at the very start, with no forces to explain it when once you eliminate God. That is the method of history. Is it God's rebuke to our materialistic sciolism which binds everything with our little cords of natural law, and with the password "Evolution" bows him out of his creation?

The rational view of miracle which I have given in this paper is really nothing new in the Christian Church. Augustine was trying to work up to a view something similar. God is the only Creator. His secret penetrating might gives everything its being by his immaculate presence. Therefore the world is full of miracles, but the world itself is the great miracle. But on account of their commonness the miracles of creation lose their charm for mankind. Therefore God allows new visible miracles to appear in nature, which are eternally present to him, but which appear as new and effective in time. These miracles appear to contradict the order of nature, but they really do not, as God is the Creator of nature and can therefore make nothing contradictory to it. "Miracles are not against nature," says Augustine, "but only against nature as it is known." In creation God did not allow all possible causes to be effective, but those that were not used then cannot contradict those that were used. Material things contain besides their visible seeds "certain secret seeds," and it is from these that the wonderful and miraculous spring. That is God's secret inner working, which goes on by the side of natural causes, just as he moved the soul innerly by the side of the word. So God

MIRACLE

creates both the ordinary and the extraordinary phenomenon. In themselves both classes of phenomena are equally miraculous, because they are both God's immediate working, though men consider only one class as miraculous (Bowne's view). Both go back to the same creative Will, and for that Will are elements of one created Nature. The distinction, therefore, between the miraculous and the nonmiraculous happening is, according to Augustine, subjective, not objective. At the bottom miracle is as natural as the natural is miraculous.[17] This attempt of the father of Catholic orthodoxy by a Higher Naturalism to solve the difficulty, in which he anticipates modern liberal views, is quite instructive.

The reasoning of Thomas Aquinas is also attractive. The divine government takes in everything that happens, so that nothing accidental does happen, and nothing outside of the "whole order of the divine government" can happen. In the system of causes, which means the world or universe, God works as the first Cause determining absolutely the long chain of causes. In this whole order God can change nothing, as he is the very one who has made the order. But instead of second causes, God can set in others. God has from the start so made the order of the world that outside of the regular second causes he can directly work. The coming in of this first cause is miracle. Miracle is in the territory of nature, but it happens beyond the custom of nature, beyond its second causes. Of course God works in the second causes, but in miracle he works directly. But not every direct gripping in of God is a miracle, but only such as deviates from the natural order.

[17] I follow Seeberg, *lib. cit.*, p. 560, where see references. For Luther, p. 561.

MODERNISM AND THE CHRISTIAN FAITH

Luther, with his customary freshness of view, won a higher outlook. The biblical miracle was a condescension to human weakness, to get Christianity started, to win a foothold for faith, and also later to confirm the preaching of the apostles, which was the important thing. But when once Christianity got started, these lower miracles are no longer needed. But God continues to bring to pass his inner spiritual miracles in the soul by Word and sacrament. These miracles are much greater than the other. Christ upon earth did only external miracles, and these for the sole purpose of creating a free path for the inner miracles. This insight into values attained at a bound by Luther is a stroke of genius, itself almost a miracle.

Before I close a word as to two New Testament miracles recently most under discussion—birth and resurrection of Jesus. Our Unitarian and Trinitarian fathers believed in both, literally. Within recent years a prejudice against the supernatural has shelved both, in the sense held in the church from the beginning till now. In my judgment, this only transfers the difficulty, does not solve it (that is, if we still occupy any kind of Christian ground). Here is the problem. Study Christ, and we find him separated in his God-consciousness not only in degree but in kind from every human being. How do we account for that? The New Testament accounts for it by his dwelling in the life of God before he came to the world; that is, by the incarnation, that is, by his miraculous birth. Modern objectors account for it simply by the Divine Spirit dwelling in him who was of ordinary earthly origin. The objection to this is: (1) It is inconsistent with the consciousness

MIRACLE

of Jesus. Every Christian knows that the Divine Spirit dwells in him, yet how different his consciousness from that of Christ! (2) It is incompetent for the result we see in the gospel and in history. (3) Or if you assume that the spirit of the Father dwelt in him in such fullness that it was competent for the result, then you have another miracle more difficult to explain, less rational, than the old one. Besides, if the Father lived in Jesus thus, why has he never lived in anyone else thus? (4) It is inconsistent with the universal belief of the first Christians, except a small section of the Ebionites. For that reason the new theory of the natural origin of Jesus does not help us. In fact, if you interpret the theory in consistency with the facts in the Gospels, you have to assume a series of miracles, just as a gasoline engine secures progress by an indefinite series of explosions.

The same in regard to the resurrection of Christ. The modern liberal who still wants to be a Christian eliminates the literal or bodily resurrection for the sake of the spiritual. That spiritual resurrection was a tremendous fact, so engrossing and compelling that the disciples and early Christians were absolutely sure that their Lord was alive, and in that faith brought home to them in visions they went forth to spread Christianity. Here, again, it is only the form of the miracle that is changed, and that change increasing the miracle and at the same time making it less rational and less believable. (1) The disciples were all Pharisees. They all believed in a future life; they all held that their Lord was living in glory the moment he passed away. They needed no visions for that, and ten thousand visions would not have changed their attitude one iota. (2) The

MODERNISM AND THE CHRISTIAN FAITH

New Testament never associates visions of ghosts with any moral or spiritual movement. An angel has a function, but ghost-revelations play no part in starting a mighty current like Christianity. They neither actually played a part, nor philosophically could they have played a part. The movement would have fizzled out as the sick dreams of enthusiasts. (3) Acknowledge whatever little discrepancies you wish in the resurrection narratives, the ghost theory does not explain the two irrefragable facts which underlie those narratives like a rock under the variations of sunshine and shower. The first fact is the empty tomb, and the second fact is the impression of all who saw Jesus that they saw him not as a ghost or vision but as a body—essentially the same Jesus that was crucified. (4) I cannot go into the passages now, but it is true that if you study the references to the resurrection of Jesus in the Acts and epistles, you will find that they generally presuppose an actual bodily resurrection and not simply a ghost resurrection. For these reasons I do not feel enthusiastic to substitute the new miracle of the present-day liberal as to the resurrection of Jesus for the old miracle of the first Christians.

I hope I have shown that the modern man, if he stands on Christian ground, has not only no need to deny his belief in miracle, but a good right even from his own point of view of reason and history to affirm it.

CHAPTER IV

JESUS—I

EVERYONE is aware of the tremendous shift of emphasis from what is called the metaphysical Christ to the moral Christ or practical Christ. The modern man is said to care nothing for questions as to Christ's being, but only for historical questions as to Christ's acts, or at most for questions as to his value. This movement, which came in with Ritschl in the seventies and eighties of the last century, has gone so far as to induce a kind of resentment to the Fathers of the church in the fourth and fifth centuries for framing their creeds in "metaphysical" language, for covering up Christ in philosophical terms, and we must now get rid of those creeds and get the everyday Christ. These objections are just as reasonable as those we might make against Jefferson for drawing up the Declaration of Independence in the language of his time tinctured with the ideas of French political philosophers. In fact, less reasonable. For, look. Arius came out in 318 with a new Christ which turned Christianity into a heathen pantheon. He raised the question not of a practical Christ who said some fine things—O no—Arius was no "modern"—but of a "metaphysical" Christ; but his "metaphysics" made Christians idolaters. The only way to meet that in the historical situation was the calling of a council. One was called, 325, at Nicæa. There the matter was threshed out, with the result we all know—the

MODERNISM AND THE CHRISTIAN FAITH

only result that was at all possible if the new paganism of Arius was to be met. Arius raised a question of being, and the church had to answer a question of being. The only question is, Did she answer it rightly or wrongly? Are the Fathers to be blamed for using the thought forms of their day any more than Lord Bacon is for not writing his essays in the language of S. M. Crothers? And yet we have the well-known comparison by Hatch of the Sermon on the Mount with the Nicene Creed. One is a law of conduct, it is said. "Metaphysics are wholly absent." The Nicene Creed is the opposite, its "metaphysical terms would have been unintelligible to the first disciples. The one belongs to a world of Syrian peasants, the other to a world of Greek philosophers."[1] But Christ penetrating Jewish law with the light of his own insight, enlarging its boundaries with daring authority, in Matt. 5ff., does not mean that he cannot also give to those same disciples glimpses of his being that are "metaphysical" enough—altogether too "metaphysical" for us to fathom—in Matt. 11. And what, perhaps, if this very repristination of his own law on the Mount, is but the pedagogical means to awaken in the dull minds of Syrian peasants this very question of being: "Who is this who says, 'But I say unto you'? Why has he this authority? Why does he speak as God? Is he, after all, the Son of God?"

For Christ himself was by no means averse to going behind value judgments to judgments of being. Who do men say the Son of man is?[2] It is as though

---
[1] *Influence of Greek Ideas and Usages upon the Christian Church: Hibbert Lectures,* 1888, London, 1890, 6th ed., 1897, p. 1.
[2] Matt. 16. 13.

JESUS—I

he said: "It is not enough for you to know God the Father. As devout Jews you already know him. He has always been known, and all things continue as before. The pagans know him, at least in part. But a new force has come into the world. I am that force. A kingdom is at the doors. I am that kingdom. The sick are healed, the poor have the gospel preached to them. I am that Gospel. It is no longer, 'Go to God the Father.' The world went—you went —to God the Father, but the world lieth in the evil one. That was not sufficient. If it had been, I would not have come. No. It is not simply, 'Go to God the Father,' but 'Come to me, all ye that are weary and heavy laden, and I will give you rest. Go ye into all the world and preach the gospel, and you will have another world.' I shall make all things new." It is as though Christ said that.

When Harnack (made von Harnack by the Kaiser in 1914, just before the war) gave his *publicum* at his University in Berlin in the winter of 1899–1900 on *Das Wesen des Christentums*, immediately published, translated in 1901 by Saunders under the title *What is Christianity?* he gave a popular putting of Ritschlianism, the modern liberalism. Among other things he told the students that Jesus himself formed no part of his gospel, that he proclaimed God and the kingdom and various fine things but not himself. Now, there is truth in this, namely, that there is nothing aggressively personal or egotistic in Jesus's preaching. His method was not always to be calling attention to himself, to make himself a hero, to secure a crowd, a following, to tell about his own history, his own relation to the Father, to the world, to the universe. In fact, quite the contrary.

MODERNISM AND THE CHRISTIAN FAITH

He was puzzlingly reticent. "Tell no man that I am the Messiah. Tell no one that I have healed you, but show yourself to the priest." When he was becoming too popular he withdrew himself to the mountain or desert. That was his disconcerting method. Why did he act thus? What was the philosophy of this reticence? Well, perhaps this: (1) It would have disrupted his plans. Sometimes it would have created a diversion to make him king, at other times it would have precipitated his crucifixion. (2) Christ did not come as an evangelist, as a Christian preacher. Others were to do the preaching. "Go ye into all the world and preach." (3) He taught by indirection, by influence, by deed, by love, by personality. He chose his disciples, we are told, "to be with him." They would find out who he was, whether he himself was part of the gospel, not by his telling them that in so many words, but by his acting and being that, and by his saying a thousand other things that meant that. You remember that was your father's and your mother's method of telling you whether they were a part of your gospel when you were between one and twenty-one. It worked with you, it worked with the disciples. After he left them *he* was their gospel. (4) There was Another who belonged to Christ's world whose very function it was to testify of him. That was the Spirit, the Comforter, the Paraclete. I do not ask now who the Spirit is, whether he is the same as God the Father as the modern liberal thinks, or another element in the life of God who has his own part in the ongoing of God's plans in the universe. I only say that it is the Spirit's place to see that Christ is not only a part of that gospel which we now call Christianity, but that he is that gospel; in fact, that he is all of it, and will remain all of it until that "far-off divine event to which the whole creation moves," when he delivers up this kingdom to God the Father. But that will be in a sense the end of the gospel, for the universe will enter into another cycle, and God will be all in all. Christ will cease to be Mediator, will cease to be Saviour, but he will not cease to be Son. His work he will change, but not his being.

So much being said for the reasons why Christ was not always preaching himself, the contention of Harnack is by no means true. Indirectly he was always his own message, his personality back of it, shining through it, making it what it was ("no man spake like this man"), giving the conviction to those who saw deepest that he alone had the words of eternal life. In fact, the words apart from the speaker were not the important thing. A good part of them were the republication of the higher messages of the Old Testament and of the Old Testament Apocrypha and of the rabbis, and can be paralleled elsewhere in Israel. They have their chief significance not in what they were in themselves, but in what they were in showing forth Jesus. And his greatest words were not this common stock of noble utterances but those special deliverances where he directly bore witness concerning himself, put himself in the place of God as the yoke-imposer, the rest-giver, and the sin-forgiver, and went forward to claims of equality with God, on which he knew his enemies would justly— from their point of view—base their accusations which must lead to his death. Yes, he was a part of his own gospel. Even in the synoptic Gospels you come occasionally to some vista into the eternal

MODERNISM AND THE CHRISTIAN FAITH

deeps, and in John's Gospel you seem to be sailing on a fathomless sea. I suppose it is the fact that this last Gospel is so full of Jesus's own personality that lends it its strange power over spiritual natures.

What is the problem of Jesus? It is not his humanity. That Jesus was a normal man is no longer in question. We take that for granted so thoroughly that it is hard for us to realize that that was the very problem in the early church. The first fight of the church was not to secure Christ's divinity or atonement, but his humanity. Was Christ really flesh and blood, actually man? That was a poser. Large sections of Christians stumbled at that. But even after the more radical of the deniers were overthrown—the fight against them is one evidence of the genuineness and early date of the seven shorter Greek Epistles of Ignatius—the shyness of thorough churchmen at Christ's complete humanity continued for a long time. Arius, the popular preacher at Alexandria, wanted to lower his divinity, but even that somber and fiery pastor of Baucalis church could not do it without mutilating his humanity; and the work of the first council of Nicæa in throwing out his doctrine was as beneficial on the side of preserving Christ's humanity as on the side most immediately attacked. Every now and then some great ecclesiastic like Apollinaris or Eutyches came out with a reconstruction of Christ which overslaughed his humanity; and even Nestorius (taking the ordinary view of his teachings), though deeply concerned to preserve the entire manhood of Jesus, so adjusted the divine and human in him as to endanger both, almost postulating two persons in him, one over against the other. Of course you can say that the regular church view, though anxiously

JESUS—I

in terms asserting his full humanity—for instance, at Chalcedon, 451—really though unconsciously denied it. I do not argue the matter. In the ancient and mediæval church there were doubtless men in whose minds Christ's divinity was so absorbing that the absolute naturalness of his humanity was lost sight of. In fact, from the fifth or sixth century on through the Middle Ages the general effect of high strained labors on Christ was to make the Son of God take the place of the Son of man. It is as Dorner says:

> The divine and human in Christ thought to be disparate, it cannot astonish us that the endeavors of the Middle Age to frame a Christology failed, and Christology failed to be a guiding light to other dogmatic labors. Mary came in the place of Christ, and the church created surrogates for Christology partly in the saints, partly in the mass. Catholic doctrine has been unable to free itself from Monophysitism in the Ego of Christ and from Nestorianism in his nature. The living Godman is pushed into the background by the worship of saints and the mass, and is snatched from us by a docetic and mythicizing doctrine of the origin, birth, and youth of Christ. Christ has again become for the mode of thought of the Middle Age an exalted God, an almighty lawgiver and judge; according to the decrees of the church there remains no essential place for his humanity. By her intercession Mary represents the divine love in human form. Indeed, the Greek Church has as little known how to find a necessary significance for the humanity of Christ, for Christ is to it preeminently only the Σοφία (wisdom), the bringer of the true knowledge, which pertains to πίστις ὀρθόδοξος (orthodox faith), for which it is evident an inspired man, and not a Godman, might have sufficed. Because the Greek and Roman Churches find no essential and permanent importance in the humanity of Christ, they ever place the divine side in a position of preponderance, and incline to a docetic treatment of his humanity.[3]

But, of course, a conscious denial of Christ's humanity

---
[3] *System of Christian Doctrine*, vol. iii, pp. 222, 223 (abridged).

MODERNISM AND THE CHRISTIAN FAITH

was never in the church's thought. And in modern times that actual humanity is an axiom. No, the humanity of Christ is not the problem. The only question now is his divinity. And in answering that question there are several factors to be considered.

1. Taking the synoptic Gospels as the sources that lie nearest to our hand, it is a fact that the divinity of Christ is the presupposition there. In source called Q, in the rest of Mark, in parts original with Matthew and Luke, nowhere is there a section which one can count out and say, "Here Christ is looked upon as a mere man." He is as divine in Q as in Matt. 16, and Luke 10. 22 is a microcosm of the fourth Gospel. The much-talked of, "Why callest thou me good?" is Christ's pedagogical method of saying: "Enlarge your ideas of God. Know what you are saying. If I am really good in the absolute sense, I must be his Son." Christ did not mean to say that he was not a good Man, for his character reveals his divinity. The familiar argument of that original and liberal thinker Bushnell as far back as 1858, that a study of Christ's character forbids his exclusive classification with man, is as valid to-day as it was then, and more so, because sixty years of research on Christ has not taken away one line of its evidence. All through the synoptic Gospels indirectly or directly the evidence of his divinity shines out. He reinterprets the law, reinvigorates or abolishes it, and in doing that he makes himself equal to the God who gave the law. He is Lord of the Sabbath, and at one stroke recovers its blessings for mankind. There is a union of love and holiness in him not only never realized before or since, but never conceivable before. Unlike all his followers, he lacks the con-

JESUS—I

sciousness not only of sin, but of the slightest moral imperfection. The kingdom he is to establish is the kingdom of God or the kingdom of heaven, but the principles of it he, and not the Father, lays down. He defines it, he rules it, in a full sense he is it, thus placing himself in the stead of God. The gospel of it is to be preached in the whole world as a testimony to all the nations, and only then shall the end come. He places himself in the middle point of history: all the law and prophets were until John the Baptist pointed to him, who is the watershed of another era, the beginning of a new world (Matt. 11. 13). Therefore attitude toward him determined one's position in the universe: "He that gathereth not with me scattereth."[4] "Men of the olden time who repented at lesser light shall condemn this generation. For this reason the Kingdom shall be taken away from you and given to another nation. For this rock is a talisman of men and of nations."[5] "All power is given unto me not only on earth (for instance, to forgive sins), but, even in heaven. He that confesses me on earth I shall confess him in heaven." The angels are not only under him, but they are his (The Son of man shall send forth *his* angels). "The greatest men of the Old Testament are related to me as slaves [δοῦλοι] to a son."[6] He not only has in himself the power of working miracle, but he imparts it to others. The Ritschlians doubt 28. 20 because it gives him the power of spiritual presence everywhere, but he already claims it in 18. 20. Besides he has proved it, and their subjective criticism dissolves before facts. He is the touch-

---

[4] Luke 11. 23.
[5] See Matt. 21. 43, 44.
[6] See 21. 33ff.

stone of eternal destiny.[7] Therefore he (not simply God the Father) shall render to every man according to his deeds, though the glory in which he shall come, he says, is the glory of God the Father, for he, and not the latter, is the judge and decider of fates. Much more than that, he himself sends forth the promise of the Father upon his disciples who must tarry till they receive that power.[8] And not in the name of God the Father, but in his name remission of sins is to be preached in all nations (verse 47). Thus, as that vast scholar and guileless and impartial spirit, the simple-hearted Dorner, said, "His disciples recognized the inner majesty of his nature ever more surely, and also received the external seal of the same in his transfiguration and resurrection, as well as in his miraculous deeds. Thus out of the lowliness of his earthly manifestation, a divine depth and height of his nature streamed forth, and this unity of the divine and human in him the disciples proclaim as the foundation of the salvation of the world."[9] One might almost eliminate the birth, the resurrection, and the ascension from the synoptic Gospels, yet from these alone a merely human Jesus is impossible. In all essentials he is as divine in these as in John. He alone knoweth the Father and the Father alone knoweth the Son, and no one shall ever know the Father except as the Son reveals him —and when that is said all is said that can be said about the divinity of Christ.[10]

Our liberal friends have met the synoptic testimony in three ways. First, they have denied it. The synoptists taught a human Jesus. I heard Weinel

---

[7] Luke 20. 17, 18. [8] Luke 24. 49.
[9] *System of Christian Doctrine*, vol. iii, pp. 166, 167. [10] Matt. 11. 27.

JESUS—I

in Bonn (he later went to Jena) in a crowded public university lecture say that the Jesus of the fourth Gospel was entirely different from the Jesus of the synoptists. Both could not be the real Jesus. *Entweder oder:* take your choice. But it seems to me that this helps only those who close their eyes to the actual testimony of the three Gospels. Then, others besides scholars have a witness here: there is the innumerable company of humble Christians in all ages and all lands who have fed their souls on these Gospels, have lived upon them and laid their heads upon them when dying, and they have never been conscious of the cleft between the Jesus of Mark and Luke and the Jesus of John: both human and both divine. Were the Gospels written for a knot of rationalists? Has the Christian democracy no witness here? Also, why should not men's understanding of Christ grow? The Lincoln of Tarbell is larger than the Lincoln of Raymond. Hampson's Wesley expanded into the Wesley of Moore, and you will never know Socrates until you have read the Mark of Xenophon and the John of Plato. How much more may this be true of One greater!

Second, our modernists have alleged interpolation of these deeper passages in the synoptists. But this is too short and easy. No one knows they are interpolations, because they are in all the manuscripts, and we are afraid to trust subjective surmises. Then the objection does not go far enough. There is an undertone through these Gospels, a key that strikes eternity, a background of divinity everywhere, an interwoven web of transcendence, which would remain. How can you get rid of that? If you read of the steam engine in Matthew, you know it is an

MODERNISM AND THE CHRISTIAN FAITH

interpolation, for the steam engine was not invented till 1655, or, better, 1699. But when you read that in his own name Christ drove out evil spirits who owned his majesty as that of the Son of God, you cannot call that passage ungenuine, for it is congruous with all the rest of the Gospel. The interpolation method would have to go so far that nothing would be left.

Third, the deeper passages are explained by a kind of indwelling of God in Christ. A part of the synoptic narrative might thus find its solution: no one would deny that God could endow a man with such spiritual power and insight that, like a better Xavier, he could do wonderful things and, like a better Edwards, throw a regnant influence out. By the power of the Spirit, who was not given to him by measure,[11] of course the Father dwelt in Christ in a wonderful way. But that does not explain Christ. All the pious know that God dwells in them, but not one of them knows that he dwells in God. That was the uniqueness of Jesus, this reciprocity of knowledge, of fellowship, of being, between God and Christ, to be explained only by the fact that n the depths of their life they were one—Father and Son. No one knoweth the Father save the Son. The endowment or indwelling theory is attractive to the modern man, but it lacks one special modern qualification—it does not explain all the facts.

2. The first literary monument of Christianity (in time) is the epistles of Paul, who within about twenty years of Christ's death sent out his first epistles. Now, even the liberal acknowledges that Paul held to the full divinity of Jesus. As one of them says:

---
[11] See John 3, 34.

JESUS—I

The Son of David, of whom even Paul incidentally speaks (Rom. 1. 3f.) is pushed back by his representation of the Son of God, of the Man from Heaven, who brings the new, the spiritual, the heavenly world. Before he took upon himself the form of a slave and came out in the image of a man, the Christ was the form of God in heaven (Phil. 2. 6f.). He is the mediator of all things, through him is the world created (1 Cor. 8. 6). This Pauline Christ is, then, a divine preexisting being, and concerning the manner of his preexistence Paul cherishes views which are closely related with those of contemporary Jewish philosophers. The divine being of whom he speaks he does not indeed call Logos; but if the word is lacking, the thing is not lacking."[12]

It is true that Wernle says that Paul looks upon Christ as "lower than God himself," but he immediately adds that he is for Paul "the God who actively works in the world," and farther on he describes Paul as holding to "the heavenly Son of God who was crucified," etc., besides making the Johannine and Pauline Christ practically the same.[13] Paul distinguishes indeed between God in the absolute sense and Christ, as in the classical passage, "Yet to us there is one God, the Father, of whom are all things, and we unto him; and one Lord, Jesus Christ, through whom are all things, and we through him."[14] But that is only to preserve the oneness of God as centering in the Father, and is not meant at all as derogating from Christ as a part of that oneness. It is disputed whether Paul actually calls Christ God. The most natural translation and interpretation of Rom. 9. 5 makes God refer to the preceding Christ, but there is a bare possibility that it is to be understood (as R. V. margin) as a doxology to God the

---

[12] G. Krüger, *Das Dogma von der Dreieinigkeit und Gottmenscheit in seiner Geschichtlichen Entwicklung Dargestellt*, Tubingen, 1905, pp.85, 86.

[13] Wernle, *Beginnings of Christianity*, tr., 1904, vol. ii, pp. 147, 148, 250, 252.   [14] 1 Cor. 8. 6.

MODERNISM AND THE CHRISTIAN FAITH

Father. But one in whom the whole fullness of the Godhead dwells bodily[15] could well be called God, and one who was in the "form" or substance of God ($μορφή$, not form in our sense of external shape, but in the Greek sense of essence or being, Phil. 2. 6), could naturally be called God. To Paul Christ's state as slave was just as truly real ($μορφή$, verse 7) as his state as God was truly real ($μορφή$, verse 6). For this reason in one breath he will call God our Saviour and Christ Jesus our Saviour,[16] and a little farther along he looks for the blessed hope and appearing (no one looked for the appearing of the Father) of the great God and our Saviour Jesus Christ, or of our great God and Saviour Jesus Christ (2. 13). Whichever we translate it, it makes Christ God or equal with God, and is blasphemy unless he was so.

Now, the significance of an almost fanatical Jew, a man who boasted of his Judaism all his life, and held it aloft as his palladium,[17] assigning divinity to Christ from the beginning of his mission to its end, taking it for granted as a part of his new heritage, with not the slightest feeling of incongruity, with no impulse to defend it or apologize for it, living in it as to the manner born, never stating it as doctrine to be believed, but always stating or presupposing it as something believed so firmly and unanimously as that the contrary never comes to his mind—this is one of the miracles of history. As a historical fact it is of overwhelming significance. Later there came to be a small section of Jewish Christians who held Jesus as a prophet alone and not as the Son of God. But Paul never heard of them. His opponents among his brother Jewish believers, against whom he con-

---

[15] Col. 2. 9.   [16] Titus 1. 3, 4.   [17] Rom. 9. 1-5; 11. 1.

JESUS—I

tended so manfully for the freedom of the Gentiles from the Mosaic law, never threw into his face his belief in Jesus as divine, for they also held it, and therefore at the apostolic council in Acts 15 neither this nor any other doctrine of Paul came up for discussion. As an American takes for granted the full right of his republic, so Paul and his contemporary Christians took for granted the full right of Jesus to divinity. After giving the correct explanation of Gal. 1. 6, 7 and 2 Cor. 11. 4, Hoennicke says:

As it never appears from the epistles of Paul that his view of the Person of Jesus was ever attacked, so there are never found there polemic discussions against the false doctrine of the Judaizers in regard to the person of Jesus. Only in a general way Paul accuses them that in a selfish way they make gain out of the word of God (2 Cor. 2. 17), that they are caught in Jewish prejudices (3. 13; 4. 4; 11. 15, 22). If against this one refers to 13. 3, where Paul says of Christ, "Who to you-ward is not weak, but is powerful in you," one can as little draw the conclusion that the Judaizers doubted this property of the Crucified. So there is not a passage in the epistles of Paul where the apostle had any strife on the nature (or essence, Wesen) of Christ. Accordingly, one ought not to speak of a "second gospel which is another" which the Judaizers proclaimed. How they individually thought of the person of Jesus is not distinctly evident from the sources. Perhaps they laid the chief weight upon Jesus' sonship of David, and emphasized his conservative attitude on the law and Judaism. That they did not place in the foreground of their preaching the saving worth of the death of Christ, that they did not share in general the significance which on principle Paul ascribed to the death on the cross, appears from Gal. 6. 12.[18] [Gal. 6. 12 may imply that, but not altogether that.]

As we go into the religious ideas of the first churches gathered in Acts we find them equally at home in

---
[18] *Das Judenchristentum im 1n. und 2n. Jahrhundert*, 1908, 209. McGiffert is to be corrected as to this. See Faulkner in *Methodist Review*, New York, December, 1912, pp. 975-977.

MODERNISM AND THE CHRISTIAN FAITH

the divinity of Christ. It was a lesson they learned easily. Jesus is exalted at the right hand of God, has received of the Father the promise of the Holy Spirit, and has poured forth that Spirit on the day of Pentecost. God hath made him Lord and Christ, or Messiah. In his name are repentant sinners to be baptized unto the remission of sins. In his name the lame are made to walk. Though he is called the Servant of God, he is in the next verse the Holy and Righteous One and the Prince of life. It is his Spirit whom Sapphira and Ananias try, and his angel who opens the prison doors. God has placed him on high as a Prince and Saviour to give repentance and remission of sins, salvation being his gift. We ourselves have witnessed these things, and so does the Holy Spirit, whom God hath given to them that obey him. For this reason Stephen saw the Son of man standing on the right hand of God, the full meaning of which the Jews knew right well, for at such a horrible blasphemy they rushed upon him and, according to their law, stoned him to death.[19] It is not necessary to go farther into Acts. Even in her swaddling clothes the church had in embryo the Trinitarian faith—the earnest of the richness and profundity of her life, of the far future that was to be hers. Paul, therefore, did not make this faith—he found it there at the start; it was not a growth except as to enlargement

---

[19] Acts 2. 23–26, 38; 3. 6. 13–15; 5. 9, 17, 31, 32; 7. 56, 57. See the interesting remark of Bishop McConnell: "Their [disciples at day of Pentecost] idea of the spiritual presence of Christ was so definitely personal as to make a beginning for that doctrine of the Trinity which has been such a sore puzzle to the theologians ever since.... The Spirit must be spoken of in personal terms. The Jesus who had been their Master was the Christ of God still living and touching their lives with direct power."—McConnell, *Personal Christianity* (Cole Lectures), 1914, pp. 30, 31.

JESUS—I

of apprehension. As his divinity was implicit in Christ's consciousness at the beginning, so it was both implicit and explicit in the consciousness of the church in these infant years.

I find interesting remarks by Pfleiderer in explaining these facts away. After speaking of the fact that Paul attributed to God redemption from sin and death by sending his Son, who was a heavenly Spirit, in the form of flesh, to overcome sin and death by his own death and resurrection, and to bring new life in the spirit of God-sonship of mankind, he says:

Since, after his conversion by the Christ-vision, Paul felt himself a "new creation," in whom the old, the flesh, had passed away and a supernatural life had been created out of the heavenly force of the Divine Spirit, so he had seen also in Christ Jesus the origin and prototype of this transformation: the Lord who according to his nature (or essence) was a life-giving Spirit, according to his origin heavenly, appeared upon the earth in the flesh to wipe out the guilt of sin by the devotion of his flesh to death, to dissolve the curse of the law, to break the power of death, and to bring to conquering rule the Spirit of righteousness and of life. Speaking psychologically, we could say: What Paul in his Christ-faith had experienced in himself: that through the giving up of the natural I the true life is won, the life of God-sonship, of peace, joy, freedom, love, inspiration, of this principle of religion Jesus was it, viz., that which Paul saw incorporated in the person of Christ Jesus and revealed typically in his sacrificial death. But this religious and moral "principle" clothed itself for Paul—under the presuppositions of that animistic popular metaphysics which had already led in Jewish theology to a hypostatizing of the divine Wisdom as a personal middle being—in the representation of a personal Spirit-being who, coming down from heaven, took on human form in order through death and the resurrection to become the beginner of a new mankind. With this method of representation the historical ground was already half forsaken, and the foundation was laid for the Gnosticizing Christ-doctrine of the later churchly dogmatics; but for Paul this hypostatizing of the Christ-spirit was only the seasonable form under which the

MODERNISM AND THE CHRISTIAN FAITH

experienced truth of his Christian faith could represent itself to consciousness, and at the same time the means to express the general, superindividual, supernational and supertemporal validity of this truth. Only at this price was the religion of Jesus to be made a universal salvation-blessing for the world, that it as a supertemporal principle should become abstracted from the individual person of the historical Jesus, and this abstraction become personified as Christ-spirit and be transported to heaven.[20]

Yes, Paul certainly saw in Jesus the origin of that new creation which he had felt and known, and Pfleiderer is right in making one source of Paul's Christology his own experience. And that Christology held its subject as divine, as there can be no "life-giving Spirit" but God. The principle and center of that new life was no other than Jesus, not only for Paul, we might add, but for all Christians. But it is not true that Paul got his Christ from Jewish theology, for the regular Jews who represented that theology rejected his Christ, and so far as there was a hypostatizing of the divine Wisdom it was neither popular (but confined to thinkers) nor animistic (but probably Greek-philosophic). But that hypostatizing is very doubtful: it was, rather, personifying through poetic realism. Paul got his Christ not from that source but from his experience, the experience of his brother Christians, the testimony of those who knew Christ, and from revelation. Nor did Paul's Christ leave historical ground. After the ascension and gift of the Spirit the reigning, living Christ was necessarily the object of faith, but that did not mean at all the separation of the historical from the living Christ. Both were looked upon by Paul and by all Christians as one and the same, as the Gospels soon

[20] *Das Urchristentum: seine Schriften und Lehren in geschichtlichem Zusammenhang*, 2 Aufl., 1902, vol. i, pp. 225, 226.

proved, which were written not so much as historical documents in our sense, but as facts necessary for a religious estimate of the glorified Redeemer. Pfleiderer is absolutely right in saying that this primitive conception of Paul, which he shared with the church, was the foundation of the later doctrine, but he is absolutely wrong in saying that that doctrine was Gnosticizing. The church's doctrine and the Gnostics' were a pole apart, but the church's and Paul's were substantially identical. It is interesting that Pfleiderer thinks that Paul's Christ was the only conception that could make Christianity a conquering religion of world-wide destination, but he seems unaware of the sad irony in the confession that the real Jesus-religion which was truth, that is, Pfleiderer's antisupernaturalistic residuum, could have no power, and the later fictitious legendary religion of Paul and the church was the only force which could win in the world. But a personified abstraction —how could that save a dying world? It was the glory of Christianity that the divinity that made the human Jesus conquer the Empire was not "abstracted from the historical Jesus" but both were one in him—the transcendental *and* the historical. Pfleiderer is right in saying a little later that the weight of the religious interest of Paul fell neither on the earthly life of Jesus in general outside of his birth and death, nor on the preexistence of the heavenly Christ Spirit, but upon the exalted life of the resurrected Christ as the "Son of God in power," the "Lord, who is that Spirit." The source of our salvation, in the nature of the case, could not be a dead Christ turned to dust in a Syrian tomb. It was the very essence of the Christian religion that the

MODERNISM AND THE CHRISTIAN FAITH

hopes of mankind should be set on the living Lord, who through the Spirit is the spring of life to all who seek him. On the other hand, the reality of Christ's incarnation, earthly life, and actual resurrection (not simply ghost visions of a floating specter, according to the "modern" theory) was absolutely fundamental with Paul, and was the necessary presupposition of the heavenly life of Christ, the reality of it and the earthly power of it. But it was not more fundamental with Paul than it was with all other Christians. Pfleiderer makes the excellent point[21] that the Gospels tended to preserve Pauline Christianity from being flattened out in vague Gnostic theories and phantasies by keeping it tied to a real history. And all illusions and fantastic religious daydreams break now as then against the solid rock of gospel history. But Paul was no less concerned in the actuality of that history. He refers to it again and again.

---
[21] Vol. i, p. 335.

CHAPTER V
JESUS—II

THE severely ethical and thoroughly Jewish Christian James, immersed in monotheism, distinguishes between Christ and God, as was ordinarily the case with the first Christians, but places Christ in a juxtaposition with God which would be blasphemy if he were not absolutely divine. James describes himself as the slave "of God and of the Lord Jesus Christ" (1. 1). He uses the word "Lord" interchangeably of the Father (1. 5, 7; 3. 9; 4. 9, 10) and of Christ (1. 1; 2. 1; 5. 7, 8, 13). Jesus is the object of faith, and is also "of glory," an epithet which associates him with the ineffable radiance of the Eternal,[1] and which no Jew could have used except of God or the Son of God. The Lord[2] shall raise up the sick. The liberal Ewald acknowledges that in Jesus Christ is not only invested "divine glory," but he is "not to be thought of at all without such divine glory; ... he is none other than the Logos; and we may add, in the sense of the whole New Testament, if he once appeared without this visible heavenly glory, yet at any moment he may now appear with it as the Judge of the world."[3] That a man steeped in Judaism as James the Just was, should have taken the divinity of Christ for granted, so that apparently Christianity could not be thought of without it, is most striking, and especially if James was, as generally held, the brother of Jesus.

---
[1] James 2. 1; compare 1 Cor. 2. 8, and Acts 7. 2.
[2] As, Christ; compare verse 14 and John 6. 39.
[3] *Old and New Testament Theology*, tr., 1888, p. 281.

MODERNISM AND THE CHRISTIAN FAITH

That Peter should have held the same is not so surprising, and yet sufficiently interesting. His first two verses have the germs of the Trinity: "Peter an apostle of Jesus Christ, to the elect . . . according to the foreknowledge of God the Father, in sanctification of the Spirit, unto obedience and sprinkling of the blood of Jesus Christ."[4] Christ is the Son of God ("the God and Father of our Lord Jesus Christ," 1. 3); it is at his revelation—not simply that of God the Father—that the proof of our faith should be found unto praise and glory (verse 7); it was his Spirit which in the prophets testified of his sufferings (verse 11); it is through his resurrection that we have a good conscience (3. 21); he is now at the right hand of God, angels and authorities and powers being made subject unto him (verse 22); God is glorified through him, whose (Christ's) is the glory and dominion for ever and ever (4. 11); God called you into his eternal glory in Christ (5. 10), as though he had no glory except in and for his Son, and it is only while you are in him that the ordinary salutation of Peace can be given (verse 14).

Whatever may be said in the famous debate on the fourth Gospel, the First Epistle of John stands on its own feet. The historian Eusebius in 324 places it among the undisputed books. But it must be remembered that in this discussion on Christ we are simply bringing in witnesses, and in any case we are sure that this whole literature belongs to the earliest age of the church, springs from its heart, and represents its veracious witness. For this tremendous epistle, in which the life of God does not pulsate but rather surges through and through like an Amazon

---
[4] 1 Pet. 1, 2.

JESUS—II

seeking the sea, let us be content to note the prologue and the closing lines:

"That which was from the beginning, that which we have heard, that which we have seen with our eyes, that which we beheld, and our hands have handled, concerning the Word of life (and the life was manifested, and we have seen and bear witness and declare unto you the life, the eternal life, which was with the Father, and was manifested unto us); that which we have seen and heard declare we unto you also, that ye also may have fellowship with us: yea, and our fellowship is with the Father, and with his Son Jesus Christ: and these things we write, that your joy may be made full (1. 1–4). . . . And we know that the Son of God is come, and hath given us an understanding, that we know him that is true, *even in his Son Jesus Christ. This is the true God, and eternal life. Little children, guard yourselves from idols*" (5. 20, 21).

From the literary point of view the Epistle to the Hebrews is the most eloquent writing in the New Testament, written in Greek only second to that of Luke, and representing a width of culture and a catholicity of background not equaled perhaps even by Paul. But the author is immersed in Christian ideas, and his culture, so far from cutting himself off from ideas which are a stumbling-block to the "modern" man, like divinity of Christ and atonement, demands these very facts which he brings out so distinctly. The Sonship of Christ is a favorite thought with him. When God "bringeth in the firstborn into the world, he saith, And let all the angels of God worship him." His angels are winds and fire, their ministries with the same swiftness, effectiveness, and

MODERNISM AND THE CHRISTIAN FAITH

power as these, but of the Son there is another word, even this: "Thy throne, O God, is forever and ever." "And Thou, Lord, in the beginning didst lay the foundation of the earth, and the heavens are the works of thy hands." Though he was Son, yet he learned obedience through suffering. But it was he (not simply God the Father) who became the author of eternal salvation to all that obey not simply the Father but him. The germ of the Trinity is also here. The blood of Christ through the Eternal Spirit offered himself without spot to God. Jesus is also eternal: the same yesterday, to-day and forever. Jesus is Lord, it is through him that we become well pleasing to God, and to him (Christ) be the glory forever.[5]

It has been said (remarks Kähler) that the Epistle to the Hebrews has been influenced by the religious philosophy of Alexandria, and it is true that there is an occasional similarity in the language with Philo, though a literary dependence has never been proved, and there might easily be in part the same presuppositions. The Logos of 4. 12 is not the same with that of Philo nor with that of John 1. The view of Christ in 1. 2f. does not spring from contemporary Jewish-Alexandrian theology, because God is here not thought of as a being who needs any mediation to get in touch with the finite, but as the living God of the Old Testament who works upon the world [notice many quotations or echoes of Old Testament in the epistle]. He proceeds not from the problem of creation or of incommunicableness of God but from the Son, the perfect mediator of revelation, in his elevation over all other mediators—proceeds from him to his position as the Lord of all and the mediator of its origin and preservation. It is his divine or superhuman being which explains the Messianic name "Son of God" as the measure of his elevation over angels and his position at the right hand of God. And as only the very "streaming forth of his glory and impress of his substance" (ἀπαύγασμα τῆς δόξης καὶ χαρακτὴρ τῆς ὑποστάσεως, 1. 3) could sit down at God's

---

[5] Heb. 1; 5. 8, 10; 9. 14; 13. 8, 20, 21.

JESUS—II

right hand, so only that High Priest could appear before God who could offer himself to God through the Eternal Spirit (9. 14, 24), and who thus without beginning and end of life has become a priest in the power of an indissoluble life (7. 3, 16). The author does not bring his Christology in as new knowledge, but as something well understood and taken for granted. He not only refers an Old Testament word of the Eternal Creator to the Son, but, according to the most probable interpretation, and even by means of Psa. 45, expressly applies to him the designation God (1. 8f.). His preexistence as Deity is alleged, and in connection with his position as Lord of the world, and with his salvation-work which began in the days of his flesh, but completed itself in glory.[6]

It is a far cry from that famous decade 1835-45 when Baur fluttered the dovecotes of the church by his portentous reconstruction of apostolic literature and history, though specially reserving the Revelation of John as an indubitable work of the apostle, to our own times—1882, when Völter divided that book into three strata or divisions (all by Christians), that by John the apostle in 65 or 66, with a supplement added three years later, and two others in 129 or 130 and 140; 1886, when young Vischer, of Harnack's seminar, came out with the view that it was a Jewish apocalypse worked over much later by a Christian, a view which fascinated his teacher Harnack;[7] 1893, when the same Völter put forth a new and larger work (*Das Problem der Apokalypse*), and increased the revisions or additions to four, the nucleus by John and the additions in the times of Titus, Domitian, Trajan, and Hadrian, who is the resurrected Nero and the number at the close of chapter 13; 1895, when Gunkel surpassed his predecessors in his

---

[6] Kähler, *Christologie, Schriftlehre*, in *Realencyklopädie*, 3 Aufl., vol. iv, p. 11.

[7] For another judgment on it see *Theologische Litteraturblatt*, 1887, pp. 153-156. In the same year (1886) Völter published a strong pamphlet against Vischer.

MODERNISM AND THE CHRISTIAN FAITH

Schöpfung und Chaos by deriving the conceptions of the book from Babylonia, and the number of the beast from the Hebrew name for the primeval chaos. Even the adventurous spirit of Baur would have been dazed at these later reconstructions of a book, which, according to a thoroughly free and impartial scholar, is one of the simplest, most transparent books "that prophet ever penned."[8] But we cannot go into this interesting territory. Everybody concedes that when Revelation first came into the hands of the Christians (say 68–93) it was their own book, penetrated with their own ideas, fears, hopes, reactions, visions, with their Master standing in its shadows "keeping watch above his own," and that Master looked upon as absolutely divine. "It ought unhesitatingly to be acknowledged that Christ is placed in the Apocalypse on a par with God."[9] "Christ is represented as divine in the strict sense of the term. He is the Alpha and the Omega, the First and the Last and the Living One, that is, the Living One in the absolute sense. He searches the reins and the hearts as God does, and gives to each according to his works. He is the Amen, the Faithful and the True, he is the Son of God, and God is his Father in a unique sense. The language of the Old Testament about God is freely applied to him. When he appears in his glory John falls at his feet as dead. He is constantly coordinated with God. The angels are his messengers, who do his bidding and receive from him praise or rebuke. He is Lord of lords and King of kings. He is also the object of worship not from men

---

[8] Reuss, *History of Christian Theology in the Apostolic Age*, vol. i, p. 370 (1872).

[9] Reuss, *lib. cit.*, vol. i, p. 398.

JESUS—II

only but from the highest ranks of created being, and that is the more significant when we observe how the angel strongly rebukes the prophet for offering him worship, since this must be reserved for God alone."[10]

Lastly, the fourth Gospel. This is so provokingly unlike, and yet in its general effect so provokingly like, the synoptic Gospels that it has been a stumbling-block to critics since Bretschneider in 1820, and especially since Strauss in 1835 and Baur in 1845. But how recent the trouble! That through the long centuries the Christian democracy should have been reading the four Gospels and should have obtained but one impression of their Hero—the Christ of Mark the same as the Christ of John, not two but one, different angles of vision of the one Person—is an historic fact that is most impressive. In fact, the synoptic Christ is so great that he is not only consistent with the Johannine Christ but he demands him. As the day advances the shadows lengthen, as the years went by the vaster he seemed who was worshiped even when on earth. But, in fact, the objections to John's Gospel rest on exaggeration or misunderstanding. Christ is no more "metaphysical" in one than in the others, and the human atmosphere, the manly traits, the matter of fact details, are as real, as insistent, in John as in the others. The sublimating of Jesus into a glorified angel was far from John, who wrote his Gospel to prove as much the humanity as the actual deity of his Master. In John as much as in the others it was the Sonship of Jesus which founded his divinity. Kunze puts this well:

---

[10] Peake, *The Person of Christ in the Revelation of John*, in *Mansfield College Essays*, presented to Fairbairn, 1909, p. 102. See Rev. 1. 4, 5, 17, 18; 2. 18; 5. 11–14; 22. 13.

MODERNISM AND THE CHRISTIAN FAITH

Also in the fourth Gospel the selfwitness of Jesus goes back entirely to the conception of the Son of God as its source and middle point. Nor for a moment does a speculative Logos conception lie at its foundation. Further, the reference of the name Son of God to the Messianic calling is held fast (1. 49; 20. 31). Especially here also the Jesus who stands before us is the man who calls himself the Son of God, and who even in the most general discussions on "the Son" and "the Father" does not speak of the hidden mysteries of the Trinity but first of himself the Son of man (5. 19ff., comp. v. 30). The man Jesus is the Son of God. In fact, with closer testing it must be said that the human form of this relation is more sharply emphasized by John than by the synoptics. Exactly as with them the communion of Jesus with God his Father fulfills itself in thanksgiving and prayer (6. 11; 17. 1), and it is an entire misunderstanding when on account of the well-known word at the grave of Lazarus it is said that Jesus prayed only on account of the people (11. 42).... Further, John shows the thoroughly personal and therefore ethical character of Christ's Sonship. Of course he does not make himself a Son by his own deed—for that would be the deepest contradiction to his being a Son, but he constantly asserts himself in his God-Sonship, in the love of his Father, through the constant never-interrupted affirmation and fulfilling of the will of God until the giving up of his life (8. 29; 10. 17; 15. 10). Even here lies the fact to which Christ constantly testifies in John that both in his having and in his acting he is determined not by himself but absolutely by God his Father. The principle that a man has nothing except what is given him from above (19. 11, comp. 3. 27), he turns without limitation upon himself. Though he dares to call and does call the greatest that God is his own, yet it is his own in that it is given him by God, by the Father who loves him (5. 20, comp. 3. 35). The life that he has in himself, the life that he is, has yet been given him by the Father (5. 26); the miracles that he does the Father gives him (5. 36); not even his word and doctrine are his own but His who sent him (7. 16; 14. 24); in fact, everything which is his is given him by his Father (17. 7).... Altogether inverted, therefore, is the view that the fourth Gospel omits the Gethsemane prayer because it is inconsistent with its Jesus picture. On the contrary, Christ speaks through the whole Gospel as the thoroughgoing law of his life,

JESUS—II

"Not my will, but thine be done." Therefore it is in this very Gospel that the modern Christology finds its best proofs.[11] [In other words, John, as Athanasius, is true to the real doctrine of Sonship, that Christ derives his divinity from God the Father, who is the eternal fountain of deity. See below, p. 108.]

It is often said that the fourth Gospel in its Logos, or Word (1. 1, 14), derives from Alexandrian Greek conceptions, and thus imports a foreign element into Christianity. This is truer on the surface than it is at the bottom. There is no doubt that in his elder years at Ephesus the author was acquainted with the Logos thought, even perhaps with that of his contemporary, the Jew-Greek philosopher of Alexandria, Philo, but it is undeniable that so far as there were historic antecedents for John's Logos they were Jewish and not Greek.[12] As the Greek language was the one common mode of intelligent intercourse throughout the whole Roman empire, so Hellenic ideas were everywhere; but Harnack is right when he says that while writers of the New Testament betray the influence of the mode of thought and culture which resulted in the Hellenizing of the East, it is equally "clear that specifically Hellenic ideas form the presuppositions neither of the Gospel itself nor of the most important New Testament writings." So far as an earlier mode of thought influences the New Testament, the latter is "determined by the spirit of the Old Testament (Psalms and Prophets) and Judaism."[13] As for Philo, his Logos has but little resemblance to John. A Scotch scholar has admirably stated the contrast, which I might thus

---
[11] *Die Ewige Gottheit Jesu Christi*, 1904, pp. 31-33.
[12] J. Rendel Harris has shown this in Expositor, London, *The Origin and Prologue of St. John's Gospel*, published separately, 1917.
[13] *History of Dogma*, vol. i, p. 48, note (tr., 1895).

condense: The Logos of Philo is metaphysical, abstract, intermediate, used by God as instrument, impersonal or personified, impossible of incarnation, never brought into relation with history any more than the incomprehensible God. The Logos of John is religious, has to do with life and history, not intermediate between God and the world, but God or toward God as agent in creation, and creator, source of all life and intelligence, personal and incarnate. "Philo affirms the absolute incomprehensibility of God; but it is the prime object of the evangelist to declare that God is revealed in Christ, and that the Logos is the unveiling through the flesh of man the self-manifesting deity. John's Logos is instinct with life and energy from the beginning, and it is the very heart of his Gospel to declare as the very center of life and history the great historical event of the incarnation which is to recreate the world and reunite man and God.... The most probable view is that Philo and John found the same term current in Jewish and Gentile circles and used it to set forth their respective ideas; Philo, following his predilections for Greek philosophy, to give a Hellenic complexion to his theory of the relation of the Divine Reason to the universe; John, true to his Hebrew instincts, seeing in the Logos the climax to that revelation of God to man of which the earlier Jewish theophanies were but partial expressions."[14]

---

[14] Alexander, article, "Logos," in *International Standard Bible Encyclopædia* (1915), iii, 1916. See the contrasts also admirably stated in Kirn, "Logos," in *Realencyklopädie*, 3 Aufl., vol. xi, pp. 602, 603, with literature in both articles. See also Gloag, *Presbyterian and Reformed Rev.*, 1898, 46ff. Aal in his *Logos*, Leipz., 1896, 204f., 213f., speaks of Philo's failure to connect Logos with Messiah, its subordination to the divine wisdom, and the impersonal nature of his being.

JESUS—II

At the close of a long life of reflection on Christ and of experience of him, helped doubtless by his written memoranda of his words and deeds, John writes a Gospel in which the human and divine in Jesus come to their full rights. Neither is shelved for the other. Beyschlag is at fault in saying[15] that Jesus rejects the inference of the Jews that he made himself equal with God in 5. 18 and 10. 33, for the point of Jesus's reply is not that he did not claim divinity, but that in whatever he claimed he did not rob God of his peculiar honor and power. His Sonship was the guarantee of both his divinity and of his rendering full honor to the Father. For that reason he not only allows Thomas's "My Lord and my God!" but praises it as a true expression of faith (20. 28f.). "The man Jesus cannot be the Son of God without being God, and he cannot be God without being from eternity."[16] And that preexistence is witnessed by Jesus in 8. 58 (compare past tense "heard" in verse 26); 16. 28; 17. 5, 24.

This will do for the New Testament. It is certainly a striking spectacle: this unanimity of judgment concerning Jesus in all this literature from Mark to John, from Thessalonians to Timothy, Peter, and Apocalypse. In these basal writings, in which the Spirit of God moves and burns in living fire, Jesus's divinity is expressed in unequivocal word. I have not even mentioned the fact that he is worshiped, or is an object of prayer and faith[17] (Christians are

---
[15] *Neutestamentliche Theologie*, 2 Aufl., vol. i, p. 253.

[16] Kunze, *lib. cit.*, p. 36.

[17] Acts 7. 59; 9. 14; Phil. 2. 10; Rom. 10. 9; 1 Cor. 1. 2. Pliny, *Ep.* 95: *Christo tanquam Deo carmina dicunt.* Perhaps the best discussion of this is T. Zahn, *Die Anbetung Jesu im Zeitalter der Apostel*, in *Skizzen aus dem Leben der alten Kirche*, 1893, 3 Aufl., 1908, pp. 271–308.

MODERNISM AND THE CHRISTIAN FAITH

those who call on the name of the Lord). Was the whole first church, Jewish and Gentile, mistaken as to this? Was their placing Christ as the center of the Christian's hopes, the end of their faith, the life of their lives, the very foundation of their whole venture as Christians, a fond thing vainly invented, a deception, a horrible idolatry? The modern so-called liberal Jesus means that. But it seems to me that this is like building a pyramid on its apex. Simply a human Jesus whether filled with God or not as little explains the history of New Testament times as it satisfies the literature of those times. Without an absolutely divine Saviour from sin in whom to trust, the movement would have lacked dynamic and the literature truth and substance. It was the certainty of salvation in him which sent that far-flung line from Jerusalem to Spain even in the first century, and which gives the sense of triumph in the literature which we feel to this hour. For him they suffered "hardship with the gospel according to the power of God; who saved us, and called us with a holy calling, not according to our works, but according to his own purpose and grace, which was given us in Christ Jesus before times eternal, but hath now been manifested by the appearing of our Saviour Christ Jesus, who abolished death, and brought life and immortality[18] to light through the gospel, whereunto I was appointed a preacher, and an apostle, and a teacher. For which cause I suffer these things: yet I am not ashamed; for I know him whom I have believed, and I am persuaded he is able to guard that which I have committed unto him against that day."[19]

---

[18] Revised Version, margin, "incorruption."
[19] 2 Tim. 1. 8–14.

JESUS—II

That I have not exaggerated the early Christians' high judgment of Jesus as divine is acknowledged by an eminent scholar of the liberal school, the late Professor Johannes Weiss (son of Bernhard), who was taken away in his prime in the early part of the Great War. He is speaking of the fact that a growth in the estimate of Christ is hardly to be traced, that it started at the full. He says:

A progressive development is hardly to be observed. In the shortest time the system of Christology is complete. Already in the New Testament lie at bottom all the chief thoughts of the later dogma, even if in part only in the germ; and all the difficulties which the later church had to carry are here to be traced.... This looking upon God and Christ side by side with each other, which corresponds exactly to the enthroning together of both, is significant for original Christian piety.... The historian must say that Christianity from the earliest beginnings, by the side of faith in God the Father showed also the worship of Christ as the form of religion which was perfectly natural to it. The ancient Christians believed themselves to be acting altogether in the sense of Christ when they worshiped him and sang hymns to him "as to God."[20]

The eminent liberal (Ritschlian) Harnack says bluntly that the "earliest tradition not only spoke of Jesus as κύριος (Lord), σωτήρ (Saviour), and διδάσκαλος (Teacher), but as ὁ υἱὸς τοῦ θεοῦ (the Son of God), and this name was firmly adhered to in the Gentile Christian communities. It followed immediately from this that Jesus belongs to the sphere of God, and that as is said in the earliest preaching known to us [the so-called second epistle of Clement], one must think of him as one thinks of God, ὡς περὶ θεοῦ. This formula describes in a classic manner the indirect theologia Christi which we find unanimously expressed in all

[20] *Christus, die Anfänge des Dogmas*, 1909, pp. 4, 5, 25.

MODERNISM AND THE CHRISTIAN FAITH

witnesses of the earliest epoch."[21] He says also that Christ "never was as θεός (God) placed on an equality with the Father—monotheism guarded against that" (p. 189), which is true in the sense that the Christians looked upon the Father as the spring of the life of the Son, and therefore held the latter subordinate to the former both in their philosophy and religion. For this reason they ordinarily kept the title "God" for the Father, and generally prayed not to Christ directly, but to the Father through Christ. But so thoroughly did Christ in their thought share in the fullness of Deity, that this custom was frequently broken into, so that both in the New Testament (see above, p. 109) and in the postapostolic literature Christ is called God and is the object of faith, prayer, and worship. Harnack also calls attention to different uses of the word "God" (pp. 119ff., 189 note 1), but it must be remembered that all the first Christians were Jews and earnest monotheists, and those who came later were the near or distant disciples of the Old Testament and abhorred idolatry; but all equally not only looked upon the Son as in theory truly divine but worshiped him with passionate loyalty as the One who filled the whole horizon of their faith.

I intended in this chapter to take up the postapostolic conception of Christ say at least till about 200, but space forbids. Suffice it to say that except a small section of the extreme Jewish Christians (Ebionites, or a part of them), who held to a human Christ only, and except a party who came out about 180 or 190 who said that Christ received divinity in part at his baptism, more fully at his resurrection

---
[21] Harnack, *lib. cit.*, vol. i, p. 186.

JESUS—II

or ascension, the general view carried on the New Testament tradition. If the reader will turn to the fourth and fifth chapters of the admirable little book on Christ by the Professors of Andover Theological Seminary, he will find an historical study of the early church view by an expert on the subject, the late Professor Egbert C. Smyth, one of the broadest, most catholic and Christian spirits of our time.[22] Harnack in speaking of this time says that the "common confession did not go beyond the statements that Jesus is the Lord, the Saviour, the Son of God, that we must think of him as of God, that dwelling now with God in heaven he is to be adored as guardian and helper of the weak and as High Priest of our oblations, to be feared as the future Judge, to be esteemed most highly as the bestower of immortality, that he is our hope and our faith."[23] This general view crystallized as a baptismal, and instruction confession between 100 and 150 in the so-called Apostles' Creed, where we have the historic faith—the Father as God and head of Deity, Jesus as his Son and our Lord, and the Holy Spirit, etc.

Where did believers get this faith? Not from Greek philosophy, which the most of them did not know. Not from pagan so-called Christs and deities, because the Christians at this time despised paganism with its gods and half-gods (much later they took over pagan customs and ideas). Not from Jewish personified Wisdom, which was too pale and far off for this vital and concrete faith in Him who was nearer to them than hands and feet. Not from the

---

[22] *The Divinity of Jesus Christ: an Exposition of the Origin and Reasonableness of the Belief of the Christian Church*, Boston: Houghton, 1893, pp. 62–132.

[23] *Lib. cit.*, pp. 189, 190.

MODERNISM AND THE CHRISTIAN FAITH

New Testament, because it antedated the New Testament and produced it. Not from theology or speculation, because it was the faith of the multitude, who were always inclined, in fact, to so emphasize the deity of their Lord that his actual life in and with the Father vanished, and Jesus and the Father became coterminous, became one and the same. No; not from these did the Christian Church get her faith in Christ. She got it from her own life, or, more correctly, she had her own life because he lived, and in her life his divinity manifested itself. He was the origin, the support, the strength of that life. Theories to explain him came and went. If the theory threatened to change the faith, it slowly disappeared. But the faith remained, because the life fed by Christ remained. "The life of the church is from the life of Christ. It believes and always has believed that in him is the Eternal Life, and that he can and does give this life to all who hunger and thirst for righteousness and for God. The divinity of Christ as a doctrine lives not only by apostolic testimony, but in this perpetuated experience."[24]

Even the so-called liberal or modern in his higher moments feels this absoluteness of Jesus as divine. "It is in accordance with the mind of Jesus," says Harnack, "and at the same time a fact of history that this gospel [whether the Gospel of Christ or the gospel concerning Christ] can only be appropriated and adhered to in connection with a believing surrender to the person of Jesus Christ. . . . The peculiar character of the Christian religion is conditioned by the fact that every reference to God is at the same time a reference to Jesus Christ, and vice versa. In

---

[24] Andover Professors (here means Smyth), *Divinity*, etc., p. 132.

JESUS—II

this sense the Person of Christ is the central point of the religion and inseparably united with the substance of piety, as a sure reliance on God. ... The Christian religion knows and names only one name before which it bows. ... Just because the Person of Christ has this significance, is the knowledge of the historical Christ required."[25] Think that through, Herr von Harnack, and you have the historic faith. Logically, Athanasius never said any more.

The youngest of that famous Nitzsch family of systematic theologians—three generations, himself of the modern school—makes the point that the "essential deliverances of faith concerning Christ spring from Christian experience, and yet not in the sense that they cannot also become the possession in possibility of those standing outside. Therefore even simply historical or scientific studies of the life of Jesus are not worthless. But it is something different to know how Jesus became the founder of the Christian religion, something else to feel him as the correlate of one's own religious self-consciousness; and that cannot come to pass unless the community of believers take hold of him as the root of their being, and the individual takes hold of him as the origin and cause of his assurance of salvation. Because in him as the representative of God, by his whole lifework, God himself perfectly makes known his gracious will of love and makes it active, because he as the revealer of God also shows the way of God in the fullness of love and holiness of his personal use of his calling, and thus evinces himself as the Son of God or as the Godman, the faith of the Christian society confesses a unique being of God in him; but this corresponds

---
[25] *Harnack, lib. cit.*, pp. 71, 72.

MODERNISM AND THE CHRISTIAN FAITH

to his self-consciousness, his ethical lifework, his moral personality. He is not only the representative of God toward man, but also the head and representative of man toward God. He is the ground of our salvation because by founding the forgiveness of sins, communication of the Holy Spirit, and with that the impartation of redeeming force to self-active life of love and moral striving, he founded the rule of God or the Kingdom of God in humanity, and placed it secure in his empire-society."[26]

Weighty words are these by Nitzsch. Study them. They show how to candid and spiritually minded Ritschlians Christ breaks down the boundaries reared by their master, and you get in its logical drive at least the historic view: "the correlate of one's religious self-consciousness;... the society of believers takes hold of him as the root of its being, and believers as both the origin and cause of their salvation;... the Godman;... the unique *being* (not simply revelation) of God in him;... he founds the forgiveness of sins;... he communicates the Holy Spirit." Who but God could do and could mean all that? And that was the Christ of the early Christians. That was the Christ they confessed, they worshiped, and for whom they died. And because they did so the society he founded and they established exists to-day.

[26] F. A. B. Nitzsch, *Lehrbuch der Evangelische Dogmatik*, 1892, pp. 454, 455.

CHAPTER VI

JESUS: QUESTIONS AND ASPECTS

Supposing there is any truth in the doctrine of the Trinity, what was the condition of the latter when the so-called second member of it was on earth? The incarnation of the Son, it is said, would make an unthinkable rupture in the life of God. Only on a false conception of the Trinity which comes to us in the wake of the modern meaning of "person." There is nothing irrational in the incarnation of that Element or Person or Moment in the rich and complex life of the Godhead which we call the Son or the Word. Such incarnation abated nothing from the infinite being of God, which flowed still full and free in the everlasting reaction of Father, Son, and Spirit. While the Son was made flesh in Jesus of Nazareth, he was still in and with God, dwelling in his bosom, even while on earth yet in heaven.[1] The incarnation was not a change in God; it was only (if I might so say) deification of man.

What about the Two Natures? It was not till October 22, 451, that we got the doctrine of the Two Natures in Christ stated with delightful fullness and mathematical precision in the fifth session of the Council of Chalcedon—so full and precise that the question involuntarily occurs to us, O Fathers of Chalcedon, who told you so much about Christ? Where did you get your rare knowledge? The same completeness of information and particularity of phras-

---
[1] Luke 10. 22; John 3. 13.

MODERNISM AND THE CHRISTIAN FAITH

ing (though the word "substance" instead of "nature)" occurs in the chantlike falsely called Athanasian Creed, with its rolling clauses so tempting to the musician. Now, over against the heresies against which these two creeds were directed even the Unitarian would say that these Fathers struck the golden mean. And it is an interesting fact that the heresies which were thrown out at the different ecumenical councils have not only no vogue to-day in the West, but no one thinks of reviving any one of them, while thousands of saints and scholars still hold to the ecumenical creeds—a striking justification of the old Fathers in the result they reached in their now much-abused creeds. Yet for me the discussions after 325 have mainly historical interest only. When once the divinity of Christ is established the other questions can take care of themselves. And this is the trend of theology, which is not interested in the Two Natures, or thinks it an insufficient formula, or beyond what is written. It is said too that psychology knows no full nature without personality, and two natures mean two persons. The Chalcedon utterance has fallen on evil days.

However, when one takes the question out of its historic frame and looks at it *de novo*, the idea of two natures is not so absurd. Did Christ have a human nature? Of course. Did he have a divine nature? All who believe in his divinity answer, "Why, certainly." Did Christ have two personalities? No one asserts it. What is a nature? An assemblage of qualities. Did Michelangelo have an artist's nature? No question. Did he have an engineer's? Look at his fortifications of Florence. Did he have the poetic nature? Read his sonnets. Byron had an animal

JESUS: QUESTIONS AND ASPECTS

nature, a poetic nature, and a patriot's nature. There is no strain on faith to say that Christ had both a human and divine nature, providing he was both human and divine. But if he was a man only—ah, there you are in another sphere. Or if he was a man filled with God, you have no problem. So was Francis of Assisi; so was Edwards. Every bush is aflame with God.

What was the basis of Christ's personality, the human or the divine? If and when he was preexistent with the Father, then the divine was the substratum; in his human life, the human. If the incarnation was real, and not docetic, the basis of the Christ on earth was human. But while this is so, it is only a half-truth. For even a superficial study of Christ reveals that his humanity, though it was as genuine as ours, was different from ours. The sources show that it was sinless, that it was the organ of the Son of God, that it was universal; in other words, it was divine. Therefore the center of his person was not human merely, nor divine merely, but human-divine and divine-human. It was humanity at its best, as it existed in God from eternity, and though absolutely real as humanity, and therefore not a veil for his divinity, was yet unique. That is the impression our sources give us. As to anything further, perhaps modesty becomes us. We can fathom no personality. Should we seek to strip the mystery from Christ's?

What was the relation of Christ to the Logos, the Word? Here perhaps I can do no better than to quote the words of an able liberal, Dr. George Harris, formerly Abbot professor of Christian theology in Andover Theological Seminary, later president of Amherst College.

MODERNISM AND THE CHRISTIAN FAITH

God reveals himself. The absolute has as a characteristic, a power, *a mode of being* [italics mine], this that he communicates and reveals himself to finite intelligences. This revealing principle or power is called the Word, which, as John says, was from the beginning with God and was God. It is the doctrine of the Logos. It was the Word or Logos through which the worlds were created, those revelations of God which have no speech nor language, whose voice is not heard, but whose sound has gone forth into all the world.... Christ is the highest revelation of God, bringing in the absolute love and goodness.... With him the Word or Logos is specially identified. All the lower revelations were foreshadowings of the highest, pointing to it and preparing the way for it, and were expressions of the revealing Word, all discerning one purpose and emanating from one mind. The same Word, or Logos, which made possible the existence of the worlds, and which was concerned in the history of the chosen people and of all peoples, was manifested in Jesus Christ, in whom the Word became flesh. The revelation is one; the purpose is one; the higher includes the lower. This view of the progressive revelation of God from power to righteousness and from righteousness to love, is in agreement with what has already been indicated of the ascending order of revelation in nature, in history, in Christ.... Several books of the New Testament begin with the truth of revelation advancing from the creation of the world to the incarnation.... They associate the very existence of the universe with redemption through Christ, boldly declaring that the world was created in and through and unto the Word or the Son, and subsists or is held together in him, who, as realizing its ends, is vitally related to its very existence.[2]

What is the Kenosis, the self-emptying of Christ? In a famous passage, Paul says (see above, p. 92): "Have this mind in you, which was also in Christ Jesus: who, existing in the form of God, counted not the being on an equality with God a thing to be grasped, but emptied [ἐκένωσεν] himself, taking the form of a servant,[3] being made in the likeness of

[2] Professors in Andover Theological Seminary, *The Divinity of Jesus Christ*, Boston, 1893, pp. 184–186.

[3] Revised Version, margin, "bondservant."

JESUS: QUESTIONS AND ASPECTS

men."[4] Was this a kenosis or emptying of the divine part of Christ, of his preexistent glory, or, after having come, an emptying in abandoning or not using the divine powers which were still his. Here again actual facts will help us. Christ did, in the opinion of the early Christians, leave the glory he had with God the Father and become poor for our sakes. Besides that, he renounced the selfish using of prerogatives which he had in essence in his earthly estate, and as an infant, child, man, illustrated the condition of one who serves. Both interpretations of the kenosis are true, then. The normal development of Jesus as a human being was itself a kenosis. Kahnis says well:

> Evidently, the fundamental failure of the old dogmatics, which it shared, of course, with the ancient and mediæval theology, was that it thought of the divine nature of Christ in full possession of its divine attributes from conception to death. What did it help that it sought to provide room for a purely human development of the human nature in the state of humiliation, while in that empty room the divine functions and attributes were always pressing? Then, 1840–60, there arose several theologians—Thomasius chief—who said that when the Logos became flesh he gave up his world or universe relations. With this was won a foundation for a truly human development. It was found that Phil. 2. 6ff. meant the kenosis of the Person of the Logos; that is, his glory, not necessarily his attributes, for reason shows that a divine being cannot get rid of himself, and the Gospels show that Jesus still had a divine consciousness, did divine works, and spoke divine wisdom. The assertion of the Kenotics that the Logos emptied himself of the Form of God (Phil. 2. 6f.), his glory (John 17. 5), and his riches (2 Cor. 8. 6) stands exegetically firm and is historically demanded. Positively, this emptying is the incarnation. As he could not, in the nature of the case, lay aside his divine nature, the emptying had to do, rather, with the use of ($\chi\rho\hat{\eta}\sigma\iota\varsigma$) than with the possession ($\kappa\tau\hat{\eta}\sigma\iota\varsigma$) of his divinity—a con-

[4] Phil. 2. 5–7.

dition of which sleep gives us analogies among men. In his slave form Jesus is essentially man, and the predicate God can belong to him only according to his latent Logos nature. The I that thinks as man can also think as a divine person. "Father, glorify thou me with the glory," etc. (John 17. 5). Christ ascribes to himself divine names, powers, rights,[5] etc.

When we leave these questions concerning Christ, which we of to-day must not despise, because some of them have cut a wide swath in history, and take up aspects of Christ, we are first struck with his position as Saviour. Everybody recognizes God the Father as Saviour, but here Christ either takes his place or he and the Father interchange or fade into each other. In a lesser way all Christians are Saviours, just as the Baptist was when he pointed to Christ,[6] and Roman Catholics ascribe attributes to Mary the Mother which makes her Saviour and God ("Have pity upon me, O great Queen, who art called the Mother of Mercy; and, according to the tenderness of that mercy, purify me from mine iniquities. . . . City of God, place thy joy in blessing her," etc.). In fact, "Saviour" was a standing title of the Roman emperor from Caligula to Constantine—Saviour of the whole Human Race—the word and idea were correct coin in that age, I mean as applied to men.[7] But even so, the thought of God or of deification of heroes or of men was included.

The surname σωτήρ (saviour) and σώτειρα (same, female) have been connected with many gods and goddesses—yes, have represented even their proper names. According to Usener, who compares the cult to that of the σώζων peculiar to inner Asia Minor,

---
[5] *Die lutherische Dogmatik*, 2 Aufl.,1875, vol. ii, pp. 81–84 (abridged).
[6] John 1. 29, 32, 36.
[7] Die Heilandsidee ist schon zur Scheidemünze geworden.—Lietzmann, *Der Weltheiland*, Bonn, 1909, p. 18.

JESUS: QUESTIONS AND ASPECTS

there lies at the bottom of this surname an independent God conception.... Everywhere Zeus, Apollos, Asclepios were worshiped as σωτήρ.... A passing view over the wide diffusion of the surname suffices to prepare for that stadium of the development with which we have to do, and for the Christian conception and the time when the Christian propaganda begins, when it is of the highest interest to notice the carrying over of the divine surname [Saviour] upon historic men, who, set in the supernatural sphere, by the conferring of this attribute became heroes or gods.[8]

Even as early as Cicero it was felt that Σωτήρ was a sacred name not lightly to be assumed. He blames Verres for taking it. "I saw him called in an inscription in Syracuse not only the patron of the island but also the Saviour (sotera) of it. How much is this! It is so great that it cannot be expressed in one Latin word. He is in truth a Saviour who has given salvation. In his name days of festival are kept."[9]

It will not be denied, I think, that in the New Testament the word "Saviour" is also a divine title and in the fullest sense. In 1 Tim. 1. 1; 2. 3; 4. 10 it is used of the Father; in 2 Tim. 1. 10 of Christ; while in Titus there is an alternation—of the Father in 1. 3; 2. 10; 3. 4, and of Christ in 1. 4; 2. 13; 3. 6. To the practical sense and spiritual insight of Luther it was one of the chief arguments for our Lord's divinity that he was Saviour and Redeemer. "The one in whom I say, 'I believe and set my trust'— that one must be God."[10] This Luther found in his own conversion—the impulse that made the Reformation, simply trusting in Christ and not in human

---

[8] Wendland, Σωτηρ, in *Zeitschrift für die neutestamentliche Wissenschaft und die Kunde des Urchristentums*, 1904, pp. 336, 337.

[9] Cicero, *In Verrem*, act. 2, book 2, sec. 63, pp. 273, 274, Long's ed. The word "salvator" was not in use in Cicero's time.

[10] Köstlin, *Luthers Theologie*, 2 Aufl., vol. ii, pp. 133, 134, with references.

doings for salvation. How many millions since then have found the same way to eternal life here and hereafter! Says Bunyan:

> After I had been in this condition some three or four days, as I was sitting by the fire, I suddenly felt this word to sound in my heart, "I must go to Jesus." At this my former darkness and atheism fled, and the blessed things in heaven were set in my view. While I was on this sudden thus overtaken with surprise, "Wife," said I, "is there such a scripture, 'I must go to Jesus'?" She said she could not tell; therefore I stood musing still, to see if I could remember such a place. I had not sat above two or three minutes, but that came bolting in upon me, And to an innumerable company of angels, and withal the twelfth chapter of Hebrews, about the Mount Zion, was set before mine eyes.
>
> Then with joy I told my wife, "O! now I know, I know!" But that night was a good night to me; I never had but few better. I longed for the company of some of God's people, that I might have imparted unto them what God had showed me. Christ was a precious Christ to my soul that night. I could scarce lie in my bed for joy and peace and triumph through Christ. This great glory did not continue upon me until morning, yet the twelfth chapter of the epistle to the Hebrews was a blessed scripture to me for many days together after this. The words are these. [He quotes Heb. 12. 22–24.] Through this sentence the Lord led me over and over, first to this word, and then to that; and showed me wonderful glory in every one of them. These words also have oft since that time been a great refreshment to my spirit. Blessed be God for having mercy on me.[11]

When the company was gone (says Charles Wesley, who was ill) I joined with Mr. Bray in prayer and the Scripture, and was so greatly affected that I almost thought Christ was coming that moment. I concluded the night with private vehement prayer. May 13th [1738]. I waked without Christ; yet still desirous of finding him.... At night my brother [John Wesley] came, exceeding heavy. I forced him (as he had often forced me) to sing a hymn to Christ; and almost thought he would come while we

---

[11] Bunyan, *Grace Abounding to the Chief of Sinners* (1666), Morley's ed., 113, 114.

JESUS: QUESTIONS AND ASPECTS

were singing; assured he would come quickly.... May 17. To-day I first saw Luther on the Galatians, which Mr. Holland had accidentally lit upon. We began, and found him nobly full of faith.... I marveled that we were so soon and so entirely removed from him [Paul?] that called us into the grace of Christ unto another Gospel [removed by High Church prejudices from the simple gospel of justification by faith in Christ alone]. Who would believe our Church [of England] had been founded upon this important article of justification by faith alone!... May 18. In the approach of a temptation, I looked up to Christ, and confessed my helplessness. The temptation was immediately beaten down.... May 19.... I received the sacrament, but not Christ.... May 21. I waked in hope and expectation of His coming. At nine my brother and some friends came and sung a hymn to the Holy Ghost. My comfort and hope were hereby increased. In about half an hour they went. I betook myself to prayer: the substance as follows: O Jesus, thou hast said, I will come unto you. Thou hast said, I will send the Comforter unto you. Thou hast said, My Father and I will come unto you, and make our abode with you. Thou art God, who canst not lie. Accomplish it in thy time and manner.... I now found myself at peace with God, and rejoiced in hope of loving Christ....[12]

[May] 14 [1738]. In the evening I went very unwillingly (says John Wesley) to a society in Aldersgate Street [London], where one was reading Luther's preface to the Epistle to the Romans. About a quarter before nine, while he was describing the change which God works in the heart through faith in Christ, I felt my heart strangely warmed. I felt I did trust in Christ, Christ alone for salvation; and an assurance was given me that He had taken away *my* sins, even *mine*, and saved *me* [echo from Luther's Preface, which emphasizes the "me" and the "mine," *personal* appropriation of Christ and assurance] from the law of sin and death.[13]

I have quoted these three celebrated accounts of conversion of men who have had immense influence in history not because of that influence, but because

---

[12] Jackson, *The Life of the Rev. Charles Wesley, M.A.*, 1841, New York ed., 1842, pp. 119-122.

[13] *The Journal of the Rev. John Wesley, A.M.*, ed. Curnock, vol. i, pp. 475, 476 (1909).

MODERNISM AND THE CHRISTIAN FAITH

those conversions through faith in Jesus are normal for practically every conversion from that of Paul till to-day. He who is Saviour is also Lord, and he who is Saviour and Lord is the Son of God. May we not, therefore, say with Peter in answer to our Lord's pathetic inquiry, "Would ye also go away?" "Lord, to whom shall we go? thou hast the words of eternal life. And we have believed and know that thou art the Holy One of God"?[14]

Is not the very idea of incarnation itself a help to faith? We need not the God of the evening star which shines cold and austere in its bitter loneliness, but the God who is the Father of our Lord Jesus Christ. The incarnation means that humanity was always in the Godhead, the eternally divine humanity. For the Christ was not only slain from the foundation of the world,[15] but he was in a sense man from the foundat on of the world. "O for a God with the touch of a man!" we all cry.

> "He who did most shall bear most; the strongest
>   Shall stand the most weak;
> 'Tis the weakness in strength that I cry for;
>   My flesh that I seek
> In the Godhead. I seek and I find it."[16]

This is the everlasting lesson of the numerous pagan attempts—some of them grotesque and detestable—to represent incarnation or earthly representation of gods and goddesses. A God who is not only infinitely above humanity, but also standard for humanity, who pulsates in our hearts and looks out of our eyes, such a God is ours; he is that or he is no God at all. The ellipse God has two foci, divinity and humanity.

---

[14] John 6. 67–69.   [15] Rev. 13. 8, marg. R. V.   [16] Browning, *Saul*.

JESUS: QUESTIONS AND ASPECTS

"The very God! Think, Abib; dost thou think,
So, the All-great were the All-loving too.
So, through the thunder comes a human voice
Saying, 'O heart I made, a heart beats here!
Face, my hands fashioned, see it in myself!
Thou hast no power nor mayest conceive of mine,
But love, I gave thee, with Myself to love,
And thou must love Me who have died for thee.' "[17]

We need not, therefore, be surprised if all genuine revivals of religion were revivals of Christ. Everything was regarded from the standpoint of Christ. Sinners as distinguished from saints or believers were those who had not yet received him as Saviour. They were "out of Christ" (compare Paul's "in Christ"). As a result so many souls were "brought to Christ." Jesus was "passing by." The converted were called "Christians." The famous tract of Newman Hall which came out of the heart of the gospel was called *Come to Jesus*. An eminent divine describes revival preaching as "Gospel preaching, that is, the all sufficiency of our Lord Jesus Christ to save even the chief of sinners, his readiness to cleanse them in his atoning blood, to clothe them with his perfect righteousness, to justify them freely, to sanctify them by his Spirit," etc.—"all this should be set forth in the most clear and persuasive manner."[18] The converts were saved not by believing in God the Father (they were already theists) but by believing in Christ. In fact, these mighty works which have Christianized not only communities but states and civilizations would have been absolutely impossible on the basis of mere theism or Unitarianism. The invitation was

---
[17] Browning, *An Epistle*.
[18] Ashbel Green, letter in Sprague, *Lectures on Revivals*, 2nd ed., 1833, pp. 347, 348.

MODERNISM AND THE CHRISTIAN FAITH

"to come and embrace the Lord Jesus Christ as offered in the gospel."[19] "Christ then appeared more lovely than the princes of this world. They sat under his shadow with great delight, and his fruit was sweet to their taste. They were feasted in his banqueting house, and his banner over them was love. They could not support themselves, many of them, under the weight of it, they were so deeply affected with it. Had not Christ put underneath his everlasting arms for their support I know not but many would have expired under the weight of divine benefits."[20] In the well-known Irish revival of 1859: "brought to the saving knowledge of Christ as his Saviour." "Oh, my sins! my sins! Lord Jesus, have mercy upon my poor soul! O Jesus, come! O Lord Jesus, come!" "No, no. No one can do me good but Jesus Christ." Passages frequently quoted were 1 John 1. 7, John 6. 37. "He saw himself to be a sinner and Jesus to be the one Mediator, and his weary soul found rest in Christ. To use his own words, he 'gave himself up, soul and body, to Jesus and trusted him with all.'"[21] How far the Reformation was a revival of religion is in dispute, but it was certainly a revival of Christ. Mary and the saints were shoved away from between Jesus and humanity, and the True Light streamed upon the world unhindered. The Methodist movement saved England from deism and a reduced Christianity. Every genuine revival is a reproclamation of Christ.

Christ as the center of devotion is another striking

---

[19] Tracy, *The Great Awakening*, 1842, p. 160.

[20] Parsons, contemporary account of revival in Lyme and vicinity, Connecticut, in 1740, quoted in Tracy, p. 144.

[21] Gibson, *The Year of Grace: a History of the Ulster Revival of 1859*, 1860, Jubilee ed., Edinb., 1909, pp. 16, 53, 203, 204, 213.

JESUS: QUESTIONS AND ASPECTS

aspect. From the flush of the church's morning till to-day Christ has been the object of prayer and praise. "They sang a hymn of praise to Christ," says Pliny, while proconsul of Bithynia in his report as to the Christians to the emperor Trajan. The Reformation started a new outburst of hymns to Christ, continued by a noble succession of German writers, and what Methodism did in the same cause is the common heritage of the Christian Church. The continuity, universality, and spontaneity of this worship of Jesus in the prayer, song, and poetry of the church is one of the most interesting things in history. Carlyle says that the "divine mystery, which lies everywhere in all beings, open to all, but seen by almost none," has been "penetrated" by the *Vates*, whether Prophet or Poet. If so, has the *Vates* been mistaken as to the mystery of Christ? "That always is his message [to tell us the divine mystery]; he is to reveal that to us—that sacred mystery which he more than others lives ever present with. While others forget it, he knows it; I might say, he has been driven to know it; without consent asked of him he finds himself living in it, bound to live in it. Once more, here is no Hearsay, but a direct Insight and Belief; this man too could not help being a sincere man! Whosoever may live in the show of things, it is for him a necessity of nature to live in the very fact of things. A man once more, in earnest with the universe, though all others were but toying with it. He is a *Vates*, first of all, in virtue of being sincere. So far Poet and Prophet, participators in the 'open secret,' are one."[22] Yes, the Christian prophets and poets know

---

[22] Carlyle, *On Heroes, Hero-Worship, and the Heroic in History: the Hero as Poet.*

MODERNISM AND THE CHRISTIAN FAITH

Christ. They have not worshiped an idol, nor erected an altar to a mistaken Galilæan enthusiast. The *Vates* penetrated him, though the world did not. "He was in the world, and the world was made through him, and the world knew him not."[23] But the flaming heart and the eye touched by the finger of God knew him.

Jesus's insight into the Father is an aspect of him that abashes us. He not only knows God through and through ("no man hath seen God at any time"), but he boasts of that knowledge.[24] He takes it as a matter of course, and speaks of it as one of the ordinary credentials of his person. Fichte says that Jesus saw the unity of the human with the divine, and that this knowledge is so wonderful that it means that he is the "only begotten and first-born Son of God, and that all ages who are capable of understanding him at all must recognize him in this character." But Jesus's insight went far deeper than that, namely, into the depths of the Eternal himself. Who could thus know God but the Son who is eternally in him and with him?

For this reason Jesus is the only one who mediates with absolute truth and perfection the knowledge of God, the life of God, the salvation of God, and union with God. Even Fichte acknowledges so much: "All those who since Jesus have come into union with God have come into union with God through him. And thus it is confirmed in every way that even to the end of time all wise and intelligent men must bow themselves reverently before this Jesus of Nazareth; and that the more wise, intelligent, and noble

---

[23] John 1. 10.
[24] Luke 10. 21, 22.

JESUS: QUESTIONS AND ASPECTS

they themselves are, the more humbly will they recognize the exceeding nobleness of this great and glorious manifestation of the Divine Life."[25] Yes, great and glorious manifestation, because he *is* the Divine Life. Therefore he can give it, because he gives himself. When we have seen Jesus we have seen the Father, and when we have Jesus we have the Father. In religious functions Jesus cannot be practically coterminous with God without being God —that is, if we are monotheists. But this functioning of Jesus as God in the religious experience of the church from the beginning till to-day is certainly one of the most impressive facts in history. To a soul so meek, so true and loyal to his Father as his, this fact must have been through these ages as gall and bitterness, if he were not in truth the Eternal Son.

Nor can the liberal and Unitarian escape. Except for the very radical, who likes to criticize Christ, Jesus practically takes the place of God.[26] They

---

[25] Quoted by Gordon, *The Christ of To-day*, 1895, p. 26.

[26] This is admitted by the rationalistic and extremely "modern" Lucius Hopkins Miller, who says: "Must not our God be like Jesus of Nazareth? He cannot be inferior to him and remain God; nor can we easily imagine a quality of life superior to that of Jesus. Thus the usual form of the problem is reversed. The modern question is not, Is Jesus like God? but, rather, Is there a God of the same quality of life as that possessed by Jesus? God is the x, the unknown quantity which we are seeking to determine, and it seems most reasonable to hold that Jesus is the known factor through which we are enabled to solve the problem."—*Our Knowledge of Christ*, 1914, p. 161. (By permission of publishers, Holt.) That is, we know God only through Jesus, which means that for practical values Jesus is God. Though Miller's "sympathies are with historic Trinitarianism" (p. 154), his book is dominated through and through by the Unitarian conception of Christ, and this admission is the more striking. He is professor in Princeton, but not in the Theological Seminary—so near and yet so far!

MODERNISM AND THE CHRISTIAN FAITH

cannot think of God, they cannot describe him, without doing so in terms of Christ. The only God they worship is the God that Jesus is. The only God they pray to is not so much the God that Jesus taught (for thousands have taught the true God), but the God every one of whose spiritual characteristics Jesus had and was. The liberals are not to be blamed for this; they cannot help it. God is a word, a concept, a flush of the sinking sun, insubstantial, afar; Christ incarnates him, brings him near, makes us to know him, to love him, to adore him, and for the very reason that for every purpose for which we need God we know that Christ is that God. We see the face of God in him and we know that we see it.

> "That one Face, far from vanish, rather grows,
> Or decomposes but to recompose,
> Become my universe that feels and knows."[27]

God as Eternal Spirit is always vanishing and appearing again in Jesus. Devout Unitarians have felt this aspect of the deity of Christ.

God as Father is the infinite deep of the Divine Being, beyond finite apprehension, beyond the reach of human thought, what no man hath seen or can see. Left here, we are in blind worship, and can only build an altar to the unknown.... But the Word is God speaking, the divine reason in self-revelation.[28] ... There are no terms employed by the apostles to exalt the Saviour that we do not need for expressing the wonderfulness of his nature. Overwhelmed by the weight of obligation laid upon us by him, no words of man's device, but such only as the Holy Ghost teacheth, can adequately clothe the sentiments of our hearts toward him; and there is no phraseology adopted by prophet, evangelist, or apostle to assert the magnitude of his office, the majesty of his person, or the momentous consequences involved in the alternative of receiving or rejecting him, that our souls do not spontane-

---
[27] Browning, *Epilogue to Dramatis Personæ*.
[28] Sears, in *Monthly Religious Magazine* [Unitarian], 1871, p. 368.

JESUS: QUESTIONS AND ASPECTS

ously fill out to the full. Does some prophet seeing in him God manifested call him "Immanuel"? Verily in him God is with *us*. Beholding in vision the miraculous establishment, the strength and wisdom, the peacefulness and perpetuity, of the Messiah's reign, does he name him Wonderful, Counselor, mighty God, everlasting Father, Prince of Peace? Amen. The prophet cannot go beyond the historian; nay, the historian and the prophet meet in the mount of holy contemplation, using the same lofty imagery to invest with superhuman attributes the peerless object of their common admiration and praise. Glorying in the regal majesty and dominion of his Lord, does some raptured saint, with his ear near to God, hear a "voice from the excellent glory" addressing the Son, "Thy throne, O God, is forever and ever; a scepter of righteousness is the scepter," etc.? Even so, Amen. *Laudate Dominum.* We rejoice, we exult; we give thanks; we chant our response with the church and say, God of God, Light of Light, very God of very God; not homoiousian with Arians, but homoousian with the Athanasians; and none shall receive a heavenlier meaning from those divinely loaded words than we. Does some apostolic seer, caught up into the heavens, hear a loud voice... saying "Worthy is the Lamb that was slain to receive," etc.? We would take up and repeat the celestial refrain, "Blessing and honor and glory and power be unto Him that sitteth upon the throne, and unto the Lamb, forever and ever.[29]"... Essential divinity in Christ is not a Person separated from the Father, another Person, but consubstantial with the Father, and revealing the whole Godhead in one glorious person.[30] ... Not much is accomplished when it is proved that Jesus is not God. When we do this, he ceases to be a central fact, a leader, a Saviour.[31] ... In days of darkest corruption multitudes have lived and died in the sanctity of a genuine faith. And what has been the doctrine which has laid hold upon them and saved them? We believe it will be found to have been the essential divinity of the Lord Jesus Christ, ... offering the Divine Person to the humble believer. This has been the saving element which no

---

[29] Rev. Dr. James W. Thompson, in *Christian Examiner* [Unitarian Quarterly Review], March, 1856, p. 185.

[30] Sears, quoted by Dorchester, *Concessions*, p. 97.

[31] Rev. Dr. Samuel P. Putnam, in *Monthly Religious Magazine*, February, 1874, p. 136.

MODERNISM AND THE CHRISTIAN FAITH

corruptions could completely overlay. It is a personal vital union of the disciple with his Saviour that causes the divine life to pass into him and transform him into the divine image, and produce a genuine righteousness. ... This has been the renewing power of Christianity, and wrought all the graces, and the righteousness, and the zeal and the piety distinctively Christian; for this is where God meets the soul and has his tabernacle with man. This is the door through which he comes and floods the heart with his strength and love. This made Methodism a saving and regenerating power,[32] etc.

The last aspect of **Christ** I have space to speak of is that of his Presence. Not only among the two or three where he promised to be, but the lonely disciple has felt him at his side. No humble and truehearted worker for him in home or foreign fields but that has known that he was not alone, but that Another has been his companion, the Son of man, perhaps the One who in the story of the Three Hebrew Heroes looked like "one of the gods" (Dan. 3. 25). This presence of Christ has been and is as real to millions of Christians as hands or feet. How do we explain it? As deception? As the result of education? But it has been too real for that, and too substantial a help not only in the crisis times of life but in the ordinary humdrum duties and temptations of the daily round. The martyrs knew this presence. "Christ suffering in him [one of the Lyons martyrs] manifested his glory delivering him from his adversary and making him an ensample for the others, showing that nothing is fearful where the love of the Father is, and nothing painful where there is the glory of Christ."[33] On account of her "communion with

---

[31] Sears, in same, 1860, pp. 106–108. I am indebted to Dorchester for these modern Unitarian quotations.

[33] Eusebius, *Hist. Eccl.*, 5. 1, 23.

JESUS: QUESTIONS AND ASPECTS

Christ" Blandina, though she suffered cruel penalties for her faith, "felt none of the things which were happening to her."[34] Of another: "And as she [Thekla] looked round on all the men there, she saw the Lord Jesus Christ sitting full opposite to her in the likeness of Paul.... I am the handmaiden of God. And he who is with me, he is the Son of the Living God; in whom I have hoped, because through him the beasts attack me not.... Our God, God of this house in which there dawned on me light from Christ Jesus, who helped me in prison,"[35] etc. "Now it is that I [Felicitas] suffer [in childbirth] what I suffer; but then [in my coming martyrdom] there will be another in me, who will suffer for me, because I also am about to suffer for him."[36] The presence of Christ with his people has been a tremendous factor in worship, life, and work. How do you account for it?

Therefore through all the ages Christians have enshrined Christ in their hearts as Lover and Lord, as practically or theoretically their God and as their exceeding great reward. From the beginning till now there has been no faltering in this loyalty. Other loyalties have changed, from this church to that, from this intellectual explanation to that, but still Jesus has been before the minds of all as the Being who fills out all their ideal of what a God should be. The Socinians and Unitarians reacted against—not Jesus, but—the Augustinian Trinity. They still wanted to keep him in their hearts as the Son of God, follow him, and him alone, in their lives, and

---

[34] *Ibid.*, 5. 1, 56.

[35] Conybeare, F. C., editor, *Apology and Acts of Apollonius and other Monuments of Early Christianity*, 1894, pp. 72, 84, 87.

[36] *Passio Perpet. et Felic.*, 5. 2.

MODERNISM AND THE CHRISTIAN FAITH

adore him as the fairest among ten thousand. That never faltering allegiance through the coming and going centuries is an aspect of Jesus in history that is impressive indeed. Some denied him in practice (Mariolatry), but they worshiped him in doctrine, others denied him in doctrine (or somebody else's doctrine), but they worshiped him in practice. And for all he took and takes spontaneously and unconsciously the place of the infinite God in the definings of the intellect and in the homage of the heart. "Show us the Father and it sufficeth us. Have I been so long time with you, and dost thou not know me, Philip?" (John 14. 8, 9.)

CHAPTER VII

ATONEMENT

I suspect that since 1600 more important books have been written on the atonement of Christ than on any other topic in theology. Why is this? Is it because that doctrine is the most open to objection, and therefore has called forth the most attacks and defenses? Is it because it is the most mysterious and profound, and therefore the most attractive to serious thinkers, or that it is, in general, the most fascinating, or the most fundamental, or what? Take Scotland alone, which according to population is of all countries in the world that in which the ablest, the most conscientious, and scholarly thinking is devoted to religious themes, and you will notice how atonement has attracted strong men. There are more than two or three books of even enduring worth. Not to go back to John McLeod Campbell's pathbreaking treatise of 1856, which lifted the whole subject into a new angle, start with Smeaton's *Doctrine of Atonement*, two volumes, 1868, 1870; follow it up with Crawford's *Doctrine of Holy Scripture respecting the Atonement*, 1871, third edition, 1880; Bruce's *Humiliation of Christ*, 1876, second edition, 1887; the able section of W. Lindsay Alexander in his *System of Biblical Theology*, 1888, until you strike the recent works of Denney, and you have a series of books which for intellectual power, scholarly equipment, and earnest reflection have never been sur-

MODERNISM AND THE CHRISTIAN FAITH

passed. Some would say that this engagement is due to the instinct or conviction that the atonement is not only historically but philosophically the storm-center of Christianity, and if that citadel is once taken, the divinity of Christ and salvation through him, objective revelation, and supernatural Christianity itself, fall to the ground. I think there is truth in this. Still, is not the question, Who is Christ? more important than, What did he do? Once establish his divinity and the historic faith in its essential features follows as a matter of course; disprove that and the house of Christianity tumbles about our ears. It becomes then only a fine morality and the best of the Oriental cults. But divinity and atonement are interwoven. They stand or fall together. If one is true, the other must be true.

The word "atonement" is used in this paper in its historic and not in its etymological meaning, not simply as external reconciliation, which offers no problem, but as the heart of the idea which is expressed by such words in Scripture as "propitiation," "expiation," "ransom," "redemption," "sacrifice." Now, the main fact which strikes one who is acquainted with the modern history of atonement when he opens the New Testament is the prominence of the fact, but the absence of philosophy or theory. The New Testament pursues the same method with God, everywhere taking for granted his existence, but entering into no discussion of his being. One might almost say it does the same with Jesus as to his absolute Divinity and his absolute humanity, but attempting no philosophy of the two. With such a background as the Old Testament how could the New do otherwise than have a stalwart and engross-

ATONEMENT

ing doctrine of atonement, which invades even the synoptic Gospels. "Even as the Son of man came not to be ministered unto, but to minister, and to give his life a ransom for many,"[1] which last clause means more than mere benevolence or service, or he would not have added a thought of such redemptive significance. O foolish men, and slow of heart to believe in all that the prophets have spoken![2] (Compare especially Isa. 53.) "Behooved it not the Christ to suffer these things and to enter into his glory?"[3] And at the Last Supper, "He said unto them, This is my blood of the covenant, which is poured out for many."[4] The Gospel of John: "Behold, the Lamb of God, that taketh away the sin of the world" (1. 29). "Therefore doth the Father love me, because I lay down my life, that I may take it again" (10. 17). "The good shepherd layeth down his life for the sheep" (10. 11). "The bread which I will give is my flesh, for the life of the world" (6. 51). Acts: "The things which God foreshowed by the mouth of all the prophets, that his Christ should suffer, he thus fulfilled" (3. 18: a divine necessity, his passion a part of the divine order of salvation; compare 17. 3; 26. 23; 3. 12; 13. 38, 39). "Take heed unto yourselves and to all the flock in which the Holy Spirit hath made you bishops to feed the church of the Lord,[5] which he purchased with his own blood" (20. 28).

If we enter the epistles and Revelation, we have such a plethora of passages that the bare mention of the references—without quoting the texts—would fill

---

[1] Matt. 20. 28. [2] Luke 24. 25. [3] Luke 24. 26.

[4] Mark 14. 24: compare Matt. 26. 28; who adds, "unto remission of sins"; Luke 22. 20.

[5] The two oldest manuscripts and other authorities read "God."

MODERNISM AND THE CHRISTIAN FAITH

a large space. It must suffice to refer the reader to some such analysis as that given by the eminent scholar Dr. Henry B. Smith—*nomen venerabile*—of Union Theological Seminary, and to quote his impartial and simple statement of the result. "This gives us the revealed facts as to the nature and relations of Christ's atoning work—no theory, no hypothesis—only an arrangement and array of the chief scriptural assertions. And it amounts to this, viz., that in Christ's death as a sacrifice for our sins, he (1) suffered and died for sin, in our stead, as a proper sacrifice: that his were the vicarious, substituted sufferings of a representative; (2) under the law, to answer the ends of the law, in some way, in our stead; (3) in order to remove its curse from us; (4) which was done by his substituted sufferings, death, and obedience; (5) and which had further the effect of a propitiation, declaring God's righteousness and reconciling man to God."[6]

In other words, even a cursory examination of our New Testament sources shows that though they had worked out no theory to cover all the facts, and cared for no theory, being too near the simplicities of sacrifice ever to think of it, they received the life and death of Christ as atonement for sin in the deepest and fullest sense, a sense which they would express in the familiar ideas of our words "ransom," "propitiation," "reconciliation." The objection of the "modern" man to these ideas would have been unintelligible to the writers. In them they were steeped. There was not a shadow of difference of judgment in the Jewish and Gentile part of the church as to

---

[6] *System of Christian Theology*, 1884, 3d ed., 1885, 4th ed., 1890, pp. 442, 461–464.

ATONEMENT

this. There was not a Christian who received Christ as King and Lord and Prophet who did not also receive him as Priest. Not a line on atonement in the New Testament is meant in refutation of any Christian view, but as simply the statement of the glory of the Christian salvation as wrought by the death of the Redeemer in that mighty expiation, and would be received as such in every society throughout the empire in which the words were read. I am not saying that these ideas were true or false; I am saying that they were Christian, and were held as such by believers of all strains in apostolic times.

That the New Testament is thus on this subject an "orthodox" book (if I might use a word everybody understands) is confessed by men who write from an absolutely "free" or "liberal" standpoint. "Faith in the atoning death" (in the New Testament), says Hase, "is a conviction of the religious feeling in which the seers express themselves of the pain and charm with which every day the celebration of the death of the Lord was celebrated. Though it is not evinced by this that the propitiation through the death of Jesus was absolutely necessary, the apostolic church felt herself reconciled (or propitiated, *versöhnt*) with God through Christ, and proclaimed this propitiation (*Versöhnung*) as the salvation of the world."[7] "The self-assertions of Jesus on his personal calling," says Lipsius, "assertions which were grounded on his consciousness of the Sonship of God as that was historically stamped in his Messiah-consciousness, for primitive Christian faith gave already to his Messianic work the threefold reference as legislation

---

[7] *Evangelische Protestantische Dogmatik*, 6 Aufl., 1870 (2nd ed., 38), pp. 201, 202.

MODERNISM AND THE CHRISTIAN FAITH

for the kingdom of God (viz., as prophet), as atoning death for the sins of the people (as priest), and as king-rule of The Messiah of Israel ascended into heaven and soon to return for the setting up of the perfect theocracy upon earth"[8] (as king).

It is indeed true that the love of God breaks forth ever and anon in the New Testament without the thought of atonement being linked with it in words. But that thought is and—with the historic lineage of writers—must have been in the background. It is as the liberal Kirn says. "The ground for the effect of Jesus' service until death is more hinted than spoken out. But in harmony with what he says elsewhere it can be found only in this that his fidelity until death fulfills the moral condition under which God's always ready forgiving grace can become effective to the many." The apparent isolation of Mark 10. 45, which has occasioned suspicions against its genuineness (F. C. Baur), disappears when we remember that the proclamation of Jesus elsewhere designates his Messianic appearance as a time of salvation (Luke 4. 21; Matt. 11. 5, 6, 25ff.; 13. 16, 17); and the guarantee of a near divine saving-deed (Matt. 5. 4ff.; 16. 27, 28; Luke 18. 7, 8). This saving proof of divine love, which begins with his works, reaches its complete climax in the new covenant which his death seals. Still less can one conclude the dispensableness of atonement from the parable of the prodigal son. It speaks only of the last ground of forgiveness, the Father-love of God, without wishing to describe the way of its historical mediation. And every Israelite knew that God's forgiveness presup-

---

[8] *Lehrbuch der Evangelische Protestantische Dogmatik*, 3 Aufl., 1893 (1st ed., 1876), p. 508.

ATONEMENT

posed the stability of his covenant grace, which must perish if God's holiness is disregarded."[9]

Of course there were different glimpses over the vast field of Christ's work. While Paul emphasizes mainly Christ's death, with which even here he connects the resurrection,[10] while with John Christ's person guarantees salvation"[11] though without neglecting his death as of important significance,[12] the Epistle to the Hebrews makes the mediatorial office of Christ, to which his sacrificial death essentially belongs (9. 15ff.), come to its conclusion only with his entrance into the heavenly sanctuary (9. 24). Other ideas also come out in setting forth the varied significance of Christ, but the student should not be forestalled in the joy of his own search in this rich pasture. Suffice it to say that the pregnant ideas which we have seen are the predominant ones in the New Testament are not only never denied but fit in readily with other views, and this could not be otherwise in a world where everyone was immersed in those ideas (sacrifice, expiation, etc.).

It is not our intention to follow the doctrine through the history of the Christian Church. Read the appropriate articles in the different dictionaries and encyclopædias and any history of doctrine. But a word must be said on the ransom to Satan theory, and on Socinus, Schleiermacher, and Ritschl on account of their influence on modern thought. The same lack of an elaborated theory which we have found

---

[9] Versöhnung, in Hauck, *Realencyklopädie f. Protestantische Theologie und Kirche*, 3 Aufl. xx, pp. 556, 557.

On this parable see the able treatment of Warfield, *The Saviour of the World*, 1915, pp. 3-33, a volume of sermons which no one should read unless he likes strong meat.

[10] Rom. 4. 25. John 2. 2. [12] John 6. 51; 12. 24.

MODERNISM AND THE CHRISTIAN FAITH

in the New Testament is true also of the so-called apostolic Fathers, though the fact of atonement is not without clear expression. It is often sought to throw discredit on the historic teaching of the church through the centuries by calling attention to the ransom-to-Satan theory, which has been called *the* theory of the church for a thousand years (though it was not), as much as to say, "Look at what fools the Fathers were, and how, then, can you expect us to respect that or any other historic theory?" Well, it is true that even Christ and the apostles were simple enough to believe not only that there were Satan and evil spirits, but that men were more or less under his power as exposed to his temptations, though one of these authorities thought that his power was so small that mere resistance would make the devil flee.[13] So they all believed that Christ's work delivered from him. But that is far from saying that Christ paid *an atonement to Satan,* which is taught first by Origen (about 230), and then as only one of the many facets of that brilliant theologian's doctrine of atonement. The idea was this: Man by his sin had given Satan a certain right or claim to hold him. Satan accepted Christ in lieu of man. Man was therefore free. But Satan was deceived by Christ's divinity, and found he could not hold him. So he lost both Christ and man. This is the famous ransom to Satan theory of which the liberals make so much. But it played a much less part than represented. For instance, it is often said that Irenæus (about 180) taught it.[14] Old Routh's golden advice,

---

[13] James 4. 7. As to whether Christ and Apostles were justified in this belief see Faulkner, in *Methodist Review,* N. Y., July, 1919, 627 f.

[14] Even Professor W. Adams Brown is misled here (in *Encyclopædia of Religion and Ethics,* vol. v, p. 643) as late as 1912.

ATONEMENT

"Verify your references," would save us much misinformation on this ransom-to-Satan business. If you will read Irenæus 5. 1, 1, and all his other references to atonement, you will find that while he teaches of course—as did all the Fathers—a rescue from Satan, he does not teach a ransom *to* Satan.[15] Augustine is said to teach it in *De Trinitate*, 13. 12–15. The nearest he comes to it is in 15, where he says that the blood of Christ was accepted by Satan, who found himself not enriched by it but bound, but he does not say that the blood was given *to him* as a ransom or price. I also turned up Leo I and Gregory I, and found, of course, Satan brought in, but this crucial part of the theory lacking—an actual ransom paid by Christ to Satan.[16] So also in Bernard of Clairvaux, *Epistolæ* 190, especially chap. 8, where Abelard is said to have denied any claim to Satan, where Bernard does not plead for such claim, much less allow that atonement was offered to him, though it is said that while "God the Father did not require the blood of his Son, he accepted it when offered," as he (the Father) "thirsted" for salvation (chap. 8, 22). Nor does the bold figure of Peter Lombard about the mousetrap and the bait mean that the death of Christ on

---

[15] Even Baur, *Die Christliche Lehre von der Versöhnung in ihrer geschichtlichen Entwicklung*, 1838., p. 43, does not affirm this, while Seeberg on Irenæus (*Dogmengeschichte*, 2 Aufl., 1908, i, p. 331, note 2) thinks that the most we can say is that God permitted himself to treat with the devil in the redemption, though even this is probably too strong as the *suadelam* (persuasion) refers not to the devil but to men. The best treatment is Sheldon, *The Atonement of the Early Church No Price Paid to Satan*, in *Methodist Quarterly Review*, New York, July, 1878 (vol. ix), pp. 504ff.: on Irenæus see pp. 507–512. See Faulkner in the same *Review*, May, 1917, pp. 459–461. There is an attempt to fairly estimate the Satan aspect in Dimock, *The Death of Christ*.

[16] Harnack has also to be corrected here (*History of Dogma*, vol. iii. p. 307).

the cross was an expiation to Satan, but has reference solely to the deception of Satan. He thought he was conquering Christ, but Christ was really conquering him.[17]

While a positive Satanward reference of the atonement was a view generally held until Anselm, there were probably not more than three or four men who interpreted it as an actual ransom to Satan, and even in these cases in connection with other ideas. That Satan was deceived and overcome by Christ and man rescued from him was often believed, and sometimes with representations grotesque if not amusing, but that the church for a thousand years held that *the* significance of the atonement was a ransom paid to Satan is a popular fiction. Like most historical legends, it dies hard.

The first to strike against the general doctrine a blow which has become a permanent force in history were the two Sozzini and their disciples (Socinians) in latter part of sixteenth, and beginning of seventeenth century. By this time the doctrine had settled down for all the churches, Catholic and Protestant, into a pretty massive form of what is called the penal satisfaction theory. Faustus Socinus had not much difficulty in showing objections. For instance, if Christ suffered punishment for sins, why are men punished for the same here or hereafter? Remission and satisfaction are mutually exclusive. Personal penalties cannot be transferred. Christ was not head of humanity when he was on earth, nor has his death exempted anyone else from death. His fulfillment of the law was only for himself, and secures

---

[17] Peter Lombard, *Lib. Sent.*, lib. 3, dist. 19, sec. 1 (Migne, tom. 192, col. 796).

ATONEMENT

exemption for no one. An equivalent by an individual can be valid only for an individual, not for the race; then if he did die as an equivalent, he would have to die an eternal death, but Christ was raised up; if it is said he is divine, then the smallest suffering would have been sufficient; but if he had been divine, he could not suffer, as the Godhead cannot suffer. If the benefits of the satisfaction are conditional, then they are not perfect. Anyhow, the doctrine blunts the conscience and leads to laxity. Besides, the Bible shows that God remits freely.

Positively, Socinus blends Christ's priestly office into the prophetic, for which office he received instruction in heaven. Eternal life is his special gift, through the spirit, which is only the power or working of God. Christ's death belonged to the prophetic office, and was a sealing of his instructions. It was necessary only in the sense of a confirmation of God's will as to salvation. It assures us of God's love, that he will give us what he has promised. Through Christ's resurrection his death assures us also of our own resurrection and eternal life, if we keep Jesus's commands. The resurrection is more important than the death; it is the "head and foundation of all our faith and salvation in the person of Christ." It will be seen that the Italian uncle and nephew (especially the latter) brought in a revolution in their doctrine of atonement. To those who could not see beneath the crasser forms of the satisfaction theory it must have come as a delightful relief.[18]

Schleiermacher worked in the same direction. Re-

---

[18] See also Faulkner, article, "Socinus and Socinianism," in Reformation year series in *Homiletic Review*, New York, June, 1917, pp. 448-453.

MODERNISM AND THE CHRISTIAN FAITH

demption is the central thing in Christianity. It is the passing from a condition of a limited to that of an unlimited God-consciousness. It realizes itself in a new community life which is that of the church as divinely founded and bound to the activity of Jesus. Though we naturally think of it as taking place in time, in the light of his eternity no activity of God can be conditioned by sin or anything else that happens in time. As a divine deed redemption is a realization of creation. The Redeemer is the historically appearing original pattern of mankind. His honor and glory we know from his activity, which we must not underestimate on account of his success (or, rather, lack of it) in the history of the church, but judge from the inexhaustible impulse which it imparts to believers. In Christ mankind, from the side of religion, is perfected; therefore we must speak of a special being of God in him. There is only one salvation—fact, Christ's person. His work is simply the outworking of the divine content of his person, the expansion of the being of God in him to a being of God in universal human nature. Sufferings and death are not causes of salvation, but only means of authentication of the sentiment and power of Christ. They are taken up as parts of his work, which at bottom is this, namely, to communicate his life. That work has no effect on God. It has to do entirely with men, whom it receives—that is, those who respond—into communion with his life. This process has two sides, the communication of the power of his God-consciousness (redemption), and the communication of the blessedness of the same (reconciliation). Atonement is simply the doing away with the evil which springs from its coincidence with the

ATONEMENT

world, and this doing away is dependent upon the strengthening of religious power (that is, redemption).

Even the liberal Kirn has to call attention to the lack in the doctrine of the brilliant Berlin preacher, professor, and theologian, who has influenced thought as few other men of his time. The blessing of the forgiveness of sins, its founding and ascertaining as a certainty, does not stand in the middle ground, but the transformation of the whole life of humanity into a share of God-consciousness. For that reason neither a transcendent reference of the salvation-work of Christ is recognized, nor its concentration in a historical act which guarantees the divine grace. I would add that from the scriptural side and from that of religious experience, his doctrine is fatally lacking. But it has been path-breaking for the newer views. For the old formula of Christ's active and passive obedience it substitutes that of his calling as redeemer (of course the meaning changed), in which Ritschl follows him as he does in so much else; for representation or substitution he places communion; and he binds closely the historical work of Christ with his continuous influence upon mankind.[19]

Though lacking in his religious genius and innerliness, Ritschl, as I said, followed Schleiermacher. Reconciliation comes after justification because the former has to do only with men, not with God. It is the subjective result of justification or the forgiveness of sins, and is simply doing away active opposition against God. Justification has to do with the Christian community, not so much with believers as such. The trouble with the old views is the incom-

[19] See Kirn, *Schleiermacher*, in Herzog-Hauck, 3 Aufl., vol. xvii, pp. 604–606.

MODERNISM AND THE CHRISTIAN FAITH

patibility of law and religion, which excludes ideas of satisfaction, punishment, etc., from atonement. There needs only an ethical ground for the forgiveness of sins, not a juristic. Even the thought of the wrath of God need not come in. For Christianity, God's nature is exhaustively expressed by love alone, wrath having only to do with the Last Judgment for those who reject the atonement. Love wants only the moral good of the person, and thinks of nothing else. Sin is principally ignorance. For forgiveness no other element need be brought in except love. No law nor other moral principle limits God in this regard. The idea of any change of God from wrath to grace (but compare Isa. 12. 1, 2), of a righteousness which hems in his grace, is excluded. Reconciliation is simply revelation, the divine love becoming effective in history. Still, no one can become certain of forgiveness except through Christ, who is a Prophet as revealing God's love, a Priest as representing man before God, and a King in the incomparable worth and success of his activity as prophet and priest. His function in the first capacity is the most important, because it assures us of God's forgiving love. By his life he shows us this, founds the kingdom of God, and invites sinners to it. In all this he represents man, who is already disposed to make God's object his own. Christ's fidelity to his calling is the means by which he both keeps himself in the love of God and opens entrance for it to his community. For he carries out this fidelity not only for himself but to draw his disciples and mankind into the same attitude to God. The climax to this fidelity is his death. We can use the common term "sacrifice," but that means nothing that has to do with law, righteousness, ex-

ATONEMENT

piation, etc., but only that Christ by this fidelity to his calling brought his community or church near to God, founded for it a new covenant with God, the blessing of which is forgiveness of sins. The community knows Christ's worth and his obedience, and by that knowledge it is justified by faith, for faith is an act of the will which affirms communion with God, and knows itself at the same time in harmony with God's object or end, that is, reconciled.

This is the boldest reconstruction of atonement ever made by a Christian theologian as part of a general system carried relentlessly through. But I must feel that the criticism of Kirn, whom I used to hear in Leipzig, and who was sympathetic to Ritschl's school, a theologian as open in mind as Christian in heart, is perfectly justified in saying that Ritschl has "limited or shortened the problem of the forgiveness of sins in a way which is unjust to both the biblical conception of God and the Christian consciousness of sin and salvation. Inasmuch as he excludes holiness from his conception of God and limits righteousness simply to God's act in bringing salvation, he covers up the cutting contradiction of man's sin with God's ethical nature. Further, inasmuch as he thinks of the death of Christ only under the point of view of obedience to his calling, he leaves out of consideration its reference to the uncovering and condemnation of sin, which is so richly and expressly emphasized in the New Testament. Ritschl does, indeed, say that the continuance in the memory of the earlier feeling of blame (or guilt), and the sharpening of that feeling in regard to the sins that have happened since, unite themselves in Christianity with the forgiveness of sins, but he omits to lay a firm foundation to this sharpening of the feeling of guilt in the explanation of the death of Jesus. Therefore we must doubt whether Ritschl in his doctrine of salvation does justice to the earnestness of guilt, or founds its abolition on a method that is convincing to a Christianly sharpened conscience."[20] With what scholarly moderateness he speaks. It is an instance of saying much in saying little.

What are the New Testament factors in atonement? (1) God as love. (2) God as righteousness, holiness, justice. (3) Sin. (4) Forgiveness or justification of the sinner. I am not saying whether these are factors in a true doctrine of atonement; the point here is that they are the New Testament factors. Atonement is a method of uniting these four facts. At the same time it would certainly be an interesting discovery to find that one of those factors is lacking in a true doctrine, to find, for instance, that righteousness is a quiescent or fleeting quality in God, or that sin is indifferent, so that he could just as well and does save the sinner out of hand, *sans plus de façons*, without more ado. For that would mean that in what is at least very near the central thing in Christianity, Christ's work for men, both Christ (Matt. 20. 28) and the apostles were misled, that is, fatally misled. If they did not know the secret of Christ, they knew nothing that we need care much for. If Paul was mistaken in Rom. 3. 21–26, we can read him still as an enthusiast whom we pity, upon whom we look down with gentle contempt from our lofty platform, but in the deep places of our lives, when our souls long for the living God and we cry,

---

[20] *Versöhnung*, in Hauck, *Realencyklopädie*, 3 Aufl., chap. xx, p. 572 (1908).

ATONEMENT

"Who shall bring us before God?" he has no message for us. He not only has no message for us then, but when he treats of other things, this $\psi\varepsilon\tilde{\upsilon}\delta o\varsigma$ $\pi\rho\tilde{\omega}\tau o\nu$, this fundamental error on the heart of Christianity, invalidates everything he says.

But there are difficulties. Yes. Was it not Butler who said in his *Analogy* that difficulties were a part of the divine order of the universe, and if there were none in Christianity, we might doubt its coming from God? Poor old Butler is superseded now, in spite of the work of Gladstone's last years, but when he said that he said eternal truth. A religion without mystery might be a clever piece of work, but it would be no religion for man because it would not be a religion. The first difficulty is the second term of the apostolic proclamation that the atonement has to do with God's righteousness. God as love can forgive for the asking or without the asking, but God as holiness—that is another matter, it is said. Now, if there is a God at all (I mean a personal God: a God who is not a person, whatever else he may be, is not the Christian's God), it is easier for me to believe that he is righteous than that he is loving. If the dread alternative were presented, "Which will you have, a holy or a loving God?" I would say, "Give us a God who hates iniquity, whether he loves the evildoer or not." A God who is love but not a consuming fire,[21] love but not light, is an impossible God, a monster in a moral universe. A God who cares much for love but nothing for justice may be a God for the Pleiades, but he is no God for our earth. The events of 1914 make one feel that all the more, but outrages against the innocent did not begin in 1914.

---
[21] Heb. 12. 29.

MODERNISM AND THE CHRISTIAN FAITH

So I agree thoroughly with some old-fashioned thinker who said, "God may be loving, but he must be holy." Now, the atonement is God's way of loving and forgiving and saving without—if I might so say—losing his self-respect. It is the price which justice pays to love or love pays to justice—for both are one in that awful Light we call God—so that salvation may come to sinners.

> Mercy and truth are met together;
> Righteousness and peace have kissed each other.
> Truth springeth out of the earth;
> And righteousness hath looked down from heaven.
> —Psa. 85. 10, 11.

It is sometimes said that love needs no atonement to forgive. That may be true of petty sins between persons. There the innocent party always hears a voice within him say, "Forgive your neighbor; you know at heart you are no better than he; if you have not offended in his way, you have in your own." But when we come to serious offenses, to mortal wounds, can anyone forgive without atonement, without the conscious or unconscious sacrifice which love pays to justice? No one, it seems to me. And the higher and holier the innocent one, the bitterer the tribute he must bring to the altar within. Every act of forgiveness of this kind whether on earth or in heaven is in its own kind and degree another Calvary, or cross erected in the soul, until it mounts up to, "The Lamb slain from the foundation of the world," "My God, My God, why hast thou forsaken me?" As his child, every soul is a miniature God. "He hath set eternity in their heart."[22] The Via Dolorosa up

---
[22] Eccl. 3. 11.

ATONEMENT

the sides of the green hill near Jerusalem which the Son of God traveled is the way which every pure heart goes whose task is forgiveness.

Twice I had occasion (in 1904 and 1908) to look upon one of the greatest pictures in the world. It was in the museum in Cologne. It was a peasant interior, partly house, partly shop, where father and son were busily plying their trade as shoemakers. The mother is standing behind the chair of the father. The door opens and the lost daughter faces the family group. Shall love triumph, or shall she be thrust out into the cold? It is a question of atonement. There is no forgiveness here out of hand. There is either a peremptory shutting the heart, as in the brother's face, perhaps in the father's, or there is atonement in the sense of the deepest theory ever devised to explain the death of Christ, as in the mother's. It was simply a picture, but the artist was a theologian. It was only a canvas, but it was the eternal drama of salvation.

What was the trouble with the cobbler and his family? If, before she entered, the girl by the waving of a magic wand could have transferred the family into a fairy world where moral laws did not run, there would have been no problem. How different then the faces of the picture! "It is not doubtful," says Fichte, "but the most certain thing there is, yes, the foundation of all other certainty, the one absolutely valid objective reality, that there is a moral world-order. What you love, that you live." The family were caught in that moral world order. The poor girl did not think she was thrusting the problem of Gethsemane on her home. In that same moral Weltordnung was Lady Macbeth caught.

MODERNISM AND THE CHRISTIAN FAITH

Doctor: Look how she rubs her hands!
Gentleman: It is an accustomed action with her to seem thus washing her hands. I have known her to continue on this a quarter of an hour.
Lady Macbeth: Yet here's the spot.
Doctor: Hark! she speaks. I will set down what comes from her.
Lady Macbeth: Out, damned spot! out, I say.... There's the smell of blood still. All the perfumes of Arabia will not sweeten this little hand.
Doctor: More needs she the divine than the physician. God, God, forgive us all.[23]

It is the genius of Shakespeare and all great artists to see that every moral act makes everything different, ourselves and the universe, that every moral act strikes chords that cease not to vibrate till they mingle for good or ill with the harmonies of the spheres. In the words of Shelley,

> "Life, like a dome of many-colored glass,
> Stains the white radiance of Eternity."[24]

You can't kill your Duncans without casting a shadow on the throne of a moral God. There is something more than the outward deed.

> Will all great Neptune's ocean wash this blood
> Clean from my hand? No: this my hand will rather
> The multitudinous seas incarnadine,
> Making the green one red.[25]

Even in larger ways atonement strikes home upon us. Everyone knows how the law of vicarious sacrifice is written across the universe. "He was bruised for our iniquities." "How one man must die for the people." Life is given up for life. Atonement is simply God coming within the sweep of his own law, bringing back his sheep fron the far mountains. Then,

---

[23] *Macbeth*, Act V, Scene 1.   [25] *Macbeth*, Act II, Scene 2.
[24] *Adonais*, stanza 52.

ATONEMENT

again, think of the sorrows of humanity. It is not necessary to ask their cause. Every heart knoweth its own bitterness. In the last analysis they all go back to sin. Anyhow they exist. Can we have a God who has not felt them, who in repose profound refuses to share them, a cross for his people but not himself?

The other difficulty is the third term of the apostolic message—sin. "You Christians make all too much of sin," the objector says; "it is not such a tragedy." Now, it is true that the Christian idea of atonement is built on the fact of sin being a horrible blot on the universe, a dreadful and hateful thing, hellish in its possibilities. Now, really, Bible or no Bible, Christianity or no Christianity, sin is just that. The newspapers teach us that every day, only remember that it is only the better classes of sins (if I might put it that way) which get into the papers. Give the editors credit for that. The nameless horrors, the blasting deeds of lust, and thousands of crimes which every day cry to heaven, the newspapers happily do not mention, partly because they ought not, partly because they dare not, and partly because these sins are hidden, not news. Whether we like it or not, these are facts. We may sympathize with Walt Whitman, who envies the cattle "so placid and self-contained," who do not "whine about their condition." "They do not lie awake in the dark and weep for their sins," and wish that man was without a conscience and more brutish than he has yet made himself, but we must take the world as it is. If hell is worse than sin has made some of the best homes and fairest parts of the world, God pity those who go there.

MODERNISM AND THE CHRISTIAN FAITH

Besides, if God is holy he is all-holy. If so, he cannot look upon sin with allowance. Then, if sin is damnable and if God is holy, punishment is not optional. It is part of the moral order of that universe of which God is the soul. But love is not an elective either. The forces of salvation are working along with those of retribution, and the Son of God who is at the heart of them is involved in their sweep. Thus we get Calvary, Vicarious Sacrifice, and the truth at the bottom of the Penal Satisfaction theory. It is not an expedient; it is not an artifice; it is not a solution of a problem; it is the Eternal Atonement, and the working out of that atonement in history, especially as summed up in one Person and in one chief sacrifice or act—the everlasting offering of the Love of God to his Righteousness, that he might be just and yet the justifier of the sinner who believes in his Son.

If we take the later discussions of atonement, or try to bring the matter under heads both scriptural and rational, we might say something like this.

(1) The atonement, since it proceeds solely from the heart of God,[26] in the nature of the case can work no change in God. Sin was not a surprise to which he had to adjust himself by a new device; it was provided for from eternity by those primal laws of being, of sacrifice, written in the nature of God and in the nature of his universe.

(2) Therefore it is the only sure anchor-ground of the sinner's hope. It is indispensable to faith because it founds forgiveness on the unchangeable and holy Will of God that is Love, and on the Love that is holy Will. Simply a process in time could not do

---

[26] John 3. 16, Luther's "Little Gospel."

ATONEMENT

that. It is just because it is an eternal process, an expression of the necessary union of holiness and love in the divine nature, that it is the perfect satisfaction of the conscience illuminated whether by natural law or by the light of the Christian revelation.

(3) The atonement rests securely and alone on Christ's Person and Work. Not on his work alone, because it is only as he expresses not the doings and sufferings of himself as a man among men in old Galilee and Judæa, but those of God, and as he represents and restores mankind to the will of God with absolute security, does the sinner have unshaken confidence in the redeeming love. "It is only because Christ is the bearer of divine life for humanity and thus its perfected head that he can guarantee the grace of God to it, and represent it before God as the creative cause of its life in conformity with God."[27] It is only because Christ is the eternal Son of God, and thus participates eternally in the atoning life of God, that he can bring salvation to the sinner with absolute certainty and fullness.[28]

(4) Christ's whole life must be taken into the account, and yet his death was the climax of his redeeming work as representing man and revealing God. It had the special significance of emphasizing the holiness of God's love, giving normal expression to the Christian judgment on sin and guilt, and thus

---

[27] Kirn, in Herzog-Hauck, *Realencyklopädie*, vol. xx, p. 573.

[28] The strong and brilliant posthumous Cunningham Lectures of the lamented Professor Denney, of Glasgow (*The Doctrine of Reconciliation*, 1918), says that when the seeking soul is brought face to face with Jesus "what he is is enough for us;" what he is, not according to any doctrine, but in the "rich and simple reality we see in the evangelists" (p. 10). True; but the doctrine is bound to come, for the Christian cannot rest till he apprehends Christ with his intellect as well as rests upon him in his heart.

MODERNISM AND THE CHRISTIAN FAITH

awakening penitence, and without all this faith in the forgiveness of sins would be a false self-confidence.

(5) While the death of Christ is the expression of God's righteousness, the newer thought rightly excludes from it God's punishment in the proper sense, or, of course, the sense of guilt. How far the marvelously profound and wide sympathies of Christ, with his delicate spiritual organization, could enter into human sin as the bearer of its curse or even in a sense its guilt, we cannot say, though modern psychology is inclined to enlarge possibilities in this field. There is a tremendously vital and vivid sense in which the innocent not only suffer with the guilty but are punished with or for the guilty. In fact, often their punishment seems keener than that of the guilty, so compelling is the solidarity of souls and so engrossing the eternal law of both retribution and atonement. But in any external or conventional sense we cannot speak of the punishment of Christ. In that case the objection of Socinus would hold, that God could not punish both Christ and the sinner. But Christ experienced the hatred of the world, the sentence of the law, and the evil that threatened humanity on account of sin. His union with us meant that.

(6) Recent discussions have brought out that we must have in mind ethical and spiritual considerations rather than legal, judicial, governmental, or such like, in our thought of atonement. We all agree. But I think the true method is the catholic one of seeking the truth in the old theories by universalizing or spiritualizing the kernel of truth in them. In other words, How do they look *sub specie eternitatis?* It may be we shall find that it is this very spiritual

ATONEMENT

or ethical content which has formed one at least of the secrets of the historic theories.

Take the so-called ransom-to-Satan theory started by Origen and Gregory of Nyssa. If there are good spirits, it is not irrational to believe there may be evil spirits (not to speak of the testimony of Scripture). And it is not irrational to suppose on account of the unity of the universe and the validity of spiritual laws in all worlds that the work of Christ made a profound impression on all beings and wrung the withers of the devil himself. So at least we hope. If the apostles were a theater-spectacle to men and angels,[29] much more may the Son's achievements have brought dismay to evil and high joy to good, spirits.

The penal-satisfaction theory is a tribute to that relentless law of justice and spotless righteousness which is the very foundation of the throne of God.[30] That is, unless it is founded on sand. Unless the atonement in some way meets this imperious claim in God it meets nothing. The New Testament ideas seem to play around this idea, its important words seem to suggest it, and it is only our modern consciousness which it disturbs, as ancient thought was very congenial to it. It is the ethical insistence on right, on purity, on goodness, it is the thought that you cannot with impunity outrage the essential nature of God. If you do, you darken the universe, you create a problem for which only God is competent.

The Grotian or governmental theory is that the chief (with some, the only) reason for atonement is the place of God as ruler, the demand of intelligent beings in all worlds that the supremacy of law be

---
[29] 1 Cor. 4. 9. [30] See Psa. 97. 2, Revised Version.

maintained, that forgiveness without atonement, even if in theory possible, would show such a frivolity of feeling toward the interests of the moral universe that the whole divine economy would break down, that atonement is necessary to preserve the unity, harmony, respect, of human beings and of all spirits. My own feeling is that as the sole and sufficient explanation of atonement this theory is superficial and inadequate, but it certainly sprang from ethical regards. Nor does it lack something of truth. God is the God of cosmos, not of chaos, of order, not of anarchy, that is, he is a ruler as well as a Father. In any important function of his relations with the world, therefore, it is inconceivable that he should act without reference to the moral harmony of the universe, to the loyal obedience and respect of all intelligences.

The moral influence theory desires, of course, also to preserve spiritual values. That there is truth in it goes without saying, but as covering the complete reality of atonement it is fatally deficient, both because it disregards most of the scriptural facts, and because it leaves out of account deeper aspects of soul, life, morals, and spiritual laws, which atonement must satisfy, besides practically making God a secondary member or silent partner of the redemption process.[31]

---

[31] On the different theories an able writer says: "The Son of God will meet the death of the cross to show us how far he will go in holy love for us. We must never cease to remember that all theories of the atonement are so many attempts on the parts of successive generations to say that God has done whatever must be done to win us. God has done all that he can do."—Bishop F. J. McConnell, *Personal Christianity*, 1914, p. 175. The author's result of this follows for Christians only, not for the world, as history shows: "Then, our moral desire is aroused to do all we can for the sake of Christ" (p. 176).

ATONEMENT

Finally, there is no doubt that there is much in modern religion that is uncongenial to ideas of atonement as set forth in the New Testament and witnessed to in the literature, hymns, ritual, and services of the church. As with some superficial Greek philosophers, so to the modern man the cross is a stumblingblock, scandal, or foolishness. But this is because either the sense of sin is lacking, or men have not come into close touch with the realities of lost souls. Christianity was not founded as a toy for dainty dilettantes who sip thoughtlessly at the banquet of life and pass tripping on their way, but for men and women who have fought the battle with the world, the flesh, and the devil, have failed, and are on the road to hell. I mean in Christ's and the apostles' thought. In other words, it is a religion of salvation from sin. It has a thousand other blessings and many secondary designs, but that is its chief mission. For that Christ came and for that the Holy Spirit was poured out. Therefore we get these profound thoughts of redemption, propitiation, sacrifice, in that first revelation. For that reason also men who have lifted the world into higher air, have exercised vast influence as saviours, set on the upward path thousands of men and women, redeemed whole sections of heathenism—Luther and the reformers (to go no farther back), the Puritans, Wesley and his preachers, Finney, Livingstone and the missionaries, Moody, and others—have all been men whose motto was,

> "Nothing in my hands I bring,
> Simply to thy cross I cling."

When the sinful soul is being pushed out toward the eternal judgment, our fine generalizations with which

MODERNISM AND THE CHRISTIAN FAITH

we as moderns comfort ourselves before the perplexity of new thought vanish, and we are helpless. An English Congregationalist, the Rev. J. Morgan Gibbon, tells of a liberal ministerial friend who was called to see a sick man in a poor quarter of a great town. After looking around the room and seeing its bare appearance the minister said: "What can I do for you? Tell me what you want and I will do my best to help you." The startling reply came, "I only want one thing, the forgiveness of my sins." All the earthly wants which appealed to the eye of the minister vanished to a soul face to face with his God, and the spiritual came uppermost. Says Gibbon: "Now, what can one do in such a case? I know of only one thing. There is only one word to be said: 'Jesus Christ died for you. Ye are made new in the blood of Jesus Christ.' " Principal Falconer tells of talking with the late eminent rationalist Pfleiderer, when the question of atonement came up, and the point was made that there was a need in man's conscience for atonement. Pfleiderer asked for an instance in real life. When one was given, the learned German replied, "If a doctrine really meets a deep human need, it must be true."

I remember when the Rev. Charles A. Berry, of Wolverhampton, came over to preach in Plymouth Church, Brooklyn, after Beecher's death. He was later invited to come as pastor, but declined, and himself soon followed into the Deathless Land. Late one night his doorbell rang. On going to the door he found a Lancashire girl, with a shawl over her head. "Are you Dr. Berry?"

"Yes."

"Then I want you to come and get my mother in."

ATONEMENT

Thinking her mother was drunk and she wanted him to go and help lead her home, he recommended the girl to get the police.

"No," she said, "she is dying and I want you to get her into heaven."

Berry was perplexed. Finally he yielded under the importunities of the girl, and went. When he got to the place he found it was a house of shame. Drinking and carousing were going on downstairs. Upstairs in a small room he found the woman dying. Berry told her of the beautiful life of Jesus, his loving ministries and example. He urged her to follow him. She shook her head.

"That's not for the like o' me. I'm a sinful woman, and I'm dying."

"It flashed upon me," said Berry, "that I had no message of hope for that dying woman, and like lightning I leaped in mind and heart back to the gospel my mother taught me. I told her of Jesus Christ, the Son of God, dying on the cross that just such as she might be saved; of his blood poured out for the remission of sins, and all the blessed truths of the old, old story. "And," he added, "I got her in, and I got myself in too."[32]

---

[32] See the valuable article by W. H. Griffeth Thomas, *The Atonement*, in *Biblical Review*, New York, January, 1918, pp. 58, 59, 67, 68. Speaking of this, I might say that the latest defense of the moral influence theory is Rashdall, *The Idea of Atonement in Christian Theology*, 1919. The deeper aspects of life do not seem to appeal to him. Much truer to reality both in Scripture and in the soul history is the last book of the lamented Denney, *Reconciliation*, 1918. The history of the doctrine can be found in Rivière, 1910, Mozley, 1915, Franks, 1917 (which needs correction in several places), and Grensted, 1920. See also W. T. Davison, *The Atonement and Modern Thought*, in *London Quarterly Review*, April, 1920, and Strong in *Church Quarterly Review*, July, 1920.

MODERNISM AND THE CHRISTIAN FAITH

And with Saint Paul and Berry I place myself with the lost woman.

> "No gate of pearl, no branch of palm I merit,
>   Nor street of shining gold.
>
> "Suffice it if—my good and ill unreckoned
>   And both forgiven through thy abounding grace—
> I find myself by hands familiar beckoned
>   Unto my fitting place."[33]

Shakespeare sings the same song as Whittier.

> "Therefore, Jew,
> Though justice be thy plea, consider this,
> That in the course of justice, none of us
> Should see salvation: we do pray for mercy."[34]

When I was in bed with influenza in the fall of 1918 I had time to review the foundations of my hope, and in my first chapel after getting out I announced this hymn as speaking my deepest thoughts for life, death, and eternity, namely, "Rock of Ages, Cleft for Me," a hymn written not in the first place for the unchurched but by a saint for saints. The flaming light of the Eternal Holiness shrivels up our excuses and palliations like burned paper, and the best man can but echo the word of Dr. Chalmers, "What should I do if God did not justify the ungodly?" This feeling is not cant or a false humility, but the question of our heart of hearts.

> "Why, all the souls that were were forfeit once;
> And He that might the vantage best have took
> Found out the remedy. How would you be,
> If He, which is at the top of judgment, should
> But judge you as you are?"[35]

---

[33] Whittier, *At Last*, stanza 4, lines 3, 4, stanza 5.
[34] Shakespeare, *Merchant of Venice*, Act iv, Scene 1.
[35] *Measure for Measure*, Act ii, Scene 2.

CHAPTER VIII

PAUL AS THE AFTER-CHRIST

ONE of the first to definitely set Paul aside as a disciple who misrepresented his Master and could not be trusted was that strange and many-sided scholar and linguist De Lagarde (died 1891, aged sixty-four), who changed his name from Bötticher in 1854, who though an Orientalist of wide repute was also a prophet, priest (in his own thought), and poet. We can get nothing trustworthy about Jesus from Paul, who says himself that he did not get his gospel from man, and who was always unauthorized and an intruder. He greatly exaggerated sin, and brought the Jewish sacrificial theories into Christianity. It angered De Lagarde when any one quoted Paul as an authority for Christ or his teachings. But the latter was equally unhappy in his selection of other disciples. Only Peter and John attained any significance, and John's gigantic exaggerations showed how little he understood Jesus.[1] Renan, of course, also could not abide Paul.

It was therefore not surprising when in 1901 (2nd ed., 1904) Wernle came out with his *Anfänge unserer Religion* to check up Paul. He complains that the apostle did not give an account of the words and deeds of Jesus, but only of the message of the crucified

---

[1] These views Lagarde brought out in 1873 in the first of his so-called *Deutschen Schriften*, on the relation of the German state to theology, church, and religion (gesammelte Ausgabe, 1886, pp. 69ff).

and risen One. The name of Jesus is in the foreground, but is it not another Jesus? Paul's theology especially is an absolutely new thing in Christianity, to be derived neither from the other apostles, nor from Judaism, nor from Jesus, but mainly from his vision on the way to Damascus and from his apologetic or preaching needs. The main point is Christ as redeemer of his people. Paul paints the world in much blacker colors than Christ in order to make his light the brighter. He brings in the idea, "Out of the church no salvation," which hitherto was only a Jewish principle. If not the creator of the Catholic sacrament doctrine, he is at least the continuer of it, and he accommodated Greek superstitions to the Supper. Jesus brought redemption to his own without describing it; Paul connected it with Jewish and Greek conceptions and bound it to the church and its institutions. And he makes faith in Jesus not faith in his whole work and passion as redeemer, but only in the cross and resurrection of God's Son. He also invented a Christology, and disconnects it from the real person and life of Jesus.

But even liberals have complained of the temperamental and contradictory in young Wernle, and his laying on the deep colors.[2] Still, Wernle admits that Paul understood Jesus better than any of his predecessors, and that Paul did not invent or discover Jesus, but that Jesus found Paul and completely possessed him. And in spite of his Christology, it is really Jesus whom he brings, and through whom he conquered the world. And Jesus was really Redeemer; here Paul was interpreter, not inventor.

[2] See von Dobschütz, *Probleme des apostol. Zeitalters*, p. 1, and Vischer, in *Theologische Rundschau*, 1905, pp. 174, 175.

PAUL AS THE AFTER-CHRIST

"The loving devotion to death whereby the Son of God redeems mankind springs out of historical reality. So Paul returns back finally to Jesus." And it was the real Jesus who shone upon him from the circle of the persecuted disciples and took him captive. His theology before conversion Paul overturned and spilled out. "There is only one Christian theology of the apostle. Every word of his letters springs from his Christian consciousness." And yet he borrows from Judaism and from Jewish apocalyptic. "The Son of God, the seed of David, prophesied by the prophets, proved to be the Son of God by the awakening from the dead—that is the old Messianic figure." His high estimation of Jesus is also Jewish. But he changed his whole Jewish platform for the Christian, and his theory of the "flesh of sin" is neither Jewish nor Greek, but an original creation. Yes, there are contradictions in Wernle. Still, there are remarkable coincidences between Paul and Jesus, and the disciple reproduces the Master with surprising fidelity, and the young Basel professor does not call the Tarsian the Second Founder of Christianity, as does Wrede.

In 1905 the Breslau professor Wrede, a brilliant and original spirit, came out with the definite discovery in his little book *Paulus* (2 Aufl., 1907) that Paul created a new religion. His doctrine of Christ which was his central idea and a new creation, and which made him the founder of orthodoxy, was Paul's chief offense. He placed as the foundation of religion the salvation-deeds of Christ, incarnation, death, resurrection, changed the simple living teachings of Jesus into a complicated piece of reflection, the piety of Jesus into another form of religion, that

MODERNISM AND THE CHRISTIAN FAITH

is, into a dogma of redemption by a history that plays its part between God and man. Paul put mythology in the middle point of religion, connected it closely with a lot of thoroughly Jewish ideas, like the general sinfulness of man or the almighty willfulness of God, the opposition between two worlds, ethical pessimism, doctrine of angels and demons, his idea of Scripture, of the Fall and its consequences, and of the future, and then placed faith in this new dogmatics before goodness of character on which alone Jesus laid weight. Paul was not a disciple of Jesus, but his creator. Not that certain precepts of Jesus were not known to him from tradition and were valid; not that there were not occasionally in Jesus slight traces of Paul's later theology; not that the development from Jesus to Paul was not inevitable, but that in all chief points the apostle struck out a new path, and in doing that founded the Christian religion.

Of course the books of Wernle and Wrede made a sensation, but their conclusions were not swallowed even by men of the left. Thus Julius Kaftan, of the right wing of the Ritschlians, came out with an able pamphlet against them.[3] Paul did indeed teach redemption, but not a doctrine in our sense, much less as an artistically constructed doctrine in Wrede's sense, *but as experience*. Not seeing this makes Wrede leave out of account Paul's doctrine of justification. Kaftan says you cannot carry out this new separation between Jesus and Paul; and this so-called Jesus religion which is now proclaimed never existed, it is a thing without a root. The gospel was never simply a teaching which Christ gave, but from its very beginning it was a gospel of a crucified and risen One.

[3] *Jesus und Paulus*, Tübingen, 1906.

PAUL AS THE AFTER-CHRIST

Not by his teaching but by his resurrection did Christ become an object of faith to his disciples and to later Christianity. Paul did not preach differently, but simply brought to full validity the gospel of Jesus. In regard to the law Paul was the truest disciple of Jesus. Of course there were differences, but history shows not a separation but close coincidence. Paul's teaching was not a "doctrine," but a reality in which he lived. Thus Kaftan.

So also the very liberal Jülicher says that Wrede did not sufficiently take account of the fact that already before Paul faith in Christ as Messiah and Saviour, in the salvation-history, was at hand. He overlooked also Paul's heart-deep piety, and in general exaggerates differences into contrarieties.[4] The Christianity of Paul grew up not on its own ground but on that of the primitive church. Paul did not set his theology in the place of the religion of Jesus, but as a wall around it. And though he made a new beginning, like many others after him, it is perversion to call him the founder of the church. Christianity has infinitely to thank him, but not for its being.[5]

Some time has passed since Wernle and Wrede so violently stirred the pool of New Testament criticism, but the question of Paul's originality is a burning one to-day. It is still fundamental with the "modern" man to eliminate Paul in his quest for Jesus, and to be impatient with what he claims the church has accepted from Paul in place of the simple Nazarene himself. In 1921 the eminent New Testament radical critic, Professor Benjamin W. Bacon,

---

[4] Article, "Wrede," in *Realencyklopädie f. Protestantische Theologie und Kirche*, 3 Aufl., vol. 21, p. 509.

[5] Jülicher, *Paulus und Jesus*, Tübingen, 1907.

came out with a book, *Jesus and Paul*, in defense of the same thesis of the transformation of Christianity by Paul. It is therefore as necessary to-day as when the ardent young Swiss Wernle and the radical Göttingen-Breslau theologian Wrede burst upon our ken with their new hypothesis—as necessary to look fairly at the question whether Christianity in its historic substance goes back beyond the great apostle to his Master.

It must be confessed that in the ordinary sense Jesus was no organizer, nor systemizer, nor theologian. Not for that did he come. His historic place or function was different. So far there is truth in Wrede. He did not come to do Paul's work. It was part of the humiliation of Christ as well as his pedagogical method to live, teach, and act under the conditions of his time and country, on the background of Palestine in A. D. 30; and it was specially his method to do *his* work and not his disciples', to lead a life of love and light, to die in order to pour out his blood of the covenant for many,[6] and to go back to the Father that the Holy Spirit might come and lead his followers into all truth. A full statement of Christianity on his part would have been premature, would have been pedagogically unwise if not worthless. "I have yet many things to say unto you, but ye cannot bear them now."[7] Has he not been saying them through the Spirit of truth ever since? His earth's method was his own—first the blade, then the ear, then the full grain in the ear.[8] Such a full statement would also have been philosophically and spiritually impossible, for Christianity was not a set of teachings by Christ. If it had been, we should

[6] Mark 14. 24.   [7] John 16. 12.   [8] Mark 4. 28.

PAUL AS THE AFTER-CHRIST

never have heard of it. There was no man with a literary bent among the disciples, and the Gospels we have are the later prompting of religious and missionary needs. There was no one to say, "Ah, look at what a philosopher and teacher we had." Christianity was not a set of instructions, though it included them, but a new life, a religion springing out of Christ's life, death, resurrection, ascension, and mediatorial activity in history through the Spirit, who works on his disciples and on the world through that life, death, etc. The only question is whether so far as Christ's teachings were concerned the apostles were true to the content and spirit of those teachings. Did they bring in a new doctrine, or did their message fit into the situation made by the historical background Christ, and was it the necessary consequence of his words and deeds?[9]

I have elsewhere shown how some of the main historic features of our religion which are a stumbling-block to the modern man go back to the message of Jesus as set forth in the synoptic Gospels, and it will be sufficient here to indicate a few points possibly not brought in there in which Paul was not an inventer nor intruder. The reader will remember Harnack's well-known assertion that the "whole of Jesus's message may be reduced to these two heads: God as Father, and the human soul so ennobled that it can and does unite with him,"[10] a pretty meager remnant, both heads in the Old Testament and even in heathenism, and so quite superfluous as the object of Christ's coming. The peculiar and far more pressing message that Christ himself is Saviour, that his

---

[9] Faulkner, "Justification," in *International Standard Bible Encyclopædia*, vol. iii, p. 1785. [10] *What is Christianity?* 1901, p. 68.

own person is part of his message, is left out, but it is Harnack, and not Himself, who leaves it out. It is not the Father simply but himself who must be loved more than father and mother, and it is for himself that the cross must be taken up in a following not of the Father but of himself (see references to all these points in note). It is confession not of the Father but of him which determines acknowledgment in the eternal world, where judgment is rendered not according to one's love of God or faith in God, but according to one's attitude to him (Christ) in his unfortunate ones. Instead of referring men to the Father, Christ forgives sins himself, and, like Paul, he reckons all men as needing this forgiveness. He prepared the way for Paul's doctrine of righteousness, negatively in demanding a humble sense of sin, inner fitness, or perfection, and positively in requiring recourse to him, and not to God the Father, by those who felt the burden of their sins, to him who was the Rest-giver, who thus takes the place of the Jehovah of the still waters and the green pastures, who restoreth my soul, an echo of Rom. 5. 1. For it was specially to those to whom, as to the awakened Paul, the law brought condemnation that he—not simply the Father—came to heal and to save. It was for sinners and to sinners that he came, just as Paul understood, and therefore as Saviour, and not simply as the preacher of God the Father, much less as a social reformer and political reorganizer. The way to this salvation was not better law-keeping, but confession of sin and trusting prayer, exactly equivalent to faith; or it was the humble heart and hunger for righteousness, also equivalent to faith. In the true spirit of Paul, Christ also teaches that he

PAUL AS THE AFTER-CHRIST

who brings the most of himself, of his own pride and works, is the least likely to obtain the kingdom of heaven. Not only entrance but the final reward itself is of grace, also in the spirit of Paul, in anticipation of whose message was the promise of paradise to the penitent robber. At the beginning the message sounded out, "Repent ye, and believe the gospel," the gospel which was summed up in Christ, who would gather the poeple not directly to God the Father but to himself (see reference). All this means that faith in himself, in him as the Son of God, of which faith he speaks with anxiety (faith in God the Father he and all who heard him took for granted) and the presence of which he greeted with joy. And no sooner was his person as the Son of God rightly estimated than he began to unfold the absolute necessity ("must," $\delta\epsilon\iota$) of his death and resurrection. In the evening before he was to be offered up he brings out the significance of that death, not as martyrdom, not as witness to his teaching, not as showing how we should die, but as covenant blood shed for ($\dot{\upsilon}\pi\grave{\epsilon}\rho$, for the sake of, sometimes, instead of) many, in fact the giving up of his soul as a ransom for ($\dot{\alpha}\nu\tau\grave{\iota}$, instead of) many. After his resurrection he still insists that there was a religious necessity ($\check{\epsilon}\delta\epsilon\iota$) to suffer these things, and to enter into his own glory (a word that has to do with the ineffable effulgence of the Eternal God himself).[11] Paul could hardly have expressed the fact of atonement through Christ's death better than the latter does in Matt. 20. 28; 26. 28. With

---
[11] Matt. 10. 37–39; 16. 24–27; 10. 32; 25. 35ff.; 9. 2–6; 6. 12; 5. 3; 5. 6, 8, 20, 48; 11. 28; Mark 2. 17; Matt. 9. 13; Luke 15. 7; 15. 2; 7. 39; 19. 7; Matt. 11. 19; Luke 18. 13; Matt. 5. 3, 6; 18. 3, 4; Mark 10. 14; Matt. 19. 30; 20. 1–16; Luke 24. 43; Mark 1. 15; Matt. 23. 37; 16. 13–16; Luke 18. 8; Matt. 8. 10; Mark 14. 24; Luke 24. 26.

MODERNISM AND THE CHRISTIAN FAITH

this whole foundation, could the Christian doctrine of salvation take any other course than that it actually did take? Ihmels is right, therefore, in holding that Paul's proclamation was continuous with the self-witness of Jesus, which pointed as a consequence or development to the witness of Paul.[12] There was no serious teaching of the apostle which was original with him, which did not have distinct premonitions in Jesus.

The discovery by the liberal, therefore, of a different gospel in Paul than in Christ as to the divinity of Christ, atonement, salvation, justification, and the ordinary elements of Christian teaching, is the discovery of a mare's-nest.[13] If we had the synoptic Gospels alone, there is not one essential element of our religion as Paul conceived it that is not already there in the germ. For this reason the radical or consistent Unitarian has very little more patience with those Gospels than he has with Paul. Or he explains the deeper parts of them away as themselves Pauline, as showing a later deposit, as interpolated, as anything to get rid of them as a witness for Christ. Is the trouble with the Gospels or with his own presuppositions? Luke was the friend of Paul, but if there is a human Gospel in the world it is Luke's. But the divine parts are there too. Mark represented Peter, another circle, but the objectionable elements are in Mark too. There is no recourse. In order to get rid of the deeper things in the Gospels which have Paul in their roots you would have to lay them waste with a plowshare of criticism as deep

---

[12] *Realencyklopädie f. Protestantische Theologie und Kirche*, vol. 16, 490 (3 Aufl.). See Faulkner in *International Standard Bible Encyclopædia*, p. 1785 (vol. iii).

[13] Read especially the objective putting of Jesus's teaching by Ihmels in *Neue Kirchliche Zeitschrift*, 1906, 456ff. (*Jesus und Paulus*).

PAUL AS THE AFTER-CHRIST

as the shell-holes of war-torn France of 1914–18. The residuum left would present some beautiful thoughts, but as a force for redeeming and converting the Roman world or for explaining Christianity as a dynamic for righteousness it would be nil.

I think Paul's own witness is not to be despised. No one accuses him of dishonesty or of self-deception. Did he think he was innovating on Jesus? On the contrary, he gloried in being not simply the servant, but the slave, of Jesus. He loved him, he followed him, and it was the ambition of his life to witness for him, to speak his thoughts, to have his spirit, to represent his mind. To have brought in another gospel than Christ's would have killed him with chagrin and remorse. Paul himself was not conscious of any such lapse from Christ.

What about his contemporaries? His friends certainly never threw in his face any betrayal of Christ. Did his enemies? Outside of the Gnostics, who taught another gospel with a vengeance (see Epistle to the Colossians), Paul had two kinds of enemies. There were those who fought him for not insisting on circumcision for the Gentiles. But we don't know that they ever alleged Christ for their side as over against Paul's. Then there were those who were nervous over the method of Paul's Gentile mission and not clear as to his treatment of the Jews, in which the question of circumcision and other Jewish matters were mixed up. These were moderate enemies (in fact, they could hardly be called enemies) and the apostles themselves were at first a mild section of them. But did any of these allege betrayal of Christ by Paul, departure from Christ's preaching, or anything of the kind? Our sources do not so inform us.

MODERNISM AND THE CHRISTIAN FAITH

So far as we know there was not a single objector who ever appealed to Christ on any subject as over against Paul. And as to his main witness on those fundamental things which have made Christianity what it has been through the centuries from Jesus till to-day, there is not a scintilla of evidence that he was ever accused of departing from his Master.

What were the sources of Paul's knowledge of Christ and Christian things? There was, first, the common information possessed by every intelligent person who had anything to do with Palestine, and especially any Jew who would naturally be interested in an alleged Messiah. Besides, Paul had been a fierce persecutor, and was therefore intensely concerned to know whom and why he was persecuting. He was no amused observer standing aloof in indifference as to the new faith, but his whole soul was wrapped up in knowing and fighting it.

There was, second, his intercourse with Ananias and other disciples at Damascus, with disciples at Antioch, with apostles and others in Jerusalem, what he learned in Arabia, etc., and it is not to be supposed that so wide-awake, inquisitive, eager spirit would not exploit his opportunities to the utmost. It is true that he celebrates his independence ("Neither went I up to Jerusalem to them that were apostles before me," Gal. 1. 17), but he is speaking here of his call to be an apostle, which depended not on authorization from the twelve, which he did not seek. As to general knowledge, his fifteen days with Peter in Jerusalem (verse 18) would not be misspent.

But, third, Paul himself brings in revelation here as a source of his truth. He glories that his gospel was not after man, nor did he receive it from man,

PAUL AS THE AFTER-CHRIST

nor was taught it, but it came through revelation of Jesus Christ (verses 11, 12). Of course revelation would not give him the facts of Christ's life and teaching, because it is not the substitute for inquiry and study, nor the abettor of laziness. On all these things God's method is, "Come and see," "Seek and ye shall find." What revelation gave was his good tidings, that alone, the substance of his religious message. Now, it is not to be assumed, I think, that that revelation would contradict another, or contradict what Christ and the apostles taught, for there is likely no schism in God. At least it is not to be assumed without evidence. Of course in methods, ways, expression, in the periphery of Christianity, in matters not at the heart and therefore not included in the revelation, there will be differences of judgment, opinion, approach, due to education, environment, etc.; but if Paul spoke the truth in claiming this source of his glad tidings, it is probable that his Teacher or Inspirer and Peter's were (or was) not at sixes and sevens.

Fourth, even liberal critics admit that Paul's Damascus vision was one chief source of his gospel or of his revelation. If that vision was from God, and if Christ was from God, I hardly think there was any essential departure in Paul's gospel from that of Christ and his apostles.

Fifth, the Old Testament has an important place as a common fountain for both Jesus and Paul. There was hardly an element in the religious testimony of both for which they did not either appeal to the Old Testament or for which the Old Testament could not be appealed to. Paul was insistent on this. It is as though he said: I am not foisting on you, my brother Jews, a lot of new ideas from foreign sources, but everything in my gospel—the Christ as divine, as Son of God, atonement, his life, death, resurrection, ascension, salvation as a free gift from God, justification by faith alone—all these and other things are in your own prophets and psalmists, if you would but open your eyes and see. And so, although Christ corrected, enlarged, or spiritualized the law, he felt himself bound up in God's bundle of life which we call the Old Testament, and, so to speak, to have stepped out of it to call his people back to a true appreciation of it.

No, Paul was not the creator of Christianity. He took no laurels from his Master; but, he might be called the second founder of it. He broke in on paganism in Asia and Europe with a strategic knowledge of great centers, with a statesmanlike adaptation of means and ends, and yet with a zeal, fiery force, and intellectual and spiritual power, which made the second epoch of Christianity and assured it its final triumph. He interpreted Christianity to both Judaism and paganism, and he interpreted both to Christianity, and so laid down the bridge on which Jew and Greek could go over into Christ. He explained and defended our religion, and presented it in that shape which made it intellectually reasonable and evangelistically effective.

Paul was neither the "Second Founder of Christianity" nor did he teach "another gospel" than that of Christ. But he was the deepest and richest in spirit among the first witnesses of Christ. That is the reason why among all the New Testament men he comprehended most deeply the nature of Christ and the peculiarity of the Christian religion, and that he created, on the other hand, formulas and combinations which were new in relation to tradition. That expresses the peculiarity of his thought-world.

PAUL AS THE AFTER-CHRIST

One can call Paul the first theologian, for it is the task of theology to create for the revelation of Christ forms of expression pertinent to the times and effective. But Paul was more than a theologian and less: more, for he had experienced revelation itself; less, for he had never deliberately striven for a whole view of Christianity. The deeper and richer a spirit is, the more original will be his understanding of revelation, but the brighter will his whole thought-world express the fundamental tendency of the revelation. There is no man in history of whom that is true in the measure it is of Paul. He proclaimed *his* gospel, and yet it was Christ's gospel. Every thought of this infinitely versatile and rich spirit had only *one* object, namely, to get hold of the revelation of Christ in its depth. "I live, yet know I, Christ lives in me." The fundamental thoughts of Christianity received through Paul for all time their standard expression.[14]

Or, if I might quote from F. W. Orde Ward, B.A.: "St. Paul was the sole apostle with a cosmopolitan mind, who could be and was all things to all men, without compromising the great Christian truths. He was invincible, because he knew that he was really possessed with the spirit of Jesus, who spoke and lived and worked through him. *Christus auctor ecclesiæ, Paulus ædificator, Christus creavit, Paulus disposuit.* ... He always gave the glory to God, and confessed his work was Christ's and not his. He felt the dignity of the divine commission, and was consequently proud and jealous not for himself, but for the honor of the Master whom he served so faithfully and so long. His sympathy covered a multitude of sins and embraces every sinner—at a time when men and women alike knew how to sin." (It is one of the objections to Paul in favor of Christ that the former had a much more pessimistic view of human nature, a more somber view of sin and of

---
[14] R. Seeberg, *Paulus und Jesus*, in *Aus Religion und Geschichte*, Leipz., 1906, vol. i, p. 102.

actual sins. It is true that Paul wrote Rom. 1. 18–32, sufficiently frank, but Jesus said those terrific words in the twenty-third chapter of Matthew concerning the most respectable and supposedly pious people in the world. I suspect that Paul did not have, however, the fine feeling of Jesus concerning children, though in that Jesus was nineteen hundred years ahead of his time. But that Jesus did not share Paul's view of the so-called fall of man and its consequences is impossible, because Christ was nursed on the Old Testament, and all its main religious ideas and history he took over as a matter of course, while he had no more occasion to be always referring to those ideas and history than a professor of church history has to be proving to his students the existence of God. Paul never went quite so far as John 8. 44. O no; Jesus was no liberal on sin. Besides, he swung the thunderbolts of hell too often for that.) "But in the worst he [Paul] saw a potential Christ, he saw a spark of the heavenly fire and the divine image. The way in which he absolutely identified himself with his Lord, he who was once a blasphemer and persecutor and the arch-enemy of the infant church, we know, because it is recorded in his epistles. But the secret of his Christianity, or the abolition and regeneration of his own personality in the personality of his Saviour, is a secret still to most people. And those who do know it cannot reveal it."[15]

---

[15] Ward, *Christ and St. Paul the Epi-Christ*, in *The London Quarterly Review*, July, 1919, pp. 50, 52.

NOTE.—There is a rich literature in this field of Paul and Jesus. The best list is in Machen, *Jesus and Paul*, in *Biblical and Theological Studies* (pub. on 100th Anniversary of Founding of Princeton Theological Seminary), New York, 1912, pp. 547, 548. Vischer gives interesting review from liberal side in *Theologische Rundschau*, 1905, 129ff.,

PAUL AS THE AFTER-CHRIST

173ff., 1908, 301ff. To Machen's list must be added the able work of Walther, *Pauli Christentum Jesu Evangelium*, Leipz., 1908 (51 pp.). I give the liberal Deissmann's conclusions. "In speaking," he says, "of the two dominant personalities of the creative epoch of Christianity, I do not speak of Jesus as first and Paul beside him as second. To place them thus side by side would be unhistorical—a modern collocation. Their historical position is: Jesus the One, Paul the first after the One, the first *in* the One. From the personality of Jesus there went forth the decisive impulse, the effects of which are felt to this day; historically speaking, Jesus is the origin of our religion. The historical significance of Paul is that by insisting on the cult of the ascended Master he preserved what was precious for men's souls in the revelation of Jesus, saved it from being narrowed to the national religion and sacrificed to legalism, and secured it to the heart of the people forever. [I might correct Deissmann here that Paul did not "insist on the cult of the ascended Master" in the usual sense of those words. Christ was to him no new demigod whose cult must be propagated, but Christ was to him the Son of God to be worshiped by the church as a matter of course, and all the apostles insisted on this according to their measure and opportunity, and, of course, never found fault with Paul as to this. Paul saved Christianity from being narrowed into a national religion not only by the place Christ had in it but by his principle that pagan Greeks should not come into Christianity by way of Judaism, a program indorsed by the apostolic council of Acts 15.] He gave to the cult of Christ at once its popular shape and the outline of its world wide organization. The structure of their inner lives is alone sufficient reason to prevent Jesus and Paul from being ranked together. With Jesus all is bedrock, resting on nothing but himself. But Paul's masonry needed foundations. Paul is great, but he is great in Christ."—Deissmann, in *The Expositor*, London, 7th series, vol. vii, 1909, pp. 215, 216. Even Alfred Seeberg (younger brother of the eminent theologian of Berlin, Reinhold; Alfred died during the Great War) admits that a firm connection exists between the apostolical proclamation and the traditional material which forms the foundation of the synoptic Gospels. See *Theologisches Literaturblatt*, 1912, p. 60. The admirable discussion of Feine should also be read, *Jesus Christus und Paulus*, 1902, *Das Christentum Jesu und das Christentum der Apostel in ihrer Abgrenzung gegen die Religionsgeschichte*, 1904, and *Paulus als Theologe*, 1906. See the valuable book by Moe, *Paulus und die evangelische Geschichte*, Leipz., 1912. On account of space I have made this survey too brief. See also W. H. Johnson, in *Princeton Theological Review*, 1907, pp. 399–422, Vos, in same, pp. 496–502, and W. C. Schaeffer in *Reformed Church Review*, 1910, pp. 450–468 (Did Paul understand Jesus?).

CHAPTER IX

TRINITY

I HAVE always felt some sympathy with Unitarians in their revolt of the eighteenth and early nineteenth centuries. To preserve Christianity as monotheism and yet to swallow the conventional doctrine received from Augustine, Aquinas, and the Reformers was a hard pill. What helped us to do it perhaps was the knowledge that all these teachers were as earnest monotheists as ourselves, and out of respect to them we gave the doctrine the benefit of the doubt. Of course there were many other factors which gave birth to modern Unitarianism, but a too tritheistic Trinity was one of them. Thus, in his celebrated Jared Sparks ordination sermon, preached in Baltimore in 1819, Channing describes what a stumbling-block the doctrine was. He says:

In the first place, we believe in the doctrine of God's unity, or that there is one God, and one only. To this truth we give infinite importance, and we feel ourselves bound to take heed lest any man spoil us of it by vain philosophy. The proposition that there is one God seems to us exceedingly plain. We understand by it that there is one being, one mind, one person, one intelligent agent, and one only.... We conceive that these words could have conveyed no other meaning to the simple and uncultivated people who were set apart to be the depositaries of this great truth, and who were utterly incapable of understanding those hair-breadth distinctions between being and person which the sagacity of later ages has discovered.... The doctrine of the Trinity subverts the unity of God. According to it, there are three infinite and equal persons, possessing supreme divinity, called the Father,

TRINITY

Son, and Holy Ghost. Each of these has his own particular consciousness, will, perceptions. They love each other, converse with each other, and delight in each other's society. They perform different parts in man's redemption, each having his appropriate office.... We have three intelligent agents, possessed of different consciousness, different wills, and different perceptions, performing different acts, and sustaining different relations; and if these things do not imply and constitute three minds or beings, we are utterly at a loss to know how three minds or beings are to be found.... We do with all earnestness protest against the irrational and unscriptural doctrine of the Trinity.... With Jesus, we worship the Father, as the only living and true God.... We challenge our opponents to adduce one passage in the New Testament where the word "God" means three persons.[1]

There are few men living to-day who do not feel the tremendous force of this appeal. They would cry, "If this is Trinitarianism, who would not be a Unitarian?" But even in Channing's day there were broad-minded Trinitarians who conceived the matter differently and from whom it was a pain for Channing to be separated. He wanted the unity of the two views emphasized. He says:

Dr. Watts and Dr. Doddridge have left us a better example [than to emphasize points of difference]. Trinitarians and Unitarians both believe in one God, one infinite self-existent mind. According to the first, this God is three persons; according to the last he is one person. Ought this difference, which relates to the obscurest of all subjects, to the essence and metaphysical nature of God, and which common Christians cannot understand, to divide and alienate those who ascribe to this one God the same perfections, who praise him for the same blessings?... According to Trinitarians, Jesus, who suffered and died on the cross, is a derived being, *personally* united with the self-existent God. According to the Unitarians, he is a derived being *intimately* united with the self-existent God. Ought this difference, which transcends

---

[1] *Works of W. E. Channing*, one vol. ed. complete, 1875 (1878), p. 371. Used by permission of The Beacon Press, Inc., publishers, Boston, Massachusetts.

MODERNISM AND THE CHRISTIAN FAITH

the conception of common Christians, divide and alienate those who love the same excellent character in Jesus Christ? ... As soon as Trinitarians attempt to show the consistency of their doctrine of three persons with the divine unity, their peculiarities begin to vanish, and in many of their writings little or nothing is left but one God acting in three characters, or sustaining three relations. ... Ought distinctions so subtle and perplexing separate those who love the same divine character? ... We all believe that the Father sent the Son, and gives to those that ask the Holy Spirit. We are all Trinitarians if this is Trinitarianism. But it is not. The Trinitarian believes [and here we get the conventional Trinity again] that the one God is three distinct persons, called Father, Son, and Holy Ghost, and he believes that each of these persons is equal to the other two in every perfection, that each is the only true God, and yet that the three are only one God. The Unitarian believes that there is but one person possessing supreme divinity, even the Father. ... [But there might be a coming together. For] what are the questions which divide them? Why, these: First, whether the One God be three distinct subsistences, or three persons, or three *somewhats, called persons*, as Dr. Worcester says, for want of a better word; and, secondly, whether one of these three subsistences, or improperly called persons, formed a personal union with a human soul, so that the Infinite Mind and a human mind ... became a complex person.

Channing called these differences "phrases," and held that they should not separate Christians. He said that Trinitarians think themselves at an immeasurable distance from Unitarians, but the reason is that they are "surrounded with a mist of obscure phraseology." Were this dispersed, they would find that they were wasting their hostility on a band of brothers.[2] But it is evident it is only with these or other explanations of the Trinity that Channing could compromise. With the ordinary doctrine he felt as inexpugnable repugnance as the most orthodox did to Unitarianism. With that repugnance we all to-day feel sympathy,

[2] W. H. Channing, *Life of W. E. Channing*, centenary edition, 1880, pp. 209, 212, 214, 215.

TRINITY

as I said, for the regular doctrine as it struck Channing and his Unitarian predecessors was another name for tritheism.

On the other hand, the substance at least of Trinitarianism made a tremendous appeal then—if it had not, we should all be Unitarians long since—and makes that appeal to-day. What is the reason?

There is, first, the New Testament testimony. It is carrying coals to Newcastle to exploit that testimony here. There are scores of passages where the Father, Son and Holy Spirit are spoken of together, which imply that they are distinct yet united and are associated together in Deity. One of these passages[3] is thrown out by the Ritschlian historians for reasons that are quite insufficient, as I have shown elsewhere,[4] but even if thus violently dealt with, the moral value of the verse is lessened but a little. In any case it must be exceedingly early, and thus is a witness to contemporary opinion in the church which associated Son and Spirit with the Father as a matter of course in the most solemn act of Christian dedication. The so-called Apostolic Benediction[5] is a Trinitarian utterance of stalwart orthodoxy, and is out of the fresh morning of the church's consciousness. I know that benediction is given in some Unitarian churches, as I heard it one Sunday morning in King's Chapel, Boston, as late as 1911, but how a Unitarian can use it is a mystery more inexplicable than the Trinity itself. Such a use must have been a bitter cross to straight-seeing Unitarians like Chadwick and Savage. But not only are there numerous

---

[3] Matt. 28. 19, 20.

[4] See *Crises in Early Church*, 1912, pp. 11-14; *Methodist Review*, New York, 1910, pp. 14-16.

[5] 2 Cor. 13. 14.

places where Father, Son, and Holy Spirit are mentioned together, but there are as numerous where each is spoken of separately under categories of divinity. Besides, they are assigned work in Christian salvation and life which belongs to God alone.

Now, these are the broad facts on the face of the New Testament to which the only pertinent answer is that the New Testament is a literature of no compelling importance to Christians. But only the most radical would give that answer, for Unitarians generally concede both the historical importance of the New Testament and its unique religious value, and they constantly appeal to it when it serves their purpose. Irrespective of any special theory of inspiration, the large and deep Trinitarian color of the New Testament can be eliminated only by the assumption that the early Christians were laboring under a deception so appalling that it renders all their other religious ideas worthless, besides making them guilty of idolatry.

Plainly, this initial Trinitarian bent to our religion never left it. There were indeed in the last part of the second century and beginning of the third a couple of interesting tendencies which came in, which arranged the factors differently. There was Patripassian Monarchianism, which appealed especially to some simple Christians who thought so highly of Christ that they made him only another form or mode of the Father—the modalistic or Sabellian Trinity which has appealed strongly to some minds. They could not think of Christ as in any secondary place, as a subsistence in God or his Son, but only as the supreme God himself. The monad God contracts himself into the Son and later enlarges himself into the Holy Spirit. Our Swedenborgian friends

TRINITY

have some such idea of the Trinity. I am sorry I cannot go with acquaintances who find their solution here. Besides being a contradiction in terms for the Son to be another form or mode of the Father, the New Testament (a) represents Christ as praying to the Father, which would be absurd on the modalistic Trinity; (b) always distinguishes between the Father and the Son; (c) represents Christ as sending the Spirit, which is absurd if they are different forms of the same thing; and (d) represents the Holy Spirit as testifying of Christ as of another. The Patripassian Monarchians or Modalistic Trinitarians are so orthodox they lean backward, but the facts of the New Testament tell another story.

At the same time that these came out, another set of men were teaching a view which in substance has been revived by our liberals in the Protestant churches. These were the dynamistic Monarchians, so called because God came down as *power* at some time on the man Jesus and endowed him for his work. After that he could be called—at least by accommodation—God. Christ was born miraculously, but that alone did not make him Messiah and God, which was done by a special descent on him, perhaps at his birth but preferably at his baptism. Our liberals change the terminology a little by saying that Christ revealed God, but the substance of the view is not changed. I do not find sufficient reasons for substituting the fascinating view of Theodotus for the Trinitarianism of the older Christians. For (1) though Christ received glory and power from God the Father, he never represents himself nor is ever represented as receiving divinity from him at any one time. (2) The history and consciousness of Christ cannot be

MODERNISM AND THE CHRISTIAN FAITH

divided into the ante-divine and the post-divine state. At his baptism he received not his Sonship, nor his divinity, nor any divine attribute, but only *testimony* as to that Sonship. (3) This view if logically carried out would make Christ's divinity the same essentially as that of all Christians, which is contrary to the consciousness and testimony of Christ and of the apostles, who knew Christ best, as well as of his followers in all ages, contrary to their devotional feelings, and to their unconquerable revulsion against bringing Christ down to the level of ourselves in regard to his relations with God. (4) "Sonship" is not a term of reception of influences, but of being. We are also, of course, sons of God, but outside of our creation we are sons in Christ and through Christ. It was ourselves, not Christ, who "received the adoption." Scripture and religious experience unite in making Christ Son in the sense of divinity, but ourselves of humanity made divine by participation in the life of God through Christ. "Now are we the sons of God"—there was a time when we were not in this sense. But Christ never began to be a Son. God's "this day have I begotten thee" is God's day, eternity's day. For these reasons I cannot feel that the dynamic Monarchians have helped me much.

It is, indeed, said that we could all be Trinitarians in the sense of the New Testament but not in the sense of later developments. That is, we could be Christian Trinitarians but not churchly Trinitarians. The Christian thought of God we receive but not the church dogma. I say "Amen" to that if the church has added anything to the Christian view which makes it another thing, but not if that view has received only scientific explanation and deepen-

TRINITY

ing by the church. It will be convenient to take R. A. Lipsius's objections here, as representing what he thinks is the Christian rather than the churchly standpoint.[6]

(1) The Church view is "simply an inconceivable mystery." But mystery is in itself no objection to a truth or fact. Every truth is a little globe of light surrounded by impenetrable mystery. (2) The Trinity doctrine "withdraws itself from every proof and understanding." Does it? (3) If the doctrine is true, the whole Heilsökonomie stands and falls with it. I agree that every doctrine of Christianity depends in whole or in part on who Christ is, and that you cannot think of Christ without sooner or later getting back into the facts of which the Trinity is designed to be the expression. (4) Therefore, not simply the denial of the doctrine, but even ignorance of it, excludes from salvation. That does not follow. "In every nation he that feareth God," etc. The honest reception of Christ secures salvation according to Christianity, whatever may be one's intellectual apprehension of him. That apprehension may be accidental, depending upon education, environment, etc., but the attitude of the soul and life is not accidental. (5) While religion attests the revelation of God in Christ and the divine life embodied in his Person, to say anything further in the direction of the Trinity as to Christ is to be metaphysical, and bring in philosophical conceptions. Very likely. Every judgment of being is metaphysical, and we can no more help forming those judgments than we can help being ourselves. In fact, Christ invited metaphysical judgments.[7] We are bound to analyze the

[6] *Dogmatik*, 3 Aufl., 1893, §§ 371ff., pp. 288ff.   [7] Matt. 16. 13.

MODERNISM AND THE CHRISTIAN FAITH

phenomenal Christ into the real Christ. The question as to the Trinity is not as to whether it is metaphysical or not, but whether it is false or true metaphysics. As to contemporary philosophy, Christians had to use the words and ideas of their age. And here the question is, Did they truly set forth Christ in that use, or did they misrepresent him? (6) Representations of the Trinity are apt to run either into modalism or tritheism. I agree. Is there not a middle way? But even a theologian so free from church tradition as Lipsius has to acknowledge that the Trinity is the expression of Christian truth. He says:

> At the foundation of the Christian faith is the Christian triad of revelation, that is, that the self-revelation of God in the Person of Jesus Christ is an actual being of God in him in objective-historical reality, and the self-communication of God in the Holy Spirit is an inner fact of the common and individual experience of the believer.
>
> The immediate presence of God as reconciling, redeeming, sanctifying power in the religious consciousness of the believer is therefore referred back on the one hand to the historical revelation of God in the Son, on the other hand to the constantly self-renewing self-communication of God in the Holy Spirit, but on both hands is founded on the eternal nature of God as absolute Love.
>
> As God as Father is the foundation of the Love which grounds salvation, which Love reveals in the Son the eternal salvation-thoughts of the Father, and as God founds in the Holy Spirit salvation-communion with Father and Son, the faith in Father, Son, and Holy Spirit is the special way in which the full religious content of the Christian idea of God lays itself out. The love of God is objectively revealed for Christian faith in the Son as the divine love that "became man," while in the Holy Spirit it is an immediate fact of subjective experience of the believer. So far now as the divine world-end according to the Christian world-view is first attained in man's salvation-life, as a real communion of the life and love of God and of man, the revelation of God in

TRINITY

the Son is at the same time the personal incorporation or "incarnation" of the eternal divine word-idea or of the divine Logos, while his self-communication in the Holy Spirit is the real presence of God as the unending administration of the Spirit in the world, or the concrete realization of the divine world-end in the finite life of the Spirit. So far the Christian salvation-experience includes perfectly the religious content of the idea of God: God's unending creative power of life and of love, fully revealing in the Son its eternal nature of the law of redeeming Love as unending world-ordering wisdom, while really actualizing in the Holy Spirit its eternal will of love in the common and individual love of men as the unending teleological principle of the world. The ontological doctrine of Trinity of the Church is only the immediate Metaphysicirung of this religious content.[8]

Well, if the doctrine of the Trinity is any more metaphysical than this statement by Lipsius of the truths of which it is the expression it is metaphysical indeed. But he is not to blame for that. Whenever you get underneath phenomena you strike metaphysics.

The work of Arius compelled the further development of the doctrine. He came out with a view of Christ which in the ostensible interest of monotheism made the beginnings of a Christian Pantheon, extended later by the Roman Catholic cult—borrowed from heathenism—of Mary and the saints. Arius led to the Nicene Creed, 325, where we meet the famous word ὁμοούσιον, of the same essence. This and other words used in the controversy have burdened the Trinity in the modern mind because (it is said) they carry us beyond our knowledge, and especially because the word "Person" suggests three Gods. But if the doctrine of the Trinity when truly understood is the only adequate explanation of the facts, it is beside the point to say that it is beyond our knowledge. And the modern meaning of "Person"

---
[8] Lipsius, *Dogmatik*, 3 Aufl., 1893, §§ 383, 384, pp. 298, 299.

MODERNISM AND THE CHRISTIAN FAITH

was not at all the meaning of those who first employed it in these discussions. This was the situation. The Sabellians used the word πρόσωπον, *persona*, "rôle," as a designation of the transient form of manifestation of God historically assumed. When the church wanted to express the fact that these so-called forms of manifestation were really forms or modes of being inherent in God, it used the word ὑπόστασις, which was at first equivalent to οὐσία, "essence." As the discussion proceeded it was felt that, as there was no intention, of course, to assert three essences, some word must be used for the divine essence and another for the different (not persons, but) modes of being of Deity. The Greek Fathers (for it was they alone who did this work, because they alone had both the language and the mental acumen and vision to do it) used the word οὐσία for the essence (*essentia*) of God and the words ὑποστάσεις and πρόσωπα (plural) for the modes or forms of being (*personæ*) of the one Godhead or divine substance. The Fathers never used the word "person" in our sense, never intended to assert three separate consciousnesses, wills, intellects, and all the other things which go to make up a person or individual, which was the form in which the church doctrine appeared to Channing and the old Unitarians. The only person in God is God himself, who realizes his being, however, not in one mode, but in a complex and rich life—Father, Son, and Holy Spirit. God the one person realized his personality not in successive modes of manifestation, which would mean growth and change in God, not in three attributes or qualities, not in three constituents of the Father, though that is near the truth, not as three species in the one genus God, as men

TRINITY

are species in the one genus man, which is tritheism, not as three quanta or different essences in which Deity is distributed—not thus does God realize his personality, but in Father, Son, and Holy Spirit and by their means. The one God finds his self-conscious and personal being not in an abstract unity, according to Mohammedanism, modern Judaism, and Unitarianism, but in the three hypostases, his unity not being separated from them but immanent in them. The three are not separate centers of self-determination (three Gods), nor three ways of revelation, for any kind of a God could reveal himself, and our God reveals himself in more than three ways or modes.

I said that Channing justly balked at the popular Trinity. This Trinity goes back to Augustine, though the popular imagination and later theological working probably made it more tritheistic, against which Augustine tried to guard. His treatise on *The Trinity* is one of the most wonderful pieces of religious literature in the world. It is resplendent with his genius and quivers with the movement of his rich spiritual life. He emphasized the solidarity of the Trinity with a vengeance. The triangle was really his symbol. Not only could one side not exist without the other, but each side is equal to the other two! "For Father, Son, and Holy Spirit together are not a greater essence than the Father alone or the Son alone, but these three substances or persons, if they are so called, are together equal to each one alone.... Neither are two something more than one."[9] From Augustine the church got the idea of the parity of the Persons, not simply as participating in the substance of Deity, but as equally furnished with all the prerogatives of

[9] *De Trinitate*, 7. 6, 11; 8. 1; 6. 7, 9; 10. 12; 6. 3, 5.

MODERNISM AND THE CHRISTIAN FAITH

God, therefore to the Unitarian three equal Gods. Augustine would have abhorred that inference, but his idea that each Person had the entire divine substance naturally led to emphasis on the three as practically three Gods. Saint Thomas Aquinas followed in his footsteps, as did the Reformers, and so that too crass Trinitarianism has come down to us, though Socinus, the high English Arians, and the Unitarians reacted against it.

But the finer and more subtle Greek intellect approached the subject differently and with juster appreciation of the unity of God. Dean Stanley once said that if John Henry Newman could have read German, modern history might have been different. He could not see how anyone familiar with German theological science could become a High Churchman, much less a Roman Catholic. So we might say that if Augustine had read Greek well, the mediæval church and modern theology might have been different. Of course, these suppositions are vain. The Latin inheritance and language would probably have overborne Greek knowledge and Greek inwardness. Athanasius guarded monotheism both more scripturally and more philosophically just than Augustine. He made the center and heart of Deity God the Father, the one God finding its unity not in a solid Trinity but in the Father. "And since Christ is God *from God* and the Logos, Wisdom, and Power of God [italics ours], therefore one God is proclaimed in the Holy Scriptures. For the Logos, being the Son of the one God, is referred back to him from whom he is, so that the Father and the Son are two, yet the monad of divinity is unseparated and undivided. Thus there is one original source of

TRINITY

divinity [the Father] and not two original sources, and hence there is a monarchy. [But Christ is not a demigod for] the essence and the nature are one."[10] The Trinitarian relations are with Athanasius, as with Augustine, eternal and founded in the divine nature, but the spring or nucleus of that nature is God the Father. "Just as a river springing from a fountain is not separated from it, although there are two forms and two names, so neither is the Father the Son nor the Son the Father."[11] The Son derives his life from the Father, but he derives it not by an historical movement but by an immanent process. It would have been a solecism both to the Greek mind and Christian consciousness of Athanasius to think of God as gaining an increment of power and glory competent to beget the Son; therefore he could never have been a Unitarian. It would have been an equal solecism for him to have made that Son equal to the Father according to the symbol of a triangle, because, while the Son is of the same essence with the Father, he is by the very fact of being a Son eternally subordinate to him and dependent on him; therefore Athanasius could never have been an Augustinian Trinitarian. The source or ruling principle ($ἀρχή$) of the Trinity, the fountain ($πηγή$) of it, is the Father,[12] and thus Athanasius gives forth as almost axiomatic with Christians: "And thus there will be proclaimed in the church one God, the Father of the Logos,"[13] reminding us of the similar axiom of Saint Paul: "To us there is one God, the Father, of whom are all things, and we unto him; and one Lord, Jesus Christ, through whom are all things,

---

[10] *Contra Arianos oratio*, 4. 1.
[11] *Expositio Fidei* 2. *C. Ar. or.* 3. 4.
[12] *Ad Serapionem*, 1. 28.
[13] *Ad Epictetum*, 9.

MODERNISM AND THE CHRISTIAN FAITH

and we through him,"[14] which does not mean that both Paul and Athanasius could not on occasion call Christ God, because both did, not out of courtesy or accommodation, but as recognizing realities of Sonship. Perhaps you might call Athanasius a Trinitarian-Unitarian and Augustine a Unitarian-Trinitarian,[15] and the orthodox would say that the danger of the one was toward subordination, and the liberal would say that the danger of the other was toward tritheism.

I do not claim that the old Unitarians would have clung to Trinitarianism if the Athanasian or older Greek variety had been explained to them, though it is historically certain that it was the Latin Trinity at which they stumbled. Perhaps also psychological explanations would not have helped them. Still, such explanations are interesting. Take the human personality. The spirit or diviner part, the intellect, and the sensibilities and emotions, are so emphasized in some that they seem to become separate subsistences or persons, even in the same individual. Take three circles of being as wide apart as music, philosophy, and history, and yet Professor John Fiske lived at different times in each one, three persons in one man. There is a group-individual like Andrew Lang. Goethe was an eminent instance of a man who seemed to dwell in many personalities, so complex and many-sided his nature, like God dwelling in three modes or points of being. Gladstone as theologian, as ecclesiastic, as Greek or Homeric scholar, as statesman,

---

[14] 1 Cor. 8. 6; compare 1 Tim. 2. 5.

[15] I think I am indebted to the late Professor Paine, of Bangor Theological Seminary, for these terms. See his slashing book, *A Critical History of the Evolution of Trinitarianism*, Boston, 1900.

TRINITY

is another instance. I do not speak simply of aptitudes or a clever facility of nature, but of diversity and breadth of personality that suggest different persons or hypostases in one man. Then a man can devastate or destroy one or more of these realms of personality till he is reduced to simplicity of being, like the Mohammedan God. He becomes, say, pure intellect, the sensibilities, the spiritual or higher nature, and the large humanity dying out, as with Charles Darwin, whose intellect destroyed the spirit; or as with Edward Irving, with whom the emotional and spiritual swallowed up the rest and wrecked his work. On the other hand, how large, rich, and normal the trinity of intellect, spirit, and sensibility with Edwards and Wesley, especially in the latter, whose personality ranged through so many elements or hypostases of being.

Or, take the strange revelations of abnormal personality. It has been shown that in the same individual may live or may seem to live two or three separate persons, or that the same consciousness may clothe itself successively with the mental and moral feelings and thoughts of different individuals. The last quarter of a century has revealed a rich field here to the psychologist.

I do not say that these instances of either normal or abnormal man are closely analogous to the Trinity. What I do say is that personality is too mysterious and complex a quantity to allow us to measure God's with our yardstick, and to say, "There can be no Trinity in him."

Speaking of personality, it is an interesting question how there could be any movement in the life of God, any action and reaction, if his unity is simple

MODERNISM AND THE CHRISTIAN FAITH

and not complex. It is specially interesting to ask how the absolute monad shut up in his frigid loneliness and reduced to a mathematical point could have any of the social attributes which Christians have attributed to him—truth, justice, righteousness, benevolence, love. These attributes hang in the air or live as in a vacuum except when God is Father and the giver of his Spirit. I do not mean by this that the "social Trinity" is to be conceived after the manner of men, only that God is and must be conceived as having in himself sources of life and communion. "We cannot conceive God as personal," says Garvie, who wrote such an appreciative study of Ritschl, "without conceiving him as difference in unity. We cannot think of him as conscious without the distinction of subject and object, as truth without the knowing and the known, as holiness without the purpose and the realization, as love without the loving and the loved. But the difference must also be ever the expression and realization of unity."[16]

Recent Ritschlian theologians in America—as, for instance, Dr. Henry Churchill King—have repeatedly objected to the social Trinity. I have no interest in defending it. If you carry it out too far, it would land you into tritheism. But it is no more than fair to say that when rightly expressed it makes a legitimate and even an attractive appeal. Society is certainly a necessary element in the universe, especially among intelligences, and may it not therefore rest back upon some element in God, be the expression of his life? Then, how can that life function at all if it is a simple monad with no interactions of

[16] *Handbook of Christian Apologetics*, 1915, pp. 157, 158. Charles Scribner's Sons, publishers. Used by permission.

TRINITY

personality? Besides, human beings lend analogies. The more comprehensive and complete the endowments the more they shape themselves into rudimentary personalities. The painter who is also an architect and a poet is like three persons, and between the three communion or society is possible, in fact inevitable. He has the beginning of three consciousnesses, three wills, and a fullness of emotional and intellectual life impossible to the less amply equipped man who lives in the solitariness of a single power. This is one of the benefits of education: it increases the personality, which in its intercommunion of attainments is the reflection of the large fellowship of Father, Son, and Holy Spirit.

But we touch our hearts more nearly when we say that the Trinity is a truth of Christian experience. And this in two aspects.

(1) It is undeniable that it is the bridge of salvation over which God travels to meet us. If sin and sorrow had never visited this planet, we would doubtless have looked into the heart of God by beatific vision and in that sight found our joy, but it is sin which has brought the fullness of God to us in his threefold perfection. For it is as John says: "Of his fullness we all received, and grace for grace."[17] "Apart from the revealed activity of God toward the world there is no mention [in Scripture] of the Logos, and apart from the historical salvation there is no mention of the Son as a Moment of the divine self-life. Also God in his relation to Christ can be designated as well God (John 17. 3; 20. 17) as Father (1 Cor. 8. 6)."[18]

---

[17] John 1. 16. Margin, "grace upon grace."

[18] Kirn, article, "Trinität," in *Realencyklopädie* (Herzog-Hauck) 3 Aufl., vol. xx, p. 113.

MODERNISM AND THE CHRISTIAN FAITH

It is as poor, miserable sinners that we have come to know the Father's love, the Son's grace and salvation, and sanctification and consolation in the Holy Spirit's communion. In other words, the Trinity is especially a truth of revelation conditioned by the Great Salvation. But that revelation does not make the Trinity; it only shows it.

(2) Is there a nearer experience? Wesley quotes a Roman Catholic saint, De Renty, as saying, "I bear about with me the daily experience of the Trinity," and he adds, "I think this is an experience only of the perfect, not of babes in Christ." (I quote from memory.) In the case of Christ the matter is not so difficult. It is the experience of millions that, believing in—not God the Father but—Jesus, they have forgiveness of sins and new life. This is as certain to them as any experience can possibly be. Not only so, millions have the experience of companionship with Jesus, of a lifting up of the soul, of consolation and strength which they refer to him and not to the Father, and which they rightly refer to him, just as Paul did. We may deny the source of these blessings, or say that they really came from the Father. But if the affirmations of these Christians are uncertain when they testify of things which have repeatedly entered into the very texture of their being and are a part of their daily life, how much more uncertain are our denials who profess from the start to know nothing on the subject. As to the Holy Spirit the matter is less clear. It is through the Holy Spirit that the light and truth of God reach the soul, but how to tell whether that light comes directly from the Father or through or by the Holy Spirit must be left to the revelation in the Scripture

TRINITY

and to those general considerations which make the Trinity the most rational explanation of God.

That the Trinity is the only adequate statement of the Christian redemption as experienced is admitted by an eminent liberal, Professor Paul Lobstein, of the University of Strassburg. To comprehend the meaning and value of this doctrine, "it is necessary to start from the redemptive work in which the Son of God appears" and from the Spirit's spiritual regeneration, and the doctrine is the "most complete and profound" expression of those facts. The doctrine "has its root in piety, in the inner religious experience of the Christian brought into contact with the prior and higher facts of a divine manifestation in humanity. In Jesus Christ God is revealed to us as our Father, and the Holy Spirit bears witness to our spirits that we are children of God. The union of God with humanity in Jesus Christ and by the Holy Spirit, or God manifesting himself in Jesus Christ through the Holy Spirit—that is the divine revelation affirmed by the Christian consciousness by virtue of an experience which science has not created, which it can neither demonstrate nor refute, and upon which criticism has no hold." Lobstein holds that the New Testament has "nothing on the subject of a trinitarian distinction in the divine essence," and that is true so far as an affirmation of that distinction in so many words is concerned, but he does hold that that Testament teaches a "religious, historical, economic triad." Saying so much, we are bound, it seems to me, to press back to a Trinity of being, for we cannot think of God's revelation of himself as being less than he really is in himself, or other than he is. Even Garvie says: "All certainty and confidence would be lost in the religious life if God in himself can be thought of as other than he makes himself known to be in his revelation. If he is revealed temporally as Father, Son and Spirit, then he is eternally Father, Son, and Spirit."[19] But Lobstein concedes that the Trinity has not the less an assured and rightful place in Christian truth because it is based on the doctrine of salvation, as such a conception "demands not less imperiously that we shall make the doctrine of the Trinity the supreme and necessary crowning point of the dogmatic structure." That doctrine "unites in a rich and luminous expression, in a concise formula appropriate to the needs of teaching and the cult, the totality of the divine factors of salvation and of the new life."[20]

Before I close, a word or two on the further history might be welcome. In the interest of monotheism Schleiermacher reacted toward Sabellianism, but his conception goes out toward pantheism. In fact, it seems to me that the only alternative to the Trinitarian is either the deistic notion of a barren God or the pantheistic notion of a nonpersonal God, and Schleiermacher looks toward this last. He makes God self-identical in act and being, which makes the universe another name for God, and destroys the Christian thought of creation as a work of God in and for and by his Son. That God has revealed himself, however, in Son and Spirit, Schleiermacher holds fast, his religious nature and his reverence for history demanding this.

---

[19] Garvie, *Handbook of Christian Apologetics*, 1915, p. 157. Charles Scribner's Sons, publishers. Used by permission.

[20] Lobstein, *Introduction to Protestant Dogmatics*, tr. A. M. Smith, 1902, pp. 256-259. Chicago University Press. Used by permission.

TRINITY

Rothe agrees so far as to make Father, Son, and Spirit have to do only with the world of revelation, but still the Trinity is a part of the being of God, as only thus can God be personal. Sartorius worked the matter out from the standpoint of love (1851). God is personal love. But love must have its object, otherwise it is egoism. I demands a Thou. Without a duality God is absolute Egoism. The Father must, in the nature of his being, concentrate the whole majesty of his Godhead in a second self-consciousness, the Son. The reciprocated love between these two unites in a third hypostasis, the Spirit, which is, so to speak, the connecting link, and thus the circle of the life of God is complete. Ritschl, starting from an arbitrarily limited conception of knowledge and a superficial conception of being, waved the Trinity aside as of no concern of ours. He has given the cue to many—not to all—liberals, but I feel that this is an inconsequential attitude for a theologian, who should not only concern himself with the surface of his subject, but imitate the Spirit, who searcheth all things, yea, even the depths of God.[21] Ritschl's more spiritual disciples have shown a finer appreciation of their task. Heinrich Schultz went forward to think the eternal unfolding of God's being in Word and Spirit as lying at the foundation of his historical indwelling in Christ and of the Christian society.[22] While Julius Kaftan thought that the Trinitarian expressions in the New Testament are assertions of faith only in so far as they have reference to the historical Christ and the historical communication of his Spirit, yet he by no means was satisfied with

---
[21] 1 Cor. 2. 10.
[22] *Lehre von der Gottheit Christi*, chap. xxviii, p. 610.

MODERNISM AND THE CHRISTIAN FAITH

an economic Trinity, but saw in both that and the immanent Trinity in content congruent sides or considerations of the same subject. "What appears to us as successive in time [God in Old Testament, Christ, the Spirit], that we behold as a timeless fact in God himself."[23] And the late lamented theologian of Leipzig, Otto Kirn, of the same general liberal school, says distinctly that if "it belongs to the essence of faith to apprehend something sacred in the secular, the eternal in the historical, then the religious understanding of the salvation-history can fulfill itself only in this way, namely, that we see in the Person of the Redeemer and the possession of the Spirit by the church the eternal self-revelation and self-communication of God. Every view lower than this is lacking in religious confidence and clearness. The same Christ who as founder of a new religious universal life belongs to mankind and its history, belongs at the same time to the eternal life of God, whose full revelation never to be surpassed he is. The Spirit in whom we call on God as Father and through whom we are transformed in the image of Christ, belongs even as well to the unfolding of our personal life in time as to the self-unfolding of God, who desires to fill his personal creatures with his presence. Because we perceive in the historical salvation-revelation an eternal divine effect, there arises for us also the task to coordinate every other self-revelation of God with the historical Redeemer and every other self-communication of God with the Holy Spirit."[24] The Trinity of our faith and of our love, the Trinity of

---

[23] *Dogmatik*, 4 Aufl., § 21.

[24] Kirn, Article, "Trinität," in *Realencyklopädie*, 3 Aufl., vol. xx, pp. 121, 122.

TRINITY

our hymns and of our devotion, the Trinity of our study and of our meditation, is the Trinity of revelation, and not the Trinity of speculation or of à priori reasoning. But the human mind as God made it is bound to press back the facts to their last ground, to the Trinity as it is in God. An eminent Unitarian scholar, Professor Dr. James Drummond, had the frankness to concede that there were "elements in Christian experience which necessarily resulted" in this doctrine, and that whatever foreign forms influenced the terminology we must admit, he says, the "reality of the fundamental Christian facts which imparted to the doctrine all its religious vitality."[25] Yes, fundamental Christian facts gave the doctrine its vitality in the early church when she sang the Gloria Patri, and will they not give the same vitality after another two thousand years? Though we might say with the modest and shrinking young Melanchthon in the first edition of his *Loci:* Mysteria divinitatis rectius adoraverimus quam vestigaverimus.[26]

---

[25] *Via, Veritas, Vita: Hibbert Lectures,* 1894, p. 203.

[26] Plitt-Kolde, *De Loci Communes Melanchthons in ihrer Urgestalt,* 3 Aufl., 1900, p. 60.

CHAPTER X

RITSCHL OR WESLEY?

RITSCHL goes back immediately to Kant, Wesley's contemporary (1781, first great book, died 1804), and therefore a little survey of German thought from Kant is advisable. Kant held that we can have no certain knowledge of God, the world, the soul, immortality, etc., but only practical or regulative knowledge. We can know only by experience and experiment, and this gives us sensations or mediate knowledge, not immediate, not the reality of the thing behind the sensations, not the thing in itself. God and religion have moral or practical basis, not a theoretic or actual basis, and cannot, therefore, be absolutely necessary or certain. Morality, however, is necessary, and that takes the place of religion with Kant. "As the rationalist said that revealed religion was unnecessary, for he could demonstrate a better one on grounds of reason, so Kant says that both revealed and natural religion are unnecessary, for morality is sufficient."[1] "Morality does not need religion at all," says Kant, "but by means of the practical reason is sufficient for itself." Kant held to a strict morality himself, but since he did away with the bases of religion in any profound sense, young Germany can be excused not only for taking it for granted that religion is played out, but for thinking that he lays quite unnecessary stress on morality. Ritschl got his idea that we can know

---
[1] Carr, *Development of Modern Religious Thought*, Boston, 1895, p. 181.

RITSCHL OR WESLEY?

nothing of the nature of God, for instance, whether there is a Trinity in him or not, that we can know nothing of the preexistence of Christ, whether Christ is essentially divine, what is his relation to God as to his inner being, and all such deeper questions—Ritschl got this from Kant. He also got his idea of the kingdom of God from Kant. "The church," says Kant, "could best be compared to a household, under a common though invisible Father, in so far as his holy Son, who knows his will and also stands in blood relationship to all its members, occupies the place of the Father in the family, so that he makes the Father's will more distinctly known to the members, and therefore they honor the Father in the Son, and so enter among themselves into a voluntary, universal and permanent union."[2] This kingdom is a purely moral one, however, Kant throwing out every trace of supernatural ideas, like forgiveness of sins, a divine Saviour, influence of that Saviour on the soul, prayer, means of grace; these things are simply superstition, and a religion of reason is to take their place. Ritschl took over too much of Kant here also.

Kant's influence on Germany and in fact, on philosophical students of all lands has been immense, and the weakness of positive Christianity resulting from that influence can easily be imagined.

Hegel (active 1800–31) approaches religion from a different angle. We have the idea of absolute being. God is that idea. God is thought. That thought going out of itself is the creation of the world, and being a necessary action is eternal, therefore the world is timeless or eternal, though in thought God is before it. In this idealized precreative inactivity

---
[2] Quoted by Carr, p. 187.

MODERNISM AND THE CHRISTIAN FAITH

God is Father; in his going out in thought which actualizes itself in the world he is Son; knowing himself in the Son, and returning in love reconciled unto himself, he is the Spirit. Religion is a man's spirit's knowledge of itself as spirit. Revelation is man's knowledge of himself, which is knowledge of God. Christ, the Bible, miracles, etc., are all of inferior importance. The spiritual is higher than all these, and can be proven only in itself and through itself. What we call the witness of the Spirit is only the response of the soul to what it thinks is truth. Hegel often uses the historic Christian words, but he evaporates them of their historic content, in this respect being followed by Ritschl. Hegel also had an immense influence in Germany and far beyond, and that influence certainly as a general fact undermined the historic faith. Occasionally a man is found who follows some of his ideas toward essential Christianity, and claims that those ideas even gave the surest basis for that Christianity (like Professor J. McBride Sterrett, formerly of the Episcopal Divinity School, Faribault, Minnesota), but it is undeniable that the general trend of Hegel's influence and its logical trend was hostile to Christianity of Christ and apostles.

An influential name in this dechristianizing of Germany is Röhr (died 1848, when Ritschl was twenty-six years old), court preacher in Weimar and general superintendent of the Evangelical Church of that province, who followed in the footsteps of the older rationalists like Wolff, Semler, Reimarus, Lessing, and Kant, and tried to popularize the last named philosopher's views. Röhr taught that reason is the only authority in religion, and its only aim is morality, which is the chief thing which commends Christianity to man. Christology should be discarded. The church's view of Christ is legendary, speculative, and a later growth, and should be thrown out, and the morality of Christ substituted. The influence and position of Röhr will be brought home to us if we should think of Bishop Simpson proclaiming far and wide throughout Methodism the broadest Unitarianism. With such influences at work in Germany, it seems a miracle that there is as much evangelical Christianity as there is.

The work of Röhr, the preacher and Church administrator, was much helped by Paulus, the theological professor (Heidelberg, died 1851), who also carried out Kant's rationalistic moralism, reducing Christianity to morality and Christ to an ethical ideal. The miracles are, of course, discarded or explained away. The angels at birth of Christ were phosphorescent appearances, Christ's healings were through remedies not mentioned, Lazarus was in a lethargic sleep, the transfiguration was the effect of sunlight on suddenly awakened persons, or an optical illusion, and Christ was simply a noble man teaching fine morality.

There was one man who set himself against this tremendous trend toward the destruction of Christianity in Germany, the brilliant preacher and theological professor of Berlin, Schleiermacher (died 1834), but the power of that trend can be seen by the way it overthrew the positive elements of Schleiermacher's own faith. It is well known that he tried to bring back the German people to religion by showing them that religion was not something far off and hard to grasp, but was simply the feeling of dependence. In fact, almost any feeling is religion. He says:

MODERNISM AND THE CHRISTIAN FAITH

"Your feeling, in so far as it expresses the common being and life of yourself and of the ALL, in so far as you hold its particular elements as an activity of God in you, mediated by the operation of the world upon you—this is your piety. . . . There is no feeling which is not religious unless it indicate a diseased abnormal condition of life."[3] Hegel remarked that according to this a dog was more religious than a man, for his mental life is all feeling. Schleiermacher said that the essence of religion is this: "that we are conscious of ourselves as absolutely dependent, or, what expresses the same thing, as in relation to God."[4] But this is not the same thing, for a man may feel in some relation to God, but that relation may be opposition, independence, hatred, indifference. And since a feeling of dependence may be universal, all religions are on the same plane. Schleiermacher acknowledges this, and asserts that all religion is equally true, only some religions are less noble expressions of man's nature. You will notice the pantheistic element here. So also in his claim that to a religious man everything is a miracle on its religious side: "The more religious you are the more miracle you will see everywhere." Revelation is not a special communication of truth to Isaiah or Paul, but "every original and new communication of the universe to man is revelation. Every intuition and original feeling proceeds from revelation." So also with prophecy: "Every religious anticipation of the other half of a religious event, one half being given, is prophecy." It will be seen, then, that Schleiermacher was not untouched by the Zeitgeist. In fact, Zeller says that he was almost a pantheist.

[3] *Reden*, Berlin ed., 1878, p. 40. [4] *Der Christliche Glaube*, § 4, p. 14.

RITSCHL OR WESLEY?

"God and the world are according to Schleiermacher only different expressions of equivalent value. God is not an almighty will outside and above the world, who produces effects in it; he is only the infinite essence of the world itself.... He did not believe in the creation of the world in time, nor that God interrupts the order of nature by miracle, or that the will is above natural necessity."[5] We should not aim at personal immortality, but at sinking ourselves in the all, our personality in the infinite.

This tendency to pantheistic absorption is found in his method of proof of Christianity. With Ritschl he held that natural theology has no place, nor can you appeal to rational grounds to prove that God exists, that Scripture is inspired. To take the place of these Schleiermacher appealed to the Christian consciousness. Why is Christ sinless? Why is he divine, so far as he is divine? Because I find him such in my Christian experience.[6] "Christian articles of faith," he says, "are the conceptions of the religious states of the Christian mind, expressed in language."[7] "Who is Jesus Christ? The revealer of God, the Saviour. Why? Christian consciousness declares it. How does Christ reveal God and save men? Christian consciousness has no answer, and it is unnecessary to raise these questions."[8]

Ritschl followed Schleiermacher also in his emphasis on the Christian community. It is not that we simply believe in Christ and thus find peace, but that peace is ours because we are members of the Christian community. But this consciousness cannot flow from the church itself, says Schleiermacher, because

---
[5] *Vorträge*, i. p. 204, quoted by Carr, pp. 220, 221.
[6] Carr, p. 225.   [7] *Der Christliche Glaube*, § 15.   [8] Carr, p. 226.

MODERNISM AND THE CHRISTIAN FAITH

the church is composed of erring and sinful persons; therefore the Christian consciousness finds its source in the founder of the community—Jesus. Sin is that which hinders the development of the God-consciousness in the soul. Redemption is the influence of the Redeemer working through the church which brings the believer into unity and harmony with God.

In regard to Christ Schleiermacher argues for his sinlessness in this way: In the Christian society the believer finds himself brought into God-consciousness and toward moral perfection. How is this done? Not by the society itself, for this is imperfect. Then it must be by its founder, who is therefore sinless. Is Christ also divine? Only in this sense that he had a perfect God-consciousness. Not in his pre-existence, not in his miraculous birth, not in his oneness with God in his essential nature, for these have no meaning, but in his God-consciousness alone. Any man who can reach to his God-consciousness is as divine as he is. Christ's redemption is not atonement, is not reconciliation, but is a work by which he imparts to the believer his own God-consciousness. This is done not through faith in him but through the society or church. There is no Holy Spirit, or, rather, the Holy Spirit is the influence of the Christian community. "Under the expression 'Holy Spirit' is understood the living unity of the Christian community as a moral person."[9] Here also Ritschl followed him. Salvation is not salvation from sin through faith in Christ, but is that righteousness which though imperfect is reckoned ideal by the Judge, which we get through our relation with the Christian community or church, and the church gets that power to make

---
[9] *Der Christliche Glaube*, § 116.

RITSCHL OR WESLEY?

us righteous through the influence of Christ's perfect example.

It was Schleiermacher who saved Germany from infidelity, but in doing that he threw overboard so much that what was left was hardly worth saving. There was scarcely a doctrine as Christ and apostles taught it which this great preacher and professor did not explain away or give away. His influence has been immense in German thought. When he, in some respects, the greatest Christian teacher of Germany in the nineteenth century, thus eviscerated the contents of the gospel, can we wonder that Ritschl, who followed in his footsteps and in those of Kant, fell short of the message of Christ, Paul, and Wesley?

Placing the names of Wesley and Ritschl in juxtaposition might be unjust to both. Not only as to the time in which they lived (Ritschl was born thirty-one years after Wesley died), but their whole equipment, motive, and mission were different. While Wesley was an educated man and an accomplished linguist, he was not a scientifically trained theologian, nor did he profess to be. He was a practical reformer, an evangelist, a religious leader, and he became a theologian (so far as he was one) as a result of his mission, not as the first impulse of his being. Ritschl was a theologian and theological teacher pure and simple, nothing more, nothing less. As such he received the usual education of a German expert in the theological department of different German universities (Bonn and Halle) and immediately became a theological professor (Bonn 1846–64, Göttingen 1864–89), and so continued to the end of his life in 1889. It is acknowledged on all hands that he was one of the ablest and acutest theologians in the history of the world. While

MODERNISM AND THE CHRISTIAN FAITH

his chair was systematic theology, like all Germans in this department he was thoroughly at home in historical and exegetical theology. He devoted his life to only one thing—teaching and writing theology. When he prepared his great work on reconciliation and justification, he devoted one volume to the history of the doctrines, another to the exegesis of the biblical basis, and only the third volume to the exposition of the doctrine itself and of related doctrines. His first three books were in historical theology, and as to the last of these three, *Die Enstehung der altkatholischen Kirche*, 1850, second edition much revised and enlarged, 1857, though it is out of print and expensive (as I found when I bought it), it remains one of the greatest books in church history of the nineteenth century. It is nothing against Wesley that he had little of this masterly equipment. First, he was born in a church which has never been famous for its theologians. The men of this type in the seventeenth and eighteenth centuries in England were mainly Puritans, and they were cast out by an intolerant Anglicanism. Besides, the Church of England was such a theologically inchoate, Janus-faced, comprehensive affair, and so nearly allied to the state and controlled by it, that there were few stimuli to the growth of theologians. Then, there was no one man at the birth of the church who, like Luther, worked as a driving impulse to the study of theology. Luther was not himself a scientific theologian, but his theological influence was most impelling. In fact, I am inclined to believe that between the death of Saint John and the birth of Wesley there is no man whose influence theologically has been so fructifying. He had too by his side a man whose mental training

RITSCHL OR WESLEY?

and scientific apparatus for systematic theology was unsurpassed, and who therefore supplemented Luther in this field. No such men appeared at the beginnings of the English reformation. I dare say one single university in a little German town produced more theologians in a hundred years than all the schools in England in three hundred. Second, Wesley's interest in theology was practical, not scientific. His genius was missionary and reforming, not intellectual. One cannot be both a theological professor and an itinerant evangelist. Third, he did not have a theological education. I think most—not all—of the theological professorships in Oxford post-dated Wesley.

But I do not mean by this that Wesley had no interest in theological truth, did not seek it, or did not attain it. Just the contrary. Probably there was no man in his day who was more keenly alive to religious truth than was Wesley, or more insistent in pursuing and publishing it. His well-known utterances about the catholic terms of admittance into his societies—absence of almost all theological tests—have led some to think that he was indifferent to theological correctness. One does not have to read his *Journal* or other writings long to be disabused of that impression. His first conferences were taken up with theological discussions. His sermons were largely doctrinal, and many of them he published immediately either separately or together, as he later made them a test of the soundness of his preachers. He read diligently theological books, and wrote books himself to refute theological errors. And those who remember the words of the Lord about hiding these things from the wise and prudent and

MODERNISM AND THE CHRISTIAN FAITH

revealing them unto babes need not be reminded of the fact that it is quite possible for an earnest seeker for the truth like Wesley to find it when learned theologians miss it. Besides Christ said, If any man willeth to do his will, he shall know of the teaching; and certainly no one strove to do that will more strenuously and longer than Wesley. We need not assume, therefore, that the poorly equipped (scientifically) Wesley failed in his grasp of Christianity, and has to be corrected in essentials by the richly equipped Ritschl.

But why do we bring Wesley and Ritschl together? For the best of reasons. The latter is threatening to drive the former out of business. That is, since about 1890 the ideas of Ritschl have been slowly penetrating English-speaking lands and modifying former beliefs. His books and those of his disciples have been translated, earnest propagandists have defended his views in pamphlet, article, and book; others have taken them up and reshaped them, so that there can be no doubt that one cause for the tremendous liberalizing influence which since the last twenty-five years has wrought a sea-change in the beliefs of evangelical ministers has been the trend which has gone forth from the potent name of Ritschl. Not only so, theological seminaries in America are filled with professors who have either sat in the Ritschlian lecture rooms in Berlin, Marburg, Göttingen, etc., and have come back devotees of the faith, or they have imbibed at Ritschlian springs nearer home. Now, as a thorough carrying out of Ritschl's principles would emasculate evangelical Christianity, especially the Methodist branch of it, it is not without reason that I have asked the question, Shall we leave Wesley for Ritschl?

RITSCHL OR WESLEY?

What, then, did Ritschl teach? And here I have to say that although I have read hundreds of pages of Ritschl's own writings and those of both his German and English expositors, I find it difficult to understand him. Nor am I alone in this. His own style is not at all clear. Neither his sentences nor his ideas are lucid. His expositors are at sea. You read Professor Swing, and Ritschl is evangelical, sound, thoroughly Christian, apparently the first really Christian theologian that God ever made.[10] You read the late Professor Orr, and in all Ritschl's main teachings he is one of the most subtly dangerous teachers of modern times.[11] You read Hermann, and you find him a great and noble Christian teacher,[12] Dieckhoff, and it runs, "The break of the theology of Ritschl with the faith of the church is a radical one."[13] You read Garvie's able books,[14] and you are left swinging in the air. Ritschl is largely right and largely wrong. Between Ritschl's own obscurity and long-drawn-out definings, and the opposing interpretations of commentators and opinions of counsel, you are at a loss to know whether he is a new god in Olympus or an adversary who has come among the sons of Elohim to accuse the theologians. One says he believes in the incarnation and the divinity of Christ, another that he does not. One affirms that his theory of value judgments is

---

[10] *The Theology of Albrecht Ritschl*, New York, and London, 1901.

[11] *The Ritschlian Theology and the Evangelical Faith*, London, 1899; *Ritschlianism: Expository and Critical Essays*, London, 1903.

[12] *Der Evangelische Glaube und die Theologie Albrecht Ritschls*, Marburg, 1890, 31 pages; *The Communion of the Christian with God*, Edinburgh, 1906.

[13] *Die Menschwerdung des Sohnes Gottes: ein Votum über die Theologie Ritschls*, Leipz., 1992, pp. 15, 16.

[14] *The Ritschlian Theology, Critical and Constructive*, Edinburgh, 1900, 2nd ed., revised and enlarged, 1901.

MODERNISM AND THE CHRISTIAN FAITH

one of the happiest discoveries in theology, another that it undermines the faith. Some claim that his throwing out what he calls metaphysics from theology is the best advance since Luther, whom he follows in this, and others rejoin that he throws out a true metaphysics and keeps a false one, while Kähler takes a middle ground: "It is all right that Ritschl threw out metaphysics, if he had not also thrown out with it so much of truth"; that is, he cast out the child with the bath. Most of those who do not follow Ritschl have welcomed his emphasis on the kingdom of God, but Lemme, in his able pamphlet, says that his idea of the Kingdom is not that of the gospel, but of Kant.[15] Amid these contrary voices, let us try to get hold of Ritschl's teachings, especially on those cardinal doctrines which were the heart of Wesley and the driving forces of his movement.

That movement was soteriological, not in the first place theological in the strict sense. It came round to God and Christ and Spirit by way of salvation. Speaking historically, Wesley and his coworkers first saw the lost state of England—sin everywhere, even in the church and especially among depraved peoples. And it was damnable, here and hereafter. Who can save? Christ only. Who is Christ? The eternal Son of God. Why can he save? Because, being thus

[15] Lemme, *Die Prinzipien der Ritschlshen Theologie und ihr Werth*, Bonn, 1891, pp. 44, 45, and p. 49. The difficulty of understanding Ritschl and differences of opinion as to what he taught are due to the fact that some themes he did not discuss, being as he said, beyond our knowledge, he not accepting the Bible light, that he deals more largely in criticism than construction, and that especially in later editions of his great work, and in his *Unterricht in der Christlichen Religion*, 1875, 5 Aufl., 1895, "by a wavering (or hanging-in-the-air) treatment he conceals rather than makes plain his opinion."—Frank, *Geschichte und Kritik der neueren Theologie*, 4 Aufl., 1908, pp. 317, 318.

essentially divine, he came among men to save, and did save them all in possibility by laying down his life for them, and thus paying a ransom for them to the everlasting holiness, which they had outraged. How can he save? By their faith in him as Saviour. How far can he save? To the uttermost as to the worst sinners and to the uttermost as to the completeness of the salvation. How do the saved show themselves as saved? By a holy life of devotion and love to Christ and service to men, of self-denial, evangelistic zeal in saving others, Christian work and social enthusiasms. How do they know themselves saved? Because the Holy Spirit witnesses to their spirits that they are the children of God. Let this suffice. These were the characteristic, the central, things of Methodism. Now, let us see how Ritschl takes these things.

Ritschl does not proceed from sin, but from weakness or dependence. The great thing is not to save a man from sin, but from limitation. Man needs to be elevated over the world as part of a divine kingdom. "The idea of God and the world-view conformable to it," he says, "has everywhere this significance, to help man over the contrast between his natural position and his spiritual self-feeling, and to secure him an elevation or freedom over the world and the usual intercourse with it." When man feels his dependence upon God, then he gets his free self-determination in detachment from the world. To do this he must have faith, but this faith is not trust in Christ for salvation, but is impulse or power, will, and then representation or imagination. There is no such thing as a fundamental racial weakness or sin. Of course there are individual sins, and if a man

MODERNISM AND THE CHRISTIAN FAITH

holds out finally in deliberate preference to sin rather than God, he will be blotted out, but there is no wrath of God against sin. In the Methodist sense there is no such thing as salvation in Ritschl; neither the word nor thing hardly occurs in his writings. Forgiveness occurs, and it means bringing home to a man the fact that God loves him, so that unburdened of any feeling of guilt he may mount up to an independent position in the kingdom of God. Justification occurs, but it means the same as forgiveness, namely, a creative act of God's will, a synthetic judgment, that God in his love for man, and for the final object of his kingdom, in which he wants man's cooperation, steps in to forgive man as a pure act of will, and for the exercise of that act there is nothing either in sin, in God's nature, nor in man's feeling of guilt that interposes any obstacle.[16]

It is not necessary to say that with this doctrine of sin and salvation, not only would Methodism never have been heard of, but Christianity likewise. You cannot conceive of an evangel without a vital message as to sin and salvation, and if you could, such an evangel would be worthless—worthless because it does not fit the facts of life. There is sin as guilt and damnable, and there is salvation as a cleansing tide which by faith in Christ alone, on the background of Calvary, brings the sinner into communion with God.

Christ alone. Ritschl had a high opinion of Christ. He repeatedly refers to him as divine, and speaks of his divinity. In this sense he undoubtedly worked

---

[16] Mielke, *Das System Albrecht Ritschl's dargestellt, nicht kritisirt*, Bonn, 1894, p. 33. See *Unterricht*, § 35, *Rechtfertigung und Versöhnung*, vol. iii, p. 316.

RITSCHL OR WESLEY?

as a conservative force in Germany. Christ mediates —and he alone—God to us. He is the perfect and final revelation of God. If even another should come as great as he, he would not be as great, because he would be after Christ in time and thus in a sense dependent on him. God has given him rulership over the world, and he reigns in glory now. For all believers he has the value of God, and though he is not God, he may be worshiped. As to his preexistence we know nothing at all. All we know is his temporal existence, and it is beyond our province to say anything about his relation to the being of God. We do not know anything about God's nature except that he is grace and love and Lord, and as we see these in Christ we may honor him as God, and especially as he has been called by God as the final end of his kingdom, and as he carried out that calling with perfect self-devotion and mastery of the world. He overcame everything and turned everything as a means to his glory. And thus he works to-day upon the Christian society, and for that society exercises a world lordship. We therefore can predicate divinity (*Gottheit*) of him. In doing this the two significances of Christ, as the perfect revealer of God and the revealed original pattern of spiritual world rule, are brought together. That is all we can say of Christ. When we declare that there is in God a Trinity, that Christ is essentially one with the Father, that he existed with him in eternity, we go beyond our knowledge. His preexistence is simply ideal in the mind of God, and thus eternally existing for God, but not really existing in the being of God. He is, of course, the founder and Lord of the Christian society. He alone, that is, the revealed love of God in him, gives

MODERNISM AND THE CHRISTIAN FAITH

to every member of the society the impulse to love, which enables him to act consistently with the final end of the kingdom of God. Ritschl did not affirm nor deny the miraculous birth.

Now, in a country where rationalistic principles are constantly minimizing the supernatural elements of Christianity this view of Ritschl is to be welcomed. It saves a more or less divine Christ for many. But for those who know the Christ of the Gospels, of the apostolic church, and of Christian experience, it comes short. It is a cold and calculating limitation on the boundless passion which the first Christians threw into their predicates of their Lord. He was not simply the lord of the kingdom who realized the object of the kingdom and inspired them to realize it too—he was just their Lord and their God. You can always distinguish a Ritschlian from an early Christian—the former never uses the word "God" of Christ, it is taboo, like meat on Friday to a Roman Catholic, while the ancient Christian called Christ God and worshiped him as God. But what I insist on here is that that Ritschlian Christ was not only not the Christ of Wesley, but that if he had been, you and I would not be here to-day. Wesley called dying men to believe on the ever-living Christ, who through the Spirit was at their side begging for admission into their hearts to save and rule and dwell in them as God. Only thus could the movement start, only thus could it go on conquering and to conquer, and only thus did it start and go on. So with every other evangelistic agency. You cannot save lost men with a Unitarian God. Men already nursed by Christian civilization may want no other, but the sinner cries out for a God with the touch of a man. He cannot believe in the God of the Northern Lights, but only in Him who said, "Thy sins, which are many, are all forgiven." If to-morrow you blot out the absolute divinity of Jesus, the next day you would have to close every Salvation Army hall in Christendom, every mission in home and foreign lands, and every church where the demons of greed and lust and hate are being cast out.

To this general view corresponds the Ritschlian doctrine of the work of Christ. But before I speak of this I should say a word on sin.[17]

How slightly Ritschl heals the hurt of the world can be seen in his doctrine of sin. With him sin is simply "lack of honor and trust toward God," and is judged by God as ignorance. There is no fall, and therefore no inheritance of the results of that fall. Though he speaks of a "kingdom of sin," he refers merely to the sum of individual sins small and large which men commit against society, against the moral precepts of Christ, or against the honor of God. He says: "Sin is an apparently unavoidable creation of the human will under the given conditions of its development, but in consciousness of our freedom and independence is reckoned by us as guilt.... The possibility and probability of sinning is founded in this, that the human will which should determine itself after the known good is an always becoming quantity (*grösse*) with whose activity there is not bound from the beginning a perfect knowledge of the good." But a sinless development of every man is also possible. The consciousness of guilt in conscience is only a result of education and society.

---
[17] For further exposition of Ritschl on Christ see Faulkner, *Methodist Quarterly Review* (Nashville), April, 1920, pp. 289ff.

MODERNISM AND THE CHRISTIAN FAITH

Evil in the world is not a punishment of sin, but proceeds from the course of nature, and is only limitations on our freedom.[18] With such a shallow and atomistic or mechanical conception of sin as this it is evident there is no place for atonement or salvation in the New Testament sense. Now we can better appreciate Ritschl's doctrine of the work of Christ.

The words "redemption" (*Erlösung*) and "atonement," or "reconciliation" (*Versöhnung*), are used, but it is characteristic of Ritschl and his school to use historic Christian words without their historic content. Now, there can be no objection to that if their historic content is false, and his new meaning is true. Otherwise, there is serious objection. In this case I regret I cannot go with Ritschl. I admit there have been mechanical and overwrought theories brought in to explain the reconciliation wrought by Christ. Just as likely as not I could not swallow Wesley's view without some grains of salt. But for all that, atonement is atonement. It has a Godward aspect. It is not only the reaching down of God to save; it is the self-propitiation of a righteous God so that he can save and—if I might so say—maintain his self-respect. Now, consciously or unconsciously, the sinner feels the necessity of this. At the background of his faith there is always a cross lifted up. But even more, the saint feels the necessity of it. It is not poetry; it is the deepest expression of his heart of hearts:

"In my hand no price I bring;
Simply to thy cross I cling."

Now, Ritschl has eviscerated from the Christian

---
[18] Claravellensis, *Die Theologie Ritschls und d. Christliche Wahrheit*, 1891, pp. 63–94.

RITSCHL OR WESLEY?

religion an objective atonement, and so his minimizing doctrine here meets his minimizing Christology. There is no sin that needs atonement, for sin is only mistake, and so far as it is anything else it calls not for atonement but only for judgment; there is no righteousness in God that needs atonement, for God in all his relations is only love. The atonement is simply God's declaration through the life and teachings of Christ that he loves men and thus calls them to embrace their highest good, that he forgives them, that they have no guilt that he (God) needs to reckon with, but that they can immediately become members of his kingdom. Forgiveness of sins is connected with the calling of Christ as declarative of God's love, but it is not connected with the work of Christ as the expression of God's nature any farther. The calling of Christ is to teach men that they should have the same relation to God that he has. This lack in Ritschl is fundamental. It is another Christianity than that taught even in Mark's Gospel, and it is another world than that in which moved Paul and the early Christians. And if Methodism had been Ritschlian in this regard, it would have been a pale and sickly growth, helpless before the seething mass of the world's corruption.

What is faith with Ritschl? Here I quote Mielke, who has given a reliable statement of his views, and who as a Ritschlian himself has not given them any unfavorable turn. Says Mielke:

> The form in which sinners appropriate justification is faith. To understand this rightly it is necessary to keep in mind that religious apprehension (*Erkennen*) or faith moves in direct value judgments. This truth first discovered by Luther was not acknowledged by the Catholic Church, which explained faith as a holding

MODERNISM AND THE CHRISTIAN FAITH

for true the articles of faith, whether as understanding the articles (*fides explicita*) or holding them as true without understanding them (*fides implicita*), by which faith is lowered to a degenerate kind of knowledge. Luther so far broke with this false idea of faith as to make faith chiefly trust in the grace of God. But as a farther achievement of faith he considered a consent to the articles of faith. This double form of faith, which later found its expression in the words of Johann Gerhard, "faith is not only knowledge (*notitia*) and assent, but also trust (*fiducia*)," has been held up to this day by orthodox Lutheran theologians —yet so that the more valuable part of faith as trust has been derived from faith as assent to the Holy Scriptures, or to the articles of faith, by which the lower part is shoved in the foreground, and in all public controversy is alone emphasized. Over against this confusion it is now with all emphasis pointed out [by Ritschl] that Christian faith consists simply in trusting upon God's grace. Faith in Christ is this, that one appropriates in trust the worth of the love of God revealed in Christ's work for our reconciliation, a trust toward him which subordinates itself to God as his, and our Father, wherein one is certain of eternal life and blessedness. Faith is thus a function of the will, a new direction of the will to God, which is called out by the reconciliation. As effective—from the worth of the merciful will of God —to induce sinners to convinced trust for their own blessedness, a trust which masters all motives of life and subordinates itself [to God], it steps in the place of the mistrust bound up hitherto with the feeling of guilt. It is included in this faith which restores communion of man with God that the believer directs his will constantly upon the final end (*Endzweck*) of God and Christ. Therefore faith falls within the circumference of love.[19]

On Ritschl's doctrine of faith I would say: (1) It is most praiseworthy to throw overboard once and for all the Catholic idea of saving faith as belief in the doctrines of the Church, an idea which did cling more or less to orthodox Lutheranism. (2) It is praiseworthy to bring back Luther's idea of faith

---

[19] Mielke, *Das System Albrecht Ritschl's dargestellt, nicht kritisirt*, pp. 38, 39 (see his references).

RITSCHL OR WESLEY?

as trust in the grace and love of God in Christ. So far Ritschl's faith is Gospel truth. (3) But it lacks the religious motive and destination of Luther, Paul, and Wesley. With these faith was trust for salvation from sin, from the law as condemning, from death and hell. When that is accomplished, the sinner takes his place as a matter of course in the kingdom of God, and realizes for himself and others the objects of that kingdom. With Ritschl faith is a new direction of the will toward God called out by the work of Christ, by which we subordinate ourselves as Christ did to God and become convinced of our blessedness. Here, again, when you have the moral man penetrated more or less by the Christian atmosphere he breathes, Ritschl's faith may lift him a little higher, but for sinners on the way to Damascus, ah! that is another problem! A flower or beautiful twig is all right in its place, but for a man falling over a precipice it is poor support. The faith that saved the world and the faith that made the Reformation and Methodism was quite another thing. Ritschl's faith is the airy bridge you cast over the gulf for the feet of children and the lightly stepping dude; New Testament faith and Wesley's is the mighty structure firmly grounded on the Rock of Ages which the true engineer builds for the tramping millions of sin-scarred men and women.

Speaking of the New Testament brings up Ritschl's doctrine of Scripture. He had no doctrine of Scripture. He held firmly to the view that the New Testament as a whole was a genuine product of apostolic times, and gives a true account of the history and beliefs of those times. That was all that he wanted. Compared with later literature, the New Testament is

MODERNISM AND THE CHRISTIAN FAITH

the source of our knowledge of Christian revelation, not because it is inspired, but because it is early. So much we must be thankful for. If the chief object of the Bible is to testify of Christ, as Luther rightly held, then a main interest is secured even if the Bible is no more than an authentic account. But Ritschl lost much both out of his theology and his life by closing his eyes to the deeper view of Scripture. The New Testament is, as a matter of fact, much more than merely a reliable record. It teems with the life of God. Its inspiration, its spiritual power and illumination, its doctrinal clearness, satisfactoriness, depth, its religious beauty and reasonableness, its ethical purity, consistency, and appeal—all these not only set it apart among sacred books, but prove it the vehicle of the Spirit in mighty fashion. Because he could not see this, there is a profound lack on the scriptural side in Ritschl's theology. Even so appreciative an expounder as Garvie often has to call attention to this. In my judgment it is a fatal lack. If you are going to have a theology which will be not only true but living, not only living but powerful, you must have one whose roots are watered by the word of God which liveth and abideth. For that reason I think that Wesley still makes an appeal, in spite of later lights.[20]

This brings us to the Christian life. One of the outstanding merits of Wesley was to bring back the apostolic enthusiasm for Christian life and experience. The supremacy of the life hid with Christ in God, the life that we now live by faith in Christ,

---

[20] Ritschl's view of Scripture is gone into at length, with large quotations from him, in Claravallensis [a pseudonym for whom?], *lib cit.*, pp. 63-94.

RITSCHL OR WESLEY?

who yet lives in us, the light that never was on sea or land which irradiates the soul and fills it full of glory and of God, the peace that passeth understanding, the cleansing tides of Christ's love which purify the inner fountains—all these were experienced and were witnessed by the early Methodists, and gave them that swing of conquest which made them irresistible. But this did not end in experience, but was also transformed into social ministries of all kinds which brought about a new England and a new America. Only, the social reforms were the result of the inner life. Now, what was the attitude of Ritschl to the experimental side of Christianity? Reserved, critical, cold. Take, first, How do we know we are Christians?

Wesley restored Paul's doctrine of the witness of the Spirit: a direct testimony of the Spirit of God to the spirit of man. Ritschl did not believe in any Holy Spirit in the Christian sense. He defined the Spirit as: (1) The knowledge which God has of himself. (2) An attribute of the Christian society. On account of the revelation of God which Christ has made, the members of the society have the same knowledge of God and his counsel toward men which corresponds with God's own knowledge. (3) The Spirit is the same as the life or motive of Christians directed to the kingdom of God. Nor is that life changed or moved by what we call the Spirit, or by any specific power of God, but people are changed from sin to penitence, humility, and activity for the Kingdom simply by the confidence which they have in God as Father, and this confidence they get from the historical record of Jesus (see Garvie, pp. 338, 339 and references). Nothing shows the profound distrust Ritschl had for Christian experience clearer than this volatilizing of the Holy Spirit until he evaporates into a mode of knowledge, into categories of the community. Frank is perfectly right in calling attention to the violence with which Ritschl rids himself of the testimony of Scripture when the latter treats of the Spirit.[21] Explain the Holy Spirit in the life of God as you like, but unless we hold with tenacious grip that there is a Spirit who takes the things of Christ and declares them unto us, a Spirit who convicts the world of sin, of righteousness and of judgment, who makes the love of the Father and the presence of Christ a wellspring of joy as well as the dynamic of a conquering life—unless we preserve those fundamental realities in the doctrine of the Spirit we wreck Christianity as an expansive religion.

The idea of an evangel in Wesley's sense is lacking in Ritschl. That evangel according to the New Testament starts (a sense of sin being understood) from the new birth or conversion. Thence it proceeds to godly living or to Christian perfection. "So long as in man a new I, a new man, is not created by grace through the inworking of the Holy Spirit, there can be no mention of moral righteousness and perfection. But so far as I know nowhere has Ritschl designated such a conversion as necessary, not to speak of representing it as the supernatural working of the Holy Spirit. He rejects this whole conception, and confesses only the operation of the church through the means of grace. So also he designates it as a perversity to let justification have for its object holiness and good works."[22] In other words; such a

---

[21] F. H. R. Frank, *Zur Theologie A. Ritschl's*, 3 enlarged ed. Erlangen und Leipz., 1891 [1st ed., 1888], p. 111 (see also pp. 111–115).
[22] Frank, *Geschichte und Kritik der neueren Theologie*, 4 Aufl., p. 353.

RITSCHL OR WESLEY?

conquering gospel for sinners as had early Christianity, the Reformation, and Methodism would have been absolutely impossible with Ritschl.

How can we be sure of our Christian standing? In this way, says Ritschl: By justification there comes a change in the relations of the Christian. He trusts in God's all-sided care, and is penetrated with the feeling of independence from the world, of spiritual world-rule. In this activity of his faith which proclaims itself in patience in suffering and includes a power to which all powers of the world are subordinate, the believer becomes certain of the salvation guaranteed by Christ.[23] Well, that is good so far. If any man trusts in God, feels independent of the world and over it, is patient in distress, that man is to be congratulated. But I do not hear the Christian note. That certainty of salvation fits Plato and Emerson almost as well as Wesley. Here Ritschl as usual is too minimizing, too reserved and critical, too much afraid of his sources.

Ritschl is always shy of the direct gripping in of God in the souls of men. He acknowledges that Christ is now exalted, but he will not say that he exercises any activity through the Spirit on this little globe. All the way that Christ can make himself felt now is by men reading about the historical revelation in Christ. Of course we thank God for that revelation. It is of priceless value. But it is of the essence of Christianity that God has first-hand dealings with souls, that he speaks not alone in the records but in the quiet chambers of the conscience, that he comes into the life transforming it, communing with it, guiding it. That some men mistake his voice for

---
[23] Mielke, pp. 43, 44, *Recht. & V.*, iii, p. 167.

MODERNISM AND THE CHRISTIAN FAITH

the noise of the machinery of their own intellect does not invalidate the Voice, the Presence, the Glory—"the solemn awe that does not move, and all the silent heaven of love." Ritschl had perfect distrust for all manifestations of piety in the higher realms of religious experience. He disliked pietism, which saved the German Church from its spiritual torpor. Meetings like our class meetings, prayer meetings, love feasts, he abhorred. He did not believe in prayer in the sense of asking for blessings, but in the sense of a discipline in humility and patience, though he did not absolutely exclude prayer for spiritual blessings. His definition of Christian perfection was not that of Wesley—a relative perfection of love to God and man, accompanied by as perfect as possible a cleansing of the soul from sin. His definition was that we as Christians know the world as a whole, which is ruled by *one* object or end, that we distinguish our own personal worth from the world-whole, and place ourselves over it, and therefore we have the task to become a whole each in his own way. The spiritual life is a whole, is ready always in freedom directed to the final end of the good to put a limit to the impulses which strive against this final end. That overcoming of the disturbances on our religious and moral development is Christian perfection, which is consistent with actual moral imperfection. See Mielke, 50, 51 and the references. One cannot but feel that in the Ritschlian conception of Christian life and faith there is a noble moralism, but only a moralism, a better Stoicism, a moralism touched with Christian feeling and illuminated by Christian ideals. But Christianity is a religion first and last, and its religion is Christ first and last. It

RITSCHL OR WESLEY?

brings in moralism by the way, and it inevitably brings it in, and actually secures it more certainly than systems ostensibly devoted to it. But it goes by the way of Christ, his life, his cross, his resurrection, and his gift of the Spirit. Its very simplicity is its perfection, and at that simplicity Ritschl stumbled. For that reason I still prefer Wesley.

In closing my discussion of this great theologian and scholar, I have not had time to say that there was gold and silver as well as hay and stubble in what he offered. Every theologian makes his contribution to the advancing knowledge of God and his truth. It is treason in us to lie inert and content in the cradle of our fathers. But it is worse treason to forsake what they held of truth, by which truth they turned the world upside down. Their truth must be in us a living spring of activity, inquiry, search, testing, appropriation. I do not hold it against Ritschl that he limited the range of metaphysics in theology, though I think he limited it one-sidedly and used it himself sometimes wrongly. I do not hold it against him that he threw overboard the old creeds, and went back to the Gospels, though I am sorry that he did not find the whole Christ in the Gospels, and what he did find was sometimes not there. Garvie is perfectly right when he says that the men who made the ancient creeds reached the only conclusions possible for them, conclusions that were true for them and for their time, and therefore providential and historically justifiable. They were not only historically justifiable, but they were historically necessary, and saved Christian truth for their day and thus for all time. But they bind us only as to the truth they enshrine. I do not hold it against him

MODERNISM AND THE CHRISTIAN FAITH

that he denounced unhealthy pietism, if he had not swept in precious manifestations of the Christian life. His highest achievement was his recovery for theology of the idea of the kingdom of God and making that central, though it really is not central, for behind and above the kingdom is the King. His general influence against the high and dry, intolerant and know-it-all orthodoxy was beneficial. Few theologians of the nineteenth century have had more influence. His followers are in all lands. Some of them like Hermann and Kaftan and Loofs have reacted toward more Christian views, many others have left their master far in the distance in their movement to the left. The sons of Luther and Calvin can learn from Ritschl. The sons of Wesley can also take whatever stimulus he offers toward the larger light. But they have much less occasion. And if in those central verities of our Christian religion which Wesley again made regnant among men we forsake him for Ritschl, it will indeed be the Great Surrender, sad and causeless, and so far a betrayal of the faith once delivered to the saints.

CHAPTER XI

HELL

ONE of the cleverest and broadest divines of the Church of England, Archdeacon Paley (I wonder did his sarcasm about the "divine right of kings" being equal to the "divine right of constables" keep him from a bishopric) used these sensible and solemn words on the subject reluctantly chosen for this chapter: "I admit that it is very difficult to handle the dreadful subject of the punishment of hell properly; and one cause amongst others of the difficulty is that it is not for one poor sinner to denounce such appalling terrors, such tremendous consequences, against another. 'Damnation' is a word which lies not in the mouth of man, who is a worm, toward any of his fellow-creatures whatsoever; yet it is absolutely necessary that the threatenings of Almighty God be known and published."[1] No, indeed, it is not for one poor sinner to denounce the judgments of God against his brother. And were it not that future punishment is one of the cardinal teachings of our religion, recurring again and again with tireless emphasis in our sources, even given forth with unflinching frankness and unabashed terribleness of imagery by our Founder Christ, and were it not that this is also one of the doctrines at which the modern man stumbles, I would fain abstain from this dark topic. But one cannot be entirely frank with his readers and pass

---
[1] *Sermons,* Sermon 31, in *Works,* ed. Lynam, 1825, chap. iv, p. 224.

MODERNISM AND THE CHRISTIAN FAITH

over a doctrine which has caused so many searchings of heart, so many revolts from historic Christianity. In fact, a separate church or denomination has been founded on one of those revolts, and innumerable ministers and members of the so-called orthodox churches have given up entirely the common faith in this matter, or have abandoned any definite view. As one of them said to me, "We do not know what to believe on hell, and that is why we do not preach it."[2]

The event which reopened the whole subject in this generation—or should I say the preceding?—was a series of sermons preached in Westminster Abbey, London, November, 1877, in his residence as canon by Frederic W. Farrar, even then well known as an author and eloquent preacher. The echo of those sermons was heard around the world. In 1878 they were published under the engaging title, *Eternal Hope*, and sold twelve editions in one year. A burning discussion ensued in books, pamphlets, and in nearly every religious journal in Christendom. By 1881 the matter had been cleared up sufficiently for Farrar to issue another book of intense interest, especially for its side-lights on the opinions of others, *Mercy and Judgment: Last Words on Christian Eschatology*. For ten or fifteen years thereafter important books came from the press, the most of which I read at the time.[3] But the path-breaking book for the newer views was put out in London in 1869 by Andrew Jukes, *The Second Death and the Restitution of all Things*, 7th ed., 1878, and in 1877 appeared the famous *Salvator Mundi* in the same interest by Samuel

---

[2] For the relation of the pulpit to this doctrine see Faulkner in *Methodist Review*, New York, 1901, pp. 626ff.

[3] For good lists see G. W. Gilmore in the Hurst *Literature of Theology*, 1895, pp. 481, 482, 518, 520, 521.

HELL

Cox, a General Baptist clergyman, founder and first editor of *The Expositor* (London), whose expositions of the Bible are well known. Four editions of this were sold in a year. These two books were powerful solvents of the old high-and-dry orthodoxy, and paved the way for the warm rhetoric and scholarly allusions of *Eternal Hope* of the eloquent and widely read Farrar.

It was the aim of the latter to smash four elements, as he understood them, in the tradition of all the churches. (1) That the fire of hell is material. (2) That its doom is incurred by the vast majority of mankind. (3) That this doom is passed irreversibly at death on all who die in a state of sin. (4) That its duration is necessarily endless for all.[4] How far as late as 1877 these four points were held by the more enlightened in the orthodox churches might well be a question. What divine in that year believed that the pains of hell were material? How many even of Calvinists held the second proposition? As to the third, all Catholics held that only those who died in a state of *mortal* sin were lost, and all sensible Protestants held their judgment in reserve, because they said that we could not know what passes between the soul and God in the last hours and therefore could not know who dies in a state of sin. But there can be no doubt that Farrar's books came as a welcome and just relief to many hearts oppressed by the undeniably exaggerated darkness of the outlook for souls facing the other life, favored by much popular teaching up to 1877.

That the regular church teaching until about 225 took eternal punishment in some sense for granted

---
[4] *Mercy and Judgment*, American ed., p. 17.

MODERNISM AND THE CHRISTIAN FAITH

will not be disputed. The brilliant and many-sided Origen, that eager and saintly scholar of the rugged road, broke up the whole Christian eschatology as his time had received it, and branded it as a slavery to the letter. What a magnificent structure he built up instead! In the beginning all souls are in God, have their spiritual existence as parts (so to speak) of him, and the object of cosmic evolution is to restore that condition. The world process is a coming down from God and a going up to him. The work of the Logos and the saints is to loosen souls from this sensuous world, so that they can mount up again to God. There is a continuous purification of souls until they reach God as the goal of their journey. Clothed in a fine spiritual body, the good enter paradise somewhere on the earth, which is a school of souls. A stream of fire surrounds it, but the just, baptized with water and the Spirit, pass through it, receiving in it the fire-baptism. Now they see through all the riddles which have perplexed them. Then they go up to a place in the air, between heaven and earth, where they know everything which happens on earth. They advance into the invisible world, and its secrets are open to them. This is an ever-progressive celestial education, a vision of God, a return to his image. The more perfect souls instruct the less perfect, and draw them toward the divine. They learn all about the universe, for that impulse has been implanted in them by God. "World-knowledge is blessedness—how deeply does this thought shine in the Hellenic soul of Origen!"[5]

And *all* will go this way. The godless fall first into the fire of judgment. The material of it is a

---
[5] Seeberg, *Dogmengeschichte*, 2 Aufl., vol. i, p. 453 (1908).

HELL

man's own sinfulness, which torments the conscience; it is spiritual, and it is purifying. While the good mount up from sphere to sphere to God, receiving a certain purifying by their increasing knowledge, the wicked are cleansed by this intellectual fire, and after unending stages of time also reach the goal. The might of the Logos finally breaks down all opposition and annihilates the bad in the soul. Then comes the end in the Return of the Christ, the resurrection of the body, which appears as glorified pneumatic body. Souls live only in a spiritual existence in the vision of God, who is all in all. All are saved. We should naturally rest here, but Origen carries his principle of freedom so far that the end is or may be but the beginning of another vast world process. Free spirits originate new worlds, which in turn become the scenes of new tragic conflicts and new redemptions through the all-redeeming Logos. What a cycle! As the world is from eternity, so it will abide unto eternity. It is strange that Origen who made so much of freedom did not see that his philosophy is its destruction. Why should not the man who wills evil here will it forever? Why not allow him his preference?

Though Origen stood alone in these bold constructions, there were occasionally men who followed him in the Larger Hope. The celebrated preacher and bishop Gregory of Nazianzus (active 379) thought that "many might be baptized with fire in the other life, with that last, long, severe baptism, which will consume its material like hay, and take away all the frivolity of evil."[6] He speaks of a "purifying fire which has the power of doing away all evil inclina-

---
[6] *Oratio*, 29, 19.

tions" and of another "fire which does not purify but punishes, and is eternal ($διαιωνίζον$) upon the evil," though he seems to apologize for this, as though it were "more benevolent to think of this fire, in a way which is worthy of the Punisher."[7] But in an eloquent passage he shuts down hope:

> God has confined life and action to this world, and to the future the scrutiny of what has been done.... He will reason with us and oppose us, and set before us those bitter accusers our sins, comparing our wrongdoings with our benefits, and striking thought with thought, scrutinizing action with action, and calling us to account for the image which has been blurred and spoilt by wickedness, till at last he leads us away self-convicted and self-condemned.... And then what advocate shall we have? What pretext? What artifice? What device contrary to truth will impose upon the court and rob it of its right judgment, which places in the balance our entire life action, word and thought, and weighs against the evil that which is better, until that which preponderates wins the day and the decision is given in favor of the main tendency; after which there is no appeal, no higher court, no defense on the ground of subsequent conduct, no oil obtained from the wise virgins, no repentance of the rich man wasting away in the flame, no statute of limitations, but only that final and fearful judgment seat more just than fearful, or rather more fearful because just; when the thrones are set and the Ancient of Days takes his seat, and the books are opened, and the fiery stream comes forth, and the light before him and the darkness prepared; and they that have done good shall go into the resurrection of life, now hid in Christ and to be manifested hereafter with him, and they that have done evil into the resurrection of judgment, to which they who have not believed have been condemned already by the word which judges them. Some will be welcomed by the unspeakable light and the vision of the holy and royal Trinity which now shines upon them with greater brilliancy and purity and unites itself wholly to the whole soul, in which alone I take it that the kingdom of heaven con-

---

[7] *Ibid.*, 40. 36. Ullmann classes him as an Origenist, *Gregorius von Nazianz*, 1825, 2 Aufl., 1867, pp. 351, 352.

HELL

sists. The others among other torments, but especially the being outcast from God, and the shame of conscience which has no limit.[8]

His namesake, Gregory of Nyssa (bishop 372ff.), had worked out a deliberate theory of Universalism. God had created souls for the express purpose of realizing through his life perfect blessedness. But they chose evil and thwarted for the time his design. He met this by ordaining punishments, which would purge them from all evil and restore them back to their natural home, God. He would not have permitted the existence of evil at all if he had not foreseen that by redemption all rational beings would in the end attain to blessed fellowship with him. Theodore, bishop of Mopsuestia (forty miles west of Tarsus, 392ff.) also appeared to be a decided Universalist, and Diodorus, bishop of Tarsus (378ff.), is also supposed to have held the same philosophy of the universe.[9] The lofty speculator John Scotus Erigena had an occasional thought, in the same direction, but he did not deny the eternity of punishments. But outside of these half a dozen voices more or less, the impressive unanimity of a thousand years was not broken—the recognition of the darkness that settles down on the fate of the sinner according to the Scripture after the gates of the Judgment Day close behind him. Even Socinus saw but little alleviation, the only help he afforded being the substitution of annihilation for punishment in the ordinary sense, a theory with which Edward White has made us so familiar.

Schleiermacher was here a disciple of Gregory of Nyssa. We can just as well believe, he says, that

---
[8] *Oratio*, 16. 7-9, Browne and Swallow's tr., PNF, p. 250.
[9] Neander, *Church History*, Torrey's tr., ii, p. 738.

MODERNISM AND THE CHRISTIAN FAITH

all will ultimately be saved by the power of redemption as that a part will irretrievably be lost. If the first saved were brought in by the election of grace, why may not those left out be brought in by a second election? It is to him an indissoluble discord that—presuming a future life—a part of mankind will be excluded from the communion of redemption. Do the damned feel any pains of conscience? If they do, it is a sign that they are better there than here. A blessedness forfeited and felt as such by a tormenting conscience is thinkable only where there is still the capability to imagine that blessedness, yes, even to participate in it—a view in which there is truth. But Schleiermacher had a kind of deterministic or fatalistic view of the will, and a special view of the way the attractive power of the Redeemer is to work, which made Universalism easy to him. Ritschl's view of sin made him naturally inclined to the view of Schleiermacher in this also, though he thinks Scripture is not explicit, and that for those who are to perish finally, if such there be, Scripture wavers between annihilation and endless suffering.[10] A brilliant theologian of the liberal school states the matter thus:

> The reference of Christ and the apostles to the world-judgment presupposes the general idea of retribution. In a way this is realized in world-history, which contains distinct traces of the judgment of God. But the Christian consciousness cannot rest either in the general idea of retribution or in the principle that the history of the world is the judgment of the world. It demands, rather, a Last Judgment, in which the personal worth of every one is revealed, the final condition of every one is decided,

---

[10] See J. Köstlin, *Apocatastasis*, in Herzog-Hauck, 3 Aufl., i, pp. 619, 620, 622.

HELL

and the community of the saints is freed from every opposing thing. The doctrine of the final eternal loss of salvation of a part of mankind continues offensive for feeling and thought, and can be considered only *possible*, not certain. It is possible on account of the freedom of man, from which it follows that no one can be forced to holiness, that is, to communion with God and to blessedness. No one can be made holy and saved by nature-process, and it must be always possible to the will to eternally reject communion with God and thus elect loss of salvation. But it is unbiblical and untenable to think that God as foil to his holiness or as a proof of it *needs* a company of the damned. From the fact of human freedom it is equally possible that all may be saved, and there are not wanting in the Bible passages which indicate that even for the departed conversion is possible. [He refers to §63, iii, p. 607, where he gives Matt. 12. 32; 1 Pet. 3. 19, 20; 4. 6; Rev. 22. 2.] The thought of a restoration of all is therefore as justifiable a hypothesis as the thought of the final loss of salvation of a part, which the revelator calls the second death, δεύτερος θάνατος (Rev. 2. 11; 20. 6, 14; 21. 8). It is not so inconceivable as generally taken that God should only partially put through his plan of bliss. In virtue of his world government he understands very well how to put it through in spite of the apparent crossing of the same by free causes, the acts of men abusing their freedom. [He had said above that on account of this freedom the eternal loss of some is possible.] Will he in this very territory of his highest end for man be finally limited so that he cannot bless all? A third hypothesis, which, like that of restoration, includes a "united world-issue" and puts aside a part of the difficulties of the acceptance of eternal punishment, would be the perfect annihilation of the perseveringly unbelieving.[11]

What is the foundation of the Christian doctrine of eternal punishment?

First, the Scripture. Whatever our view of inspiration, the Bible is the Book of the Christian Religion, and simply as an external fact it is of appalling significance that in passages so numerous it would

---

[11] F. A. B. Nitzsch, *Lehrbuch der Evangelischen Dogmatik*, 1892, pp. 623, 624.

MODERNISM AND THE CHRISTIAN FAITH

weary you to recite them the fate of the wicked disappears in the blackness. If you will take your Revised Version and read such passages as Mark 3. 29; Matt. 8. 12; 25. 41, 46; Rom. 2. 5, 12; 3. 5; 2 Thess. 1. 9; John 12. 48, you will feel that if the writers did not intend to leave an impression of eternal loss and pain, some fearful outlook, some dread result, if they intended to teach that finally all would be well with the sinner, they certainly chose strange language to do it. It is not a question of one or two passages that you can explain away, that dropped inadvertently from the pen of the writer in a fit of absent-mindedness; it is the organ swell that dominates the whole piece; it is the ever-recurring warning; it is the "If to-day you hear his voice, harden not your hearts"; it is the "I come quickly and my reward is with me"; it is the "Beware lest there be in you an evil heart of unbelief"; it is the "Our God is a consuming fire"; it is the "Watch and pray, lest you fall into temptation"; it is the "Satan hath desired to have you, but I have prayed for you." It is like the "Watch your step" of the New York subway guards, it is like the "Don't monkey with the buzz saw" of the sawmill notice, or the placard on the New York Elevated Railroad, "Third rail: Danger." I say the moral impressiveness of that terrible unanimity is tremendous. I do not see how we can acquit the sacred writers of deception if that background of hell which they throw up is camouflage, the Black Douglass of the nursery maid. Was it not more like the seriousness of danger which was in the mind of Bishop Fowler when I heard him tell the young men of our Annual Conference, "The goblins will get you if you don't watch out."

HELL

" 'Would a man 'scape the rod?'
Rabbi Ben Karshook saith,
'See that he turn to God
The day before his death.'

" 'Ay, could a man inquire
When it shall come!' I say.
The Rabbi's eye shoots fire—
'Then let him turn to-day!' "[12]

Second, justice and righteousness. Who has implanted in the human soul that imperious demand for justice which will not down? What is it that makes us feel that there is something rotten with the universe if there is no fairness in administration of rewards, if the wicked get off as well as the good, if the adulterer and murderer are never brought to book? Hell is simply God's notice that the universe is not founded on chance, on ethical lightness, on an easy-going unconcern as to how the world wags, but on justice and the judgment of truth.

Third, conscience. Conscience is the fuel of hell; it is the fire and brimstone of the seer in the Apocalypse. It is that strange power which God has placed within us which gives the sanction to his "Don't," the "Amen" to his "Beware," the nod of assent to his "Watch." And if we refuse the warnings, if we drive on recklessly in evil ways, it brings us up with a sharp turn and tells us we have only ourselves to blame, we are getting what we deserve.

"Old man! there is no power in holy men,
Nor charm in prayer, nor purifying form
Of penitence, nor outward look, nor fast,
Nor agony, nor, greater than all these,
The innate tortures of that deep despair,
Which is remorse without the fear of hell,

---

[12] Browning, "Ben Karshook's Wisdom."

MODERNISM AND THE CHRISTIAN FAITH

> But all in all sufficient to itself
> Would make a hell of heaven, can exorcise
> From out the unbounded spirit, the quick sense
> Of its own sins, wrongs, sufferings, and revenge
> Upon itself: there is no future pang
> Can deal that justice on the self-condemned
> He deals on his own soul."[13]

Fourth, retribution. This means getting back what you have sent out, restoration, the law of cause and effect, reaping what you have sown. It is one of the most fearful laws of the universe. Nothing is lost. Everything comes back. That is hell, and that is heaven.

> "Never by lapse of time
> The soul defaced by crime
>   Into its former self returns again;
> For every guilty deed
> Holds in itself the seed
>   Of retribution and undying pain.
>
> "Never shall be the loss
> Restored, till Helios
>   Hath purified them with his heavenly fires;
> Then what was lost is won,
> And the new life begun,
>   Kindled with nobler passions and desires."[14]

The poet is contradictory here, but may be he means that even after the "new life begun" there must still be the "undying pain." Says Emerson:

> Thus is the universe alive. All things are moral. That soul which within is a sentiment outside of us is a law. We feel its inspiration: out there in history we feel its fatal strength. It "is in the world, and the world was made by" it. Justice is not postponed. A perfect equity adjusts its balance in all parts of life. Οἱ κυβοι Διὸς ἀεὶ εὐπίπτουσι,—The dice of God are always

---
[13] Byron, *Manfred*, Act iii, Scene 1.
[14] Longfellow, "The Masque of Pandora," at end.

HELL

loaded. The world looks like a multiplication table, or a mathematical equation, which, turn it how you will, balances itself. Take what figure you will, its exact value, nor more nor less, still returns to you. Every secret is told, every crime is punished, every virtue rewarded, every wrong redressed, in silence and certainty. What we call retribution is the universal necessity by which the whole appears wherever a part appears. If you see a smoke, there must be fire. If you see a hand or a limb, you know that the trunk to which it belongs is there behind.

Every act rewards itself, or, in other words, integrates itself in a twofold manner; first, in the thing, or in real nature, and, secondly, in the circumstances or in apparent nature. Men call the circumstances retribution. The causal retribution is in the thing and is seen by the soul. The retribution in the circumstance is seen by the understanding; it is inseparable from the thing, but is often spread over a long time and so does not become distinct until after many years. The specific stripes may follow late after the offense, but they follow because they accompany it. Crime and punishment grow out of one stem. Punishment is the fruit that, unsuspected, ripens within the flower of the pleasure which concealed it. Cause and effect, means and end, seed and fruit, cannot be severed; for the effect already blooms in the cause, the end preexists in the means, the fruit in the seed.[15]

We must throw arbitrariness out of our theology. No scoundrel is saved in two seconds, nor goes into the highest heaven by the turning of your hand. But can't the scoundrel be saved? Of course. But not arbitrarily. He brings himself in touch with healing forces, especially with Christ the Saviour. By his new trust in God he finds a new life working within him. It transforms him, it lifts him up, and Saul the persecutor becomes Paul the evangelist, and Newton the "slave of a slave trader" becomes the minister and author of "How sweet the name of Jesus sounds." But the law of retribution has not ceased to work. Paul's persecuting tyrannies pained

---
[15] Emerson, "Compensation," in *Essays*, Series 1, Essay 3, pp. 99, 100.

him far more after he had become a Christian than they did before. He repeatedly referred to them. Though he rejoiced in God, that rejoicing was consistent with many a secret pang which his former cruelty had caused. My father used to say, "The Christian gets his punishment in this world." Yes, and I might add, "Perhaps in heaven too." For whenever in that far future we advert to our meanness a momentary pain, a transient hell, is ours. Speaking of some recent swindle, Carlyle says in his Journal:

His [Hudson's] brother-in-law has drowned himself in York. What a world this ever is! full of Nemesis, ruled by the supernal, rebelled in by the Infernal, with prophetic tragedies as of old. Murderer Rush, Jermy's natural brother. To pious men he too might have seemed one of the fated. No son of Atreus had more authentically a doom of the gods. The old laws are still alive. [Speaking of Ireland.] Ruin and wretchedness that is prevalent there, for that seems to me the spot in our dominions where the bottomless gulf has broken out, and all the lies and delusions that lie hidden and open in us have come to this definite and practical issue there. "They that sow the wind, shall reap the whirlwind"; that was from of old the law.[16]... The universe is full of love, but also of inexorable sternness and severity, and it remains forever true that God reigns.[17] (As to the murderer.) One slight twitch of a muscle, the death-flash bursts, and he is *it*, and will for Eternity be it; and Earth has become a penal Tartarus for him; his horizon girdled now not with golden hope, but with red flames of remorse; voices from the depths of Nature sounding, "Woe, woe on him!" Of such stuff are we all made; on such powder-mines of bottomless guilt and criminality—"if God restrained not," as is well said—does the purest of us walk. There are depths in man that go to the lowest Hell, as there are heights that reach highest Heaven—for are not both Heaven and Hell made out of him, made by him, everlasting miracle and mystery as he is.[18]

---

[16] Froude, *Carlyle's Life in London*, vol. i, pp. 279, 281, New York ed.
[17] *Ibid.*, vol. ii, p. 208.
[18] *The French Revolution.*

HELL

Fifth, love. We cannot eliminate love from any part of God's dealings. Far from its being true that hell is inconsistent with God's love, it is only because God is Love that hell exists. Justice is only the other side of his love, the very attribute which gives his love worth; righteousness is the foundation on which his love rests and must rest if it is enduring. A universe where sin rages and there is no restraining hand; where deeds of lust and cruelty play the devil with the fates of the innocent and there is no recompense due, is an unthinkable universe. Love itself would commit suicide on such terms. A world that love made where no law of retribution guarded the gates of righteousness would be a contradiction, a solecism, a nightmare. Browning is right when he says, "There may be heaven—there must be hell." And he saw the eternal appeal of Dante:

> "Dante, who loved well, because he hated,
> Hated wickedness which hinders loving."

And Dante saw written over the gate of hell these words, and he never saw anything more true!

> "Guistizia mosse il mio alto fattore,
> Fecemi la divina potestate,
> La somma sapienza e il primo amore.
>
> "Justice it was that moved my Maker high,
> The power of God it was that fashioned me,
> Wisdom supreme, and primal charity."[19]

Sixth, freedom. Liberty of choice is one of the immutable principles of things. It is that which makes hell. What you desire you have, what you desire and choose and have makes *you*, and you make hell. The father can't give his son an education.

---
[19] Dante, *Inferno*, canto iii, lines 4-6.

MODERNISM AND THE CHRISTIAN FAITH

If you have no taste for music, the harmonies of Mendelssohn appeal to you in vain. God does not disinherit you, any more than the father did the prodigal son. You chose for yourself.

> "Though God be good and free be heaven,
> Not force divine can love compel;
> And though the songs of sins forgiven
> Might sound through lowest hell,
> The sweet persuasion of his voice
> Respects the sanctity of will.
> He giveth day; thou hast thy choice
> To walk in darkness still."[20]

It may not be one big choice of some dark deed, it may be the thousand little choices of the lesser good, or of the smaller sins, but they show the bent of the soul; or it may be one decisive step that puts the seal on many lesser preparatory steps, like Faust selling his soul to Mephistopheles and signing the contract with his blood—the "lurid meaning of a life which consists of innumerable individual acts." But you say, "If we are free, we may in hell choose life and thus be saved." Well, we may choose the life of God if we would. But suppose we would not. Suppose our innumerable choices here have made us into what we have chosen, so that morally we cannot help but prefer the lower. Hell is not a prison. Those who are there desire to be there—they love darkness rather than light. Hell is a state of mind.

> "Hell hath no limits, nor is circumscribed
> In one self place; for where we are is hell,
> And where hell is there we must ever be."[21]

---
[20] Whittier, *The Answer*, stanzas 9, 10.
[21] Marlowe, *Faustus*.

HELL

Our choices make our habits, our habits make ourselves, and ourselves make hell. Punishment after death "supposes the freedom of the human will, and is impossible without it. Self-determination runs parallel with hell."[22] No one has seen and expressed more vividly than Milton this psychological necessity of hell, the hell that Omar Kháyyám calls with a stroke of genius "the shadow from a soul on fire."[23]

> "Horror and doubt distract
> His troubled thoughts, and from the bottom stir
> The hell within him; for within him hell
> He brings, and round about him, nor from hell
> One step, no more than from himself can fly
> By change of place: now conscience wakes despair
> That slumbered wakes, the bitter memory
> Of what he was, what is, what must be
> Worse; of worse deeds worse sufferings must ensue."[24]

For this sober view of the destiny of the wicked as the church has—speaking generally—held it in all ages, this darker aspect as Christ left it, there have been two substitutes. The first is universal restoration, made familiar to us not only by the Universalist Church, but by individual Christian thinkers, as by Tennyson in his familiar lines in *In Memoriam*, liv. My brilliant college classmate, the Rev. Dr. Burton W. Lockhart, has found refuge in this or something like it: "I must believe that evil is essentially transient

---
[22] Shedd, *Dogmatic Theology*, vol. ii (1888), p. 715, note.
[23] "Heaven but the Vision of fulfilled Desire,
And Hell the Shadow from a Soul on fire."
—*Rubáiyát*, stanza 67, tr. Fitzgerald.
[24] *Paradise Lost*, book iv, lines 18ff. Compare the familiar but pregnant lines:
"The mind is its own place, and in itself
Can make a heaven of hell, a hell of heaven" (book i, lines 253, 254).

or mortal, or alter my predicates of God. And I must believe in the ultimate extinction of that personality whom the power of God cannot some time win to goodness. The only alternative is the termination of a wicked life either through redemption or through extinction." This is a most attractive vista, solves the problems that tear our hearts, and we are all driven to it by the passion of our souls and the theodicy of our intellects. And especially when there are passages of Scripture which in their broad sweep bear us toward some glorious goal: "The times of restoration of all things."[25] "The last enemy that shall be abolished is death."[26] "To sum up all things in Christ."[27] "In the name of Jesus every knee should bow, of *things* in heaven and *things* on earth and *things* under the earth, and that every tongue should confess that Jesus is Lord."[28] "New heavens and a new earth, wherein dwelleth righteousness."[29] And it is a sad, one might say a terrible, necessity, which compels us to turn aside from the sweet outlook of this theory and these passages, except as they fairly help us to indulge a beautiful hope, because the facts of Scripture and of life lead us to a view not quite so radiant.

What do these Scriptures mean? Do they mean, as some say, that the Bible is involved in a hopeless antinomy here, that on the question as to whether it is finally heaven or hell for lost souls, the Bible blows two ways, sometimes eternal punishment, sometimes in the end eternal glory? That would certainly be an interesting result, and yet I feel that confusion or, rather, contradiction on a stake so infinite is not

---

[25] Acts 3. 21. [26] 1 Cor. 15. 26. [27] Eph. 1. 10.
[28] Phil. 2. 10, 11. [29] 2 Pet. 3. 13.

HELL

to be accepted in a Book whose very purpose is to tell us how to save our souls, unless no other interpretation is fair. Perhaps the eminent exegete Meyer is right in saying that the allusion in these passages is not to a universal harmony that comes from a restoration of the lost, a matter not in the mind of the writers, but a harmony in and of the kingdom of God, established for the very reason that the wicked are finally excluded from that kingdom.[30] The universals of Scripture are always the universals *that are appropriate to the subject*, not absolute or mathematical universals. Whether bad men or angels who disappear from view after the Last Judgment are to come back to God in loving service would have to be specifically treated or mentioned in order for us to be sure on the strength of Scripture that they are thus to return. Or when God's judgment of sin is spoken of, then a specific statement that that judgment is only provisional or transitional would be necessary for the conclusion that it would be well with the sinner at the end.

We all feel the difficulty of eternal sin.[31] Apparently, God did not consult us about that or many other difficulties. To me the awfulness of sin with its inevitable hell is not that it is to exist in eternity but that it ever existed at all. A generation of Attila is as hard a strain on my theodicy as an eternity of hell. A God that can stand the last half of 1914— well, it is pretty hard to say what is or is not consistent with his attributes through the ages to come. If we bring our predicates of God into harmony with the facts of history, we shall be left a wide margin for the tears of Christ over the unconquerable will

---
[30] On Eph. 1. 9, 10.   [31] Mark 3. 29.

MODERNISM AND THE CHRISTIAN FAITH

("Ye will not come unto me that ye might have life") on the one hand and the Wrath of the Lamb on the other. In that infinite region I suspect that hell is possible, perhaps essential, even a spot of light in it.

It is interesting here to notice that Christian thinkers who have been the keenest in sympathy, the most earnest in deprecating the old popular exaggerations as to the future, have still not embraced Universalism, the very thing they would have gladly embraced if there had not been insuperable difficulties. Frederick Denison Maurice was one: "Can not that which is without God fix itself in misery? Has it not the power of defying that which seeks to subdue it? I know in myself that it has.... I dare not fix any limits to the power of his love. I cannot tell what are the limits to the power of the rebel will." He would not say that all would be raised out of eternal death because he did not know.[32] Charles Kingsley was another: "Your sins are killing you by inches.... Every sin you commit with your spirit... helps to destroy your spiritual life, and leaves you bad, more and more unable to do the right and avoid the wrong, more and more unable to discover right from wrong; and that last is spiritual death, the eternal death of your moral being.... The sinner always haunted by the shadow of himself, knowing that he is bearing about in him the perpetually growing death of sin."[33] The last of this celebrated triumvirate, Frederick W. Robertson, says: "There is no second spring for you—no resurrection morning of blessedness to dawn on the darkness of your grave. God has only one

---

[32] Maurice, *Life of Frederick Denison Maurice*, 1884, vol. ii, pp. 19, 20.

[33] *Charles Kingsley: His Letters and Memories of His Life.* Edited by His Wife, 1878, vol. ii, pp. 209, 210.

HELL

method of salvation, the cross of Christ. God can have only one, for the cross of Christ means death to evil, life to good. There is no other way to salvation but that; for that in itself is, and alone is, salvation. Out of Christ, therefore, it is woe to the man who reaches forth to the things which are before. To such I say: 'My unhappy brethren, Omnipotence itself cannot change the darkness of your destiny.' "[34] Lemme will not affirm eternal punishment, nor will he affirm restoration. He says the doctrine of restoration is "destructive of Christianity, and is therefore on a level with modern rationalistic attempts to resolve the peculiarities and absolutives of Christianity into the natural process of religious history. As a rule, it is observed that those who believe in the doctrine of restoration lose the earnestness and firmness of Christianity."[35] Theodore Parker rejected Christ as a teacher for the very reason that he taught eternal punishment. "To me it is quite clear that Jesus Christ taught the doctrine of eternal damnation. If the evangelists—the first three, I mean—are to be treated as inspired, I can understand his language in no other way."[36]

It is said that κόλασις, "punishment,"[37] means disciplinary or corrective punishment in classical Greek, and it is true that at a certain time in Athens a distinction was drawn between κόλασις and τιμωρία as Aristotle witnesses. Unfortunately, no weight can be attached to this, as often even in classical Greek,

---

[34] *Sermons Preached in Brighton*, New York ed., p. 68.

[35] *Endlosigkeit der Verdamniss*, u. s. w., 1900, quoted by Rishell in *Methodist Review*, 1901, p. 649.

[36] Letter to N. Adams, quoted by Dorchester, *Concessions*, etc., p. 250.

[37] Matt. 25. 46.

MODERNISM AND THE CHRISTIAN FAITH

in Hellenistic Greek, and in the New Testament that distinction had entirely disappeared.[38]

The second substitute is annihilation or conditional immortality. Though there were one or two before Edward White who ventured this solution, it was this godly and able Congregational minister in a London suburb, one of the ablest then living—the same who struck Universalism with this trenchant characterization: "Universalism with its washed-out message of general consolation, confounding salvation and damnation under one definition"[39]—who in his famous book, *Life in Christ*, 1846, rewritten 1875, and enlarged in 1878, gave the classic expression to this view once for all with a wealth of learning and argumentation which gives his book almost a solitary preeminence in the history of theology. The theory is founded on those passages in John which speak of Christ as giving eternal life and the not having Christ as death, on the literal significance of death, destruction, on the alleged falseness of the theory of natural immortality, which it is said we have borrowed from the Greeks, etc. I must confess I have never been drawn to White's theory. (1) There are millions of men who have either never heard of Christ or having heard of him have deliberately refused to receive life by faith in him—some of them men of beautiful spirit and winsome personality—of whom it is monstrous to think as being annihilated for lack of this faith. I prefer Wesley's hope of meeting Marcus Aurelius, Socrates, etc., in heaven. (2) It is evident that by eternal life Christ means not existence, but

---
[38] See S. H. Kellogg, in *Presbyterian and Reformed Rev.*, 1891, p. 564f. and Beet in *Expositor* (London), September, 1890, p. 212f.

[39] Freer, *Edward White, His Life and Work*, 1902, p. 212.

HELL

that religious and spiritual union with God through him which is the peculiar gift of Christianity. There may be another union through devotion to truth and morality, to the light as one sees it, which has the promise of life beyond, but of life of its own kind. To me it is impossible to think of immortality as something added to the soul after the exercise of so-called saving faith. The very substance of every man's life is divine, it is the mirror of eternity, and that any worthy spirit who desires immortality should fail of it in God's universe is unthinkable. Those who do not desire it, who, like Harriet Martineau, think it an impertinence—for these I have nothing to say. Perhaps the best thing to be said of them is what a French Christian replied to his infidel friend: "Probably you are right; probably you are not immortal; but I am." (3) The literal meaning of the words "death," "destroy," etc., it is impossible to carry through. I have not space to discuss the matter, but if you will read Plumptre's essay, you will see that this part of White's work is philologically unsound.[40]

So we are left with the old view which I take to be in substance that of Christ, the apostles, and saints and theologians in all ages of all churches and schools. When interpreted rationally it is to me a lesser strain on faith than annihilation, and far more in accordance with the laws of the soul and the facts of life—not to speak of the Scripture—than Universalism. Interpreted rationally: What does this catholic view involve?

---

[40] *Conditional Immortality*, in Plumptre, *The Spirits in Prison and Other Studies on the Life after Death*, 1885, pp. 312ff. See also J. Baldwin Brown, *The Doctrine of Annihilation in the Light of the Doctrine of Love*, 1875.

MODERNISM AND THE CHRISTIAN FAITH

(1) Properly speaking, according to the Scriptures, hell does not begin till after the Last Judgment. Of course for all sinners saved or unsaved punishment is now and ever, whenever memory and conscience bring a man's evil past to his mind. Punishment is not chronological. We can no more sever retribution from the soul of saint or sinner than we can sever his moral personality from him. But still God has a plan of the universe, he is a God of order, and if we take the Scripture as revealing truly in faint outlines that plan, it is evident that the fruition of our history begins after the so-called Last Day. That means a tremendous significance of the Intermediate State in God's education of the race. The details of this training are wisely left in obscurity. But that vast space is not without its uses in the divine economy. Whether those who have repeatedly and finally rejected the light here will have other chances there is a much debated question, but both Scripture and psychology speak one language—

> To-day if ye shall hear his voice,
> Harden not your hearts (Heb. 4. 7).

The fact that you heard shows that your soul's auditory nerve is still responsive. To-morrow the voice sounds, but you hear it not.

(2) There is no doubt that evil dissipates the forces of personality, and there is this much truth in the doctrine of conditional immortality. Ribot says that under certain conditions the powers of the mind dissolve toward the automatic. "One of the first signs of mental impairment is loss of sustained attention. Unity, stability, power, have ceased, and the

end is extinction of the will,"[41] or rather loss of its freedom or power. "On the principle of evolution," says Dr. Professor A. H. Strong, "abuse of freedom may result in reversion to the brute, annihilation not of existence but of higher manhood, punishment from within rather than from without, eternal penalty in the shape of eternal loss."[42] The less of personality, the less there is to suffer—possibly the soul finally so obtuse and degraded that suffering becomes impossible, at least in any sense in which a highly organized spirit would feel the boomerang which we call hell. The evil soul is like the comets which at every return to the sun "lose a portion of their size and brightness, stretching out till the nucleus loses control, the mass breaks up" and becomes "disconnected meteorites."

(3) Judas "went to his own place."[43] Hell is the place where the sinner would be. Like seeks like. The spiritual laws of the universe act as automatically and surely as the physical, and there is a spiritual gravitation which has both saint and sinner in its grip. We cannot think of God keeping anyone in heaven or hell against his will. We go to our own place.

(4) "Beaten with many stripes . . . with few stripes."[44] That means infinite variety. Hell, so to speak, shades off into heaven, or vice versa: each person dealt with with that fairness of justice we expect from the Celestial Judge, whose tribunal is guarded by a shield with two sides, justice and mercy. And may there not be improvement in one's state? If one takes his

---

[41] *Diseases of the Will*, p. 115.
[42] *Systematic Theology*, 1909, vol. iii, p. 1038.
[43] Acts 1. 25; compare 4. 23.   [44] Luke 12. 48.

retribution rightly, if one says, "Thy strokes, O righteous One, are well deserved," that very acquiescence lifts the soul into better air; at that very moment hell is and must be to us less of hell and more of heaven.

(5) Hell is only a point in God's vast cosmos. The remark of Christ, "Broad is the way that leadeth to destruction, and many are they that enter in thereby,"[45] was an historical judgment of things as he saw them and is not to be taken as the final outcome of his work, though it does, of course, express the fact that strenuous athletes after perfection are unfortunately a minority in our wayward race. Here let me quote the late Professor Shedd as an absolutely unbiased witness, the stalwart Calvinist with the marvelously trained mind, wide intelligence, and literary culture:

> Hell is only a spot in the universe of God. Compared with heaven hell is narrow and limited. The kingdom of Satan is insignificant in contrast with the kingdom of Christ. In the immense range of God's dominion, good is the rule and evil is the exception. Sin is a speck upon the infinite azure of eternity; a spot on the sun. Hell is only a corner of the universe. The Gothic etymon (Höhle Hölle) denotes a covered up hole. In Scripture hell is a "pit," a "lake," not an ocean. It is "bottomless," but not boundless ["bottomless," because sin may be of any depth]. The Gnostic and Dualistic theories which make God, and Satan, or the Demiurge, nearly equal in power and dominion, find no support in revelation. Some angels and men will forever be the enemies of God. But their number compared with that of unfallen angels and redeemed men is small. They are not described in the glowing language and metaphors by which the immensity of the holy and blessed is delineated. [He quotes Psa. 68. 17; Deut. 22. 2; Psa. 103. 21; Matt. 6. 13; 1 Cor. 15. 25; Rev. 14. 1; 21. 16, 24, 25.] No metaphor and amplification are

---
[45] Matt. 7. 13.

HELL

added [to the brief statement as to the lost in Rev. 21. 8] to make the impression of an "immense multitude which no man can number."[46]

But, dear reader, for all these alleviations—if such there be—of hell, to you and to me comes again the word,

"To-day if ye will hear his voice,
Harden not your hearts."

"Now hath my life across a stormy sea
Like a frail bark reached that wide port where all
Are bidden, ere the final reckoning fall
Of good and evil for eternity.
Now know I well how that fond fantasy,
Which made my soul the worshiper and thrall
Of earthly art, is vain; how criminal
Is that which all men seek unwillingly.
Those amorous thoughts that were so lightly dressed—
What were they when the double death is nigh?
The one I know for sure, the other dread.
Painting nor sculpture can now lull to rest
My soul that turns to his great love on high,
Whose arms, to clasp us, on the cross were spread."[47]

---
[46] *Dogmatic Theology*, 1888, vol. ii, pp. 744-747.
[47] Michael Angelo, *Sonnets*.

APPENDIX

Note A

Walter Pater on "Come unto Me."

Even Walter Pater the humanist, who had broken entirely with Christianity, came back in later years to feel the strange mystery of Him who could say, "Come unto me." In answer to the ready skepticism of the author of *Robert Elsmere* (her uncle Matthew's own niece) in her remark to Pater that historical Christianity ("orthodoxy") could not long maintain itself, expecting assent from her friend, he shook his head and looked "rather troubled." "I don't think so," he said. Then, with hesitation, "and we don't altogether agree. You think it's all plain. But I can't. There are such mysterious things. Take that saying, 'Come unto me, all ye that are weary and heavy laden.' How can you explain that? There is a mystery in it—something supernatural."[1] Yes, there is mystery in it and there is divinity in it, and of that mystery Mrs. Ward's explanation does not get to the bottom. She says that it is a lost quotation from a Wisdom book, and that it is Wisdom which is speaking, a quotation or text. But unless you say it is indeed Divine Wisdom speaking—wisdom in the new role of bearing heartbreaks, the world's sorrows and sins—you have not come far, because Wisdom, though she can give help to the inquisitive,

---

[1] Mrs. Humphry Ward, *A Writer's Recollections*, part iii. Harper & Brothers, publishers, New York city (1919). Quotations in this appendix used by kind permission of respective publishers.

APPENDIX

cannot even solve her own deeper problems, let alone carry the burdens of the heavy-laden.

NOTE B

Dr. G. A. Gordon on the *a priori* Ruling Out of the Divinity of Christ, and on Christ as the Eternal Prototype of Humanity in the Life of God, and the Resulting Kinship of Humanity with God:

The supreme divinity of Jesus Christ is but the sovereign expression in human history of the great law of difference in identity that runs through the entire universe, and that has its home in the heart of the Godhead. With this law in our thought, we dare to look into the New Testament conception of God as the Father and the Son and the Holy Spirit. In him we find eternally existing the Paternal, the Filial, and the Union of these two. Here are the differences in the ineffable community of the Godhead. Is it not conceivable that the Filial in God should have been in union with Jesus in a way unparalleled and inapproachable? Surely, it is thinkable and credible that, in consequence of his mission and relation to the world, the Deity might have been the basis of Christ's being in a manner utterly singular, and that, along with the kinship between him and us, there might be an eternal contrast. The universe is the work of God. It is not for us to say what shall be the character of creation; we must take reality as we find it, and reverently seek for insight into its mystic depths. The claim that in Jesus there is a union with God absolutely unique, is at least conceivably sound and true. The claim cannot be disposed of without consideration, it cannot be dismissed prior to examination of the fact. Jesus Christ is a fact too transcendent to be accommodated to the requirements of a given philosophy. The scheme that is to prevail, that is not doomed to a disastrous collision with reality, must grow out of the historic truth. The man who comes forward with a programme in his hand, according to which the universe must be ordered, is too ambitious. His task is too great for him. He is usurping the place of creative Wisdom. The universe is already here, ordered in terms of the Eternal Reason; and history is already here, and its evolution of the character of the Ultimate

MODERNISM AND THE CHRISTIAN FAITH

Life, and man's duty is to follow the path of the great revelation. The assertion that Christ cannot be very God of very God, in a sense infinitely beyond what may be truthfully said of all other human beings, is sheer intellectual presumption, is, indeed, dogmatism of the worst kind. . . .

All religious philosophy will admit that in God there is the Eternal Prototype of humanity. All intelligent religious thinking must recognize in the Deity an eternal basis for the nature, the advent, the career and ideal, of mankind. What possible interest can human beings have in the Infinite if society is not organized out of his life, if he is not the ground of its order and hope? Is there anything in the Infinite to account for humanity? That is the deepest question in religious philosophy, and thinkers are everywhere converging upon the conclusion that in God there is the Eternal Pattern of our race. And what is this Eternal Pattern, or Prototype, but the Son of man of the synoptic Gospels, the Only-begotten of the fourth Gospel, the Mediator of the Pauline epistles, the High Priest without descent, with neither beginning of days nor end of years, of the letter to the Hebrews, the God of God, Light of Light, begotten, not made, of the Nicene Creed, who for us men and our salvation came down, was made flesh, and became man? Granted that in all these phrases there is an effort to express the inexpressible, a framing of words to set within definite forms the unbounded and ineffable; granted that the terms are but symbolic in their force, that they but hint at the whole unutterable truth, the question comes, Is there an infinite reality behind the human symbol, is the mental effort and result a trustworthy witness to the transcendent and eternal fact? That question all religious philosophy that is not serving as its own undertaker must answer in the affirmative. And the point in Christology for the faith of to-day to master, the center round which the whole conflict of opinion is raging, is the special, unique relation of Jesus Christ to this Eternal Prototype of humanity in the Godhead. . . .

The great point, then, to be determined concerning Jesus is, whether he is the supreme and unique representative of the humanity of God, the proper incarnation of the Filial in the being of the Infinite?

Conviction upon this point can result only from serious study of the character of Jesus. In the next section of this discussion

APPENDIX

the attempt will be made to indicate the ground upon which such a conviction may be founded. Here, however, let it be remarked that, as we study Jesus in the freedom and homage of true science, we come upon the august fact that so penetrated the mind of Horace Bushnell, and to which he has given an expression so simple and magnificent, the unclassifiable character of Christ. Reason has no place for him in the purely human categories unless these are made the forms for an ideal humanity. If our human categories are the conceptions that cover actual human existence, Christ's being fills and transcends them; he is all that they require, and infinitely more. They make room for sin, and mortal ignorance, and ethical limitation in every direction, and the general sore embarrassment to which all human beings are subject. They make no room for complete holiness, absolute knowledge of moral obligation, utter ethical integrity, and the freedom of the perfect Son of God. The prophetism of Jesus; his goodness, and his power as director of our whole higher civilization; his thought, his character, his authority, cannot be put, without doing violence to fact, in the same category with those of any other leader of mankind. There is in the Founder of the Christian religion a recognizable, a demonstrable transcendence of the actual human category. He is concerned with the Deity, implicated in his nature, associated with his purpose, under his will and spirit, in a manner secret, inapproachable, ineffable. This singularity of Christ is unmistakable in the Gospels, conspicuous in the Epistles, and conclusively evident over the whole field of more than eighteen hundred years of Christian experience and history. The form of the Son of man is an eternal contrast, set in with immortal identities, to all his brethren. For the sake of the identities we must hold to the contrast. This singularity of Christ is the thing to be noted to-day; this assurance of union between God and humanity from the Christ who represents that union by the authority of a relation aboriginal and ineffable; this pledge of salvation, victorious evolution, or whatever name may be assigned it, from the Life that is human, and at the same time carries into history the secret of the Eternal Mind. This singularity of our Lord must be saved for the sake of the community with mankind that rests upon it. For I believe that only as we grasp the transcendent relation which Christ sustains to God can we retain for any length of time, and in effective living form, the other mighty insights

MODERNISM AND THE CHRISTIAN FAITH

that faith has won through him. Philosophy working upon history is to-day able to reach results similar to those revealed through the Person of Christ; but the fact must never be overlooked that philosophy did not originate the mighty truths that make us men. These truths were made known to our race by a vital process; they were brought forth by the sore travail of history. And philosophy must always be tried at the bar of history; the grand integrity of the historic reality must never be surrendered to an imperious speculative scheme. Lose out of faith the sense of the Eternal in Christ, fail to recognize in him the presence of the Absolute, miss the fact that his nature is rooted in the Deity and is part of the nature of God, and we let go the sole adequate support for belief in the consubstantiation of humanity with divinity, and the consciousness that Jesus is the moral ideal for mankind. The Christ who embodies the deepest in God, who incarnates the Eternal Filial in the Infinite, is essential to hold for the world the great convictions of the kinship between man and his Maker, and the presence in Jesus of the true and final standard of human life. If the difference in Christ to humanity is the difference of the very God, then we can believe that the identity in Christ to our race is the identity of the very God. But if the contrast in the Lord to mankind does not reach to the being of God, if it is not the manifestation of the Eternal, if it is only individual idiosyncrasy, the mere separate, highly colored envelope in which his humanity comes into the world and preserves its secrets from the vulgar crowd with whom it must be thrown together, then it follows inevitably that the kinship of Christ to his brethren does not carry us to the heart of the universe, does not go beyond the bounds of space and time. Only a Christ whose antithesis to humanity means the presence of the very God can by his union with humanity assure us of union with God. Discredit the infinite difference, and we must doubt the sublime identity. This contention will be self-evident to those who see that we owe our faith in the humanity of God and in the divinity of man, not primarily to philosophy, but to the power of the historic process. Revelation is ever through life, the apprehension of the Infinite Personality through the finite; philosophy comes afterward and finds her task. If we take Christ out of the historic process of revelation, we decapitate faith in the humanness of God and the divineness of man. We must remember

APPENDIX

the rock whence our belief was hewn, the pit whence it was dug. It was not in the world prior to Christ except in the form of intermittent prophetic dream, limited religious intuition, or vague, ineffectual philosophic fancy. It was not here as the ruling force in human civilization. The consubstantiation of man with God is the accepted and molding belief of Christendom to-day because of the revelation of the nature both of God and man made through Jesus Christ. Our whole higher faith is based upon the conviction that, inasmuch as the contrast in him to mankind means the contrast of the Absolute, the kinship in him to our race signifies the kinship of the Absolute. The historic process to which we owe our working and effectual faith may be said to consummate its service to the human spirit in the great declaration that the difference of Christ to mankind is the difference of God, and the identity of Christ to our race is the identity of God. When we ascend into the being of the Infinite upon the difference, we can with confidence descend into humanity upon the identity.—*The Christ of To-Day*, 1895, Houghton, Mifflin & Co., publishers, pp. 112–114, 115, 116, 116–121. In a letter to me in 1918, Dr. Gordon, who is a liberal thinker, says that this book—which I take to be his most widely circulated one—still expresses his convictions. See also his *Ultimate Conceptions of Faith*, 1903, pp. 290–296. Jesus's vocation is to "serve as the supreme organ of the Eternal Son in God" (p. 294). "Jesus is the sovereign historic expression of the eternal Son in the bosom of the Father" (p. 293). He accepts Origen's Trinity. "God is logically first. In himself God is eternally the Father, and the Son, and the Holy Ghost" (*ibid.*).

NOTE C

Professor George B. Foster and Dr. Gordon on Jesus.

A liberal of liberals, Professor George B. Foster, *Finality of Christian Religion* (1906), who was a radical so broad that his brother Baptists must have felt dismay when they saw him throw into the scrap heap almost every Christian doctrine which had been the glory of their church, is yet compelled

MODERNISM AND THE CHRISTIAN FAITH

to acknowledge something inexplicable in Jesus. Psychology cannot explain him (p. 265). "It is not possible to escape from the recognition of an active and creative moment in the consciousness of Jesus which, just in that account, cannot be casually explained by articulating it in the system of development" (pp. 265, 266). "The empirical inexplicability of Jesus may as well be conceded" (p. 267). "An entirely new spiritual force, not even formerly latent in the cosmic system, might appear therein" (p. 268). Permission University of Chicago Press. Says Dr. Gordon:

> All men, either in their rational endowment or in their moral character, or in both, transcend time; but Christ transcends all time. This thought after two thousand years needs no revision. His conceptions of God, of man, and human society are ultimate conceptions; intellectual power cannot go beyond them, can never even master their entire content. His spirit has upon it the mark of finality, his character is the full impression upon humanity of the moral perfection of Deity. The ultimateness of Christ's thought and the finality of his spirit differentiate his transcendence from that of the greatest and best of mankind, and ground his being in the Godhead in a way solitary and supreme.—*The Christ of To-Day*, 1895, p. 128. Permission Houghton Mifflin Company, as also selections above.

Note D

Professor Alfred Seeberg on the Primitive Conception of Jesus.

Even so liberal a scholar as Alfred Seeberg, one of the irreparable losses direct or indirect of the World War, younger brother of Professor Reinhold Seeberg, holds that while the first and simplest idea of the person of Christ was a man filled and determined by the

APPENDIX

Spirit of God, which, of course, he was, yet in apostolic times that thought enlarged itself necessarily and as a matter of course into his preexistence and postexistence, and that Jesus himself so understood and witnessed of himself. And as to his work Seeberg thinks that there was first a written or formal statement that that work consisted of a conquest of Satan and the demonic powers, which soon broadened into the idea of an offering or expiation for the sins of the world. Seeberg says that it is false to suppose that Paul brought in the redemption dogma on the simpler gospel of Jesus. Rather there was the closest relationship between Jesus, the original Christian community, and Paul; or, in other words, the apostolic teaching as a formal piece is the work of both Jesus and the community and is the foundation of the Pauline Gospel.—Seeberg, *Christi Person und Werk nach der Lehre seiner Jünger*, 1910; *Theologisches Literaturblatt*, 1910, cols. 370, 371.

Note E

Professor Erich Schaeder (modern positive) of the University of Kiel, on Christ Praying to the Father:

The divine in Jesus holds itself strictly in the frame of his *Sonship* to God. Doubtless there are points of view here which have not been duly estimated by "churchly," that is, by confessional, Christology. If they had been, one would have stood up better weaponed against the modern storm against the confession of the deity of Christ. Jesus Christ has part in the nature of God only so that he receives this part, with all that it includes as to unity of soul and will, always from God. His saving-helping aims and the powers thereto belonging come to him from God. It is in this living union of receiving and taking divine life from God that he is the Son and God his Father. For this reason he

prays to God for the reception perhaps of miracle power. Therefore, with all that he has in common with God, he is held to serve not himself, but God to live and to serve. We must out entirely with the idea that the deity of Jesus is anything personally resting in himself, which places him so to say for himself at the side of God. The deity of Jesus forms a unique life-connection of Jesus with God in which he the ever receiving One, gifted through God, is therefore the One who looks up to God and serves God. The picture of Jesus thus conceived becomes not only in content much more impressive, richer, but especially more Scriptural. And it leads to a Trinitarian conception of God which makes purer and fuller the united life-movement in the threefold God.
—*Theologisches Literaturblatt*, 1911, cols. 235, 236.

NOTE F

Bishop McConnell on Christ and the Creeds:

When we come to creed and dogma we find that these two are instruments of the kingdom of God.... The only way we can judge of the validity of belief is by noting what happens to the man who believes. The instrumental character of the creeds is very apparent as we look at the causes of their origin. The church was in danger of splitting into fragments because of lack of authoritative pronouncement on this or that, or there was required a compact shaping of the truth for fighting purposes, or for purposes of exposition. Or, we may believe the Christian community had attained through historic processes to a fresh insight which must be set forth systematically to mark an advance.... [Speaking of Christ's resurrection appearances:] The problem of Christian thinking is to express the fullness of life in Christ. It is from the point of view of those convinced of the eternal life in Christ that we read the story of the resurrection appearances. The church's appreciation of Christ, dealing with the recorded data, results in the dogma that Christ passed through death and revealed himself to his disciples in such fashion as to convince them that he liveth forevermore. In a word, the pressure of the life of Christ is the driving force in creed-making. In this or that detail the items of creed as to Christ may need improvement, but the creeds are not as likely to err from overstatement as from understatement. We have not a Christ who shrinks within the creedal

APPENDIX

phrases which we make for him, but one who outgrows the phrases.

The life of the Person is the end which we are trying to set forth All our instruments are inadequate, inadequate not so much through maladjustment as through lack of size. The great fact is Christ himself. He has been the dynamic shaping the creeds. The separate items of the creeds have been so many attempts by successive ages to put into formal terms a measure of the impact of Christ. The creeds are both results of the Personal Force which stands at the center of the Christian system, and also instruments to help us to know Christ. The Life does not shrink, but grows in size when set in the larger framework of the advancing statements of the ages. The creeds have been attempts of the church to utter for herself in compendious phrases the imprint which Christ has left on a particular time.—*Personal Christianity* (Cole Lectures), 1914, pp. 74, 75. On the divinity of Christ as larger than our definitions, he says: If we could in this life find the final meaning for the divinity of Christ, we would have in our finding disproved the divinity, for its supreme characteristic is this enormous pressure of life toward larger meanings. The real authoritative power is this compelling spiritual force.—McConnell, *Religious Certainty*, 1910, p. 170.

Note G

Dr. Horton on the Church's Loss of the Cross.

One of the bravest and most progressive thinkers of the Congregational Church in England, the Rev. Dr. Robert F. Horton, in his monthly lecture to his church, Lyndhurst Road, Hampstead, London, N. W., February 3, 1918, on the topic, "What is Wrong with the Churches?" said:

The church has for many years past been silent about sin; she has tried to give a rose-water view of life and to picture a God of infinite good nature, until the cross she preaches has become an offense again and practically meaningless. And now we have come to a point in the history of the world when the realization of evil is forced upon us; rose-water views of life have no value for us. We have no room for people who are ever expatiating on

MODERNISM AND THE CHRISTIAN FAITH

the virtue and the divinity of human nature. We have found out human nature, and the easy, comfortable Victorian age vanishes in smoke as we see what human nature can do. We find that a high and Christless civilization is more like a wild beast than man. Human nature stands before us in its hideous inhumanity and corruption, and we see the failure of the church in that the church flattered men instead of telling them what they were. The church talked softly about their virtues instead of rousing them to a sense of their wickedness. The church's failure lay exactly there—that the central truth of life, which is the cross of Christ, lost its meaning in petty phrases and empty talk about love and humanity and brotherhood. She did not teach men the truth. She went on implying that all men required was a little love to one another; she did not tell them and make them feel that what they required was holiness, goodness, the cross of Christ as the revelation of holy love, God as holy love, the sin of man, the love of God, the Son of God made sin for man, the new birth, the absolute necessity of a spiritual life that is rooted in the nature of God and is manifested in the radical change of the human heart until it becomes sweet and pure and loving. That is where the church has failed. She has taught what is not the truth of the gospel, and led men to think that it was the gospel she was preaching, and the vast failure of that invented gospel has been attributed to the true gospel, which has been forgotten or laid aside. . . . It is God's purpose in Christ, as it was shown to us at the beginning, to give us a redemption at a great cost, a reconciliation of righteousness and forgiveness, a gift to men of a power not their own, the power of an endless life. It is that which has the power of transforming the world. It is this gospel which the world wants. If it ever is to be good and happy, it must have a gospel, a great power of God that transforms human lives and gives forces to work amongst men which are not really from the earth, but are from God and from above.

NOTE H

Dr. David Smith on Atonement in the Light of the Modern Spirit.

One of the most interesting books in theology is *The Atonement in the Light of History and The Modern Spirit*, by the Rev. David

APPENDIX

Smith, D.D., professor of theology in McCrea Magee College, Londonderry (1918). For a Scottish Presbyterian divine, steeped in the study of the history of theology and of the Bible, Dr. Smith's *Atonement* is a wonderfully liberal performance. It is "modern" with a vengeance. The most of it could have been written by a Unitarian, and that is exceedingly significant for the change that has come over the Calvinism of Scotland. Judging from this book, even for so theologically backward a land as Ulster (witness the volumes of the late Dr. Robert Watts), Calvinism is dead in North Ireland and South Scotland. In the Highlands it still exists. There is one exception, however, to this prevailing non-Calvinism in Dr. Smith. The sacrifice of Christ forgives and heals by anticipation all the backslidings of the Christian. "He [Christ] forgave the sin of yesterday and the sin of to-morrow and the sin of each succeeding day to the close of our earthly pilgrimage" (p. 217). This *carte blanche* for the future sins of the Christian is splendid, but it is shattered on Heb. 10. 26 and numerous other passages of the Word. Nor is it true that the world's sins are already forgiven because they are expiated, and therefore we can say to the sinner, "Don't believe in order to be forgiven," but, "Your sin is already forgiven, therefore believe" (p. 216). This comes from the author's making "propitiation" the same as "forgiveness." Paul did not say to the Philippian jailer, "You are already forgiven and saved; simply take your forgiveness," but he said, "Believe on the Lord Jesus, and thou shalt be saved" (Acts 16. 31). Atonement secures salvation, but it does not communicate salvation. I cannot agree with Dr. Smith that "forgiveness is already a *fait accompli*" (p. 215), or that we should say to the seeker, "Believe in the forgiveness of your sins because they are forgiven." Salvation is a spiritual process, not a magical or trade exchange, and penitence and faith are not like the turning of a faucet.

The historical parts of Dr. Smith's treatise are the most valuable, though he exaggerates the prevalence of what he calls the ransom theory (the so-called ransom-to-Satan theory), and is mistaken in attributing it to the prevalence of robberies and kidnaping in the Roman empire in patristic times. It was not started till Origen came out with it (about 220), and Alexandria was a city comparatively free from marauders. It was only a small part of Origen's many-sided theory of atonement, and was due

MODERNISM AND THE CHRISTIAN FAITH

was the father that suffered most (p. 167), and it was "vicarious suffering," though not "atonement," not "sacrifice" (p. 167). "There is nothing in the parable of the prodigal son of propitiation," etc. (p. 166). Our Unitarian friends have long since not only eliminated atonement from that parable, but have declared that it is one of the best proofs that there is no such doctrine in the New Testament. But the three parables in Luke 15 were given to teach one thing, viz., that in murmuring because the publicans and sinners drew near to hear Jesus and because Jesus received and ate with them (verses 1 and 2), the Pharisees were really murmuring against the God in whom they believed, because that God was interested in that very thing, the saving of sinners, and had sent him (Christ) for that purpose. Whether this saving of sinners was not itself the expression of an atonement, the agony of a love that was redemption, and because redemption agony (the holy God bearing sin, the Lamb slain from the foundation of the world, the propitiation that in the nature of things love must offer to righteousness and vice versa), the parable does not state. It is a story, and not a didactic. Even the liberal H. A. W. Meyer says: "The interposition of this grace (for the adoption of sinners into prerogatives which belong in principle to the righteous), through the death of reconciliation and consequently the more specific definition of that confidence, Jesus leaves unnoticed, leaving these particulars to the further development of faith and doctrine after the atoning death *had taken place* [italics his]; just as in general according to the synoptic Gospels, he limits himself to single hints of the doctrine of reconciliation as seed-corn for the future" (Matt. 20. 28; 26. 28) (Com. on Luke 15. 25-32, at end).

My own feeling is that by a violent reaction against the narrow Calvinism in which he was brought up, Dr. Smith has flattened out God's nature to love merely. The sacrifice of atonement "was not *to* God, but *by* him" (p. 169). Why not both? It was "vicarious love." Why not also righteousness in the love? The atonement is "far better than a sacrifice to satisfy God's justice; it is a sacrifice to satisfy his love" (p. 170). Why limit the richness of the offering? Was it not the expression of *all* God's nature? Paul's doctrine of atonement is more comprehensive, and because so, truer (Rom. 3. 21-26).

Dr. Smith makes much of the "modern spirit." There are the "ransom theory," the "satisfaction theory," the "forensic theory,"

APPENDIX

and the "atonement in the light of the modern spirit." It goes without saying that we should interpret all of God's truth by all of God's light, and that that light is ever growing. But "modern" is a relative and ever-shifting term. In the later middle ages Ockham spoke of the "modern Platonists." Luther was a modern in part. But for how long? Until the younger Socinus (died 1604) made him an ancient. And every year since, the definition has been changing and the boundaries pushing out. To-day we are moderns, but to-morrow new ideas and new men thrust us aside as fossils. Old Unitarianism is dead—or, rather, it lives only in the evangelical Churches—the new Unitarians are "modern." This ever-shifting scene the apostolic writers saw and provided for. They felt the need of something abiding, an anchor that would hold in the flowing and ebbing tide. So they said, "Jesus Christ *is* the same yesterday, and to-day, *yea* and forever" (Heb. 13. 8). "I am [the ever-present tense] the way, and the truth, and the life" (John 14. 6). Jesus himself, his truth, his religion, his life, remain. Our grasp grows stronger, our vision clearer, our outlook wider, but it is of his fullness that we receive. Therefore the proper attitude toward the church's apprehension of him and of his truth in the past is, How much did she receive? What of truth did she get? No important idea which has been potent through centuries and nursed the saints, even though distorted and exaggerated, if founded on the Word, has been entirely false. What is the truth in it? Do not judge of him and his work by the "modern spirit," but by the Word, the whole historical apprehension, and by the ever-teaching Spirit.[1]

NOTE I

"Original Sin." "Total Depravity."
These words and the ideas commonly called up by them are the *bête noir* of the modern man. This is due to the fact that they are associated in his mind with grossly exaggerated conceptions, due partly to the fault of language and partly to actual perversions

---
[1] This note appeared originally in *The London Quarterly Review*, and is reproduced by the kind permission of the editor, the Rev. John Telford, B.A.

MODERNISM AND THE CHRISTIAN FAITH

of Scriptural truth in history (compare, for instance, Augustine and some of the Reformation creeds). But in their Christian essence what do these objectionable words and ideas mean? Original sin means that the parents of our race by voluntary transgression received a wrong bent which by natural laws they transmitted to their offspring. Depravity means the lack of the perfect image of God thus resulting, total in the sense that without the help of the Spirit of God it will issue in time in positive sin. Understood rightly there is nothing that we need be ashamed of in this part of our Christian heritage. To rightly define these ideas is sufficient. After that the history of the world is their best defense. Even the ancient Greeks and Romans had to bear their unconscious testimony. Plato says that those who are good are not so by nature, but by $\theta\varepsilon i\alpha\ \mu o i\rho\alpha$, divine fate. In his Nicomachian Ethics Aristotle assumes capacity for virtue, but recognizes universality of evil desires. Thucydides said: "It is the nature of man to sin, both in public and private." Cicero and Seneca are equally emphatic. Ovid declared, "I would be wise if I could; but a strange power bears me along against my will, desire advising one thing and reason another." *Nitimur in vetitum semper, cupimusque negata* ("We are always striving for things forbidden, and coveting those denied"—Ovid, *Amores*, pp. 3, 4, 17). In fact, when properly understood there are few truths of Christianity which are written more plainly on the human soul and in history.

Note K

Drs. Gordon, Lidgett, Kahnis, Schultz, and White on the Trinity, and Church on the Incarnation.

APPENDIX

Dr. George A. Gordon, minister of the Old South Church [Congregational], Boston:

The faith in the Trinity rests upon reason at work upon historic fact. The doctrine was a construction of the mind of the early Christian centuries, the product of metaphysical genius unequaled in the history of the church; and if to-day the great conception is coming up for rediscussion and further development, it is because that conception is fundamental not only to Christian faith, but also in the humanity that believes in itself as made in the image of God. Whatever else the idea of the Trinity implies, it certainly means that being and knowledge and love, existence and intelligence and character, are realities in God; and that the various fundamental forms of society in the earth, the essential relationships of humanity, have their Archetype, their Eternal Pattern and Causal Source, in the nature of the Infinite. *The Christ of To-day*, 1895, 3d ed. 1896, p. 100.

Dr. J. Scott Lidgett (Wesleyan Methodist) claims that our consciousness of God takes in his Trinity, inasmuch as it must correspond with the nature of God of whom it is conscious. That consciousness is threefold—of Father, Son and Holy Spirit; it holds these modes or aspects in unity: the Father is the source and goal of the religious consciousness, the Son is the law and meaning of it, and the Spirit is the impulse and inspiration of it. This doctrine is made known in the self-communication of Christ, and is a condition of the eternal perfection of God as love. —*The Christian Religion: Its Meaning and Proof*, 1907, p. 506.

K. F. A. Kahnis:

God is Urpersönlichkeit.—*Die Lutherische Dogmatik*, 2 Aufl., 1874, vol., i. p. 361.

Dean R. W. Church:

We may overlook and cloud the fact of the incarnation with subordinate doctrines, with the theories and traditions of men,

MODERNISM AND THE CHRISTIAN FAITH

with a disproportionate mass of guesses on what is not given us to know, of subtleties and reasonings in the sphere of human philosophy; we may recoil from it and put it from us as something which oppresses our imagination and confounds our reason; but we may be sure that on the place which we really give it in our mind and heart depends the whole character of our Christianity, depends what the gospel of Christ means to us.—*Pascal and Other Sermons*, 1895, pp. 182, 183.

For spiritual ministries of each so-called Person, see Holland, *Logic and Life*, 3d ed., 1885, pp. 220–224. Dr. Hermann Schultz (Ritschlian), Professor in Göttingen:

> The church doctrine of the Trinity will be the dogmatic expression of this religious fact, that God is revealed to us as our Father in Christ as his Son and through the Spirit of the Christian community as his Spirit; that is, that we have God as our Father only in his Son and Spirit. This religious fact expresses the peculiarity of Christian piety, and every weakening of the same... must be rejected.... The deity of Christ does not come into consideration as resting in itself or as comprehensible from itself. It must be from God, his revelation. Therefore a "subordination" of the deity of Christ under the deity of the Father is the necessary condition of Christian piety. Of course not in an Arian sense. For if the deity of Christ were no essential deity, only an elevated human—that is, cosmic—it could not be regarded as the object of religion nor permit an expression of faith. But in the sense of the pre-Arian Church teachers. The deity which we honor in Christ is that which goes out from the Father as the only true God, his self-revelation, which, therefore, does not have aseity [self-originated existence] in itself but only when it is considered in unity with the Father over against the world. But in this unity the Deity revealing itself in Christ is naturally included in with the aseity of the divine essence, which distinguishes it from everything created. The Deity in Christ is the *revelation* of God (Logos). With this it is consistent [is it?] that Christ as the Son of God is distinguished in the same way from God as the Christian community, namely, as a production in which God expresses his eternal essence, and that Christ himself, as he knows himself

APPENDIX

over against his own as the bearer of the divine revelation, looks upon himself over against God as a pious member of mankind. . . . The task of the Christian doctrine of God can only be this: to show how the *one* personal God without ceasing to stand over against his Christian community and Christ as their God yet can be in essence and by revelation in them so that we can worship God in Christ as the one working upon us, and know in the Spirit bearing the community ourselves penetrated by God himself and elevated over the world. . . . The revelation of God in Christ appears as the eternal revelation preceding every temporal one and conditioning it, as the revelation of God absolutely. And even so the community appears as the world-end (or object or final world-purpose), therefore the Spirit in it as the eternal power of God from which the world is to be understood. So we are led to the task to presuppose an eternal unfolding of his essence in the *one* personal God which we worship historically in Christ and in the Spirit of the community, and out of which the world and its independent life is to be understood.—*Die Lehre von der Gottheit Christi*, Gotha, 1881, pp. 605, 607, 608, 609, 610.

This is one of the best expressions on its deeper side of the Ritschlian doctrine of the Trinity ever given.

Edward White (Congregationalist), author of the famous book *Life in Christ*, 3d and definitive edition, 1878, pastor of Hawley Road Chapel, Kentish Town, London, 1852–88, died 1898, aged 79:

Orthodox Churchmen profess to be astonished at the obstinate revolt of Unitarians against the doctrine of the Trinity, as formulated in the so-called Athanasian Creed, the Quicunque vult, prepared about one hundred and twenty-five years after Athanasius died, and expressing a late Western doctrine. But who that has ever read the gospel of St. John, or one of Paul's epistles, or the Epistle to the Hebrews, can pretend that they find anything resembling those creeds on the Trinity in the writings of the chief apostles of the Gospels? In every New Testament writing, and especially in the teaching of Jesus and St. John, the supremacy of the Father and the subjection of the Son are presented as primary articles of the faith; so that instead of an incarnation of the Trinity it is always held out that it was the Word or Logos who

MODERNISM AND THE CHRISTIAN FAITH

"was made flesh," so being in the form of a Θεος [God] he thought it not a thing to be snatched at to be equal to a Θεος, but emptied himself, wherefore "ὁ Θεος [*the* God emphatically] hath highly exalted him," etc. The great Θεος, ὁ Θοες, hath "given to the Son to have life in himself," "My Father is greater than I" are words which Christ could never have spoken if (1) he were only a man, or (2) if as Λογος he was equal to the Father, of whom he says, "My Father is greater than I." ... One of the two most mischievous elements in modern and mediæval theology is the doctrine of the Trinity as taught in the [so-called] Athanasian Creed—"Three persons in one substance, equal, and coeternal." This renders unintelligible the sonship of Christ and the Incarnation of the Word, and nullifies our Lord's repeated declarations as to his relation to the Father as his agent.—From his latest notebooks in Freer, *Edward White: His Life and Work*, 1902, pp. 363, 364, 365.

NOTE L
Professor Schaeder on Beginning or Spring of the Christian Doctrine of Trinity and on other Aspects:

It is the fact of the deity of Christ [he says] which forms the decisive root-point of the original Christian faith in the Trinity. [That is, the belief in the Trinity was not a "speculative" conclusion or a "dogma," but is the necessary result of an actual fact in history and in experience.] The ground on which the Christian Trinity-faith arose was the revelation of God in the Person of Jesus Christ. It is no sense to put troubled waters of extra-Christian speculations and faith-forms through theological filters. Starting from Christ there was already the inalienable point of departure for Trinitarian faith. If in the formulating of this faith there was a kinship with extra-Christian ideas—that is something for theology to discover. But that business is subordinate to the understanding of the rise of faith in the Trinity in the personal-belonging-to God or deity of Christ.

One must concede to him (Prof. R. H. Grützmacher) that the failure of the Trinitarian baptismal formula everywhere in the New Testament except Matt. 28. 19 is not a convincing ground against its genuineness, or,—what is more important—is not convincing ground against the possibility that the Trinity of revelation confessed in this formula really formed an element of the

APPENDIX

consciousness of Jesus. The harmlessness of original Christianity over against the handing down of teaching or doctrinal formulas, its freedom of movement and lack of interest over against any doctrinal formation, can scarcely (in spite of A. Seeberg's investigations concerning a catechism of early Christianity) be strongly enough represented. Here ruled the movement and free originality which is characteristic of every classical epoch in the history of the human spirit. Also the standing-place of this revelation-history upon which Jesus is supposed to have spoken this Trinitarian confession to the God of salvation makes such a confession understandable and fit. We stand at the close of the history of the Son in its earthly aspect; his historical work is done; the period of the Paraclete begins. We can think that with the word concerning Father and Son, without whom God is not Father, Jesus united the reference to the Spirit who restores to believers the gracious presence of the Father in the Son. . . .

When in the sense of Christianity we speak of God we include everything when we speak of the penetrating all-presence of God. But even so we are certain that this God in Christ, who belongs to him, has a unique special presence in the world; that is, a gracious, reconciling, kingdom-founding presence, which he has not elsewhere. But by his exaltation Christ now belongs also to the Other World. With his personal saving life and powers he has been taken away from the trellis-work of history. Looking at this mere fact alone, it would mean an end of the grace and presence of God with its living effects and gifts. Historic reminiscences of a Christ who has been once, and then vanished from history, creates no near, reconciling, redeeming God in us. Here comes in the biblically founded confession of the Spirit of God, with which the Trinitarian faith closes. It means that just as there came out of the being or life of God a grace-bearer, the Son, the historical Christ, there also came from thence a personally effective Spirit-nature (or being); that is, personal as conscious of its end or object, which Spirit gives in history a working presence to the personal gracious life of the exalted Christ and with that also of the reconciling redeeming grace of God. [This thought has been expressed with power and beauty in the striking hymn by the Rev. Dr. William F. Warren, ex-president of Boston University and professor in the Theological School, "I worship thee, O Holy Ghost."]

MODERNISM AND THE CHRISTIAN FAITH

As to subordination, we must remember that the Son lives only through and out of the Father, and so he stands in the history of revelation as the receiver of the divine glory, who therefore for its reception or for its powers prays to God. And of the Spirit we know simply that he serves as the mediator of the grace—presence of God in Christ. If we will be true to revelation, we must maintain that the Father is in the last analysis the bearer of the divine, the Son with all his unity with God dependent on him, and the Spirit dependent on both and serving both. In the Three the Divine, the Three God, but still the three in a gradation of their life-movement over against each other. [This expresses finely not only the actual Scriptural relations, but in my judgment the true philosophy of the Trinity].—Professor Erich Schaeder, of Kiel University, in *Theologisches Literaturblatt*, 1911, cols. 205-208.

NOTE M
UNTIL HE COME

In *Crises of the Early Church*, Methodist Book Concern, 1912, chapter vi ("The Chiliastic Crisis"), this writer has given all the quotations from the pre-New Testament apocalyptic books of the Jews which speak of the coming King or Kingdom, referred to New Testament passages, and quoted in full all the passages in the post-New Testament Christian literature which have to do with the second coming or the end. Suffice it to add now that in the New Testament the comings of Christ refer to various events in his history and that of his kingdom and the world, such as the destruction of Jerusalem and the Jewish Church-State and State-Church in the year 70, possibly other catastrophes and turning points in history, the call which leaves one woman at the gristmill and takes another away, the descent of the Holy Spirit and the dispensation which that inaugurated, the various comings in his loving and saving and healing presence to those who open to him their hearts, the bringing of the gospel to a place (Eph. 2. 17) or the establishment of his kingdom in a striking manner, perhaps the summons that comes at death (compare Matt. 24. 39, 42-44, 45ff.; John 14. 3), and his second coming at the end of the world.

It is a striking fact that the finest sacramental hymn ever written ("By Christ redeemed, in Christ restored") is not by Newman or

APPENDIX

other Roman priest, not by Baring-Gould or other high churchman, but is by a Congregational layman and lawyer! It has been brought home to us here by its being given out by the president at our Supper service, and being happily wedded to Sullivan's touching and gripping music it makes a profound impression. Its pathetic cadences and rhythm remind us a little of the greatest hymn ever written, that of the Last Day, the Dies Irae (see No. 747). Rawson was a pious poet and solicitor of Leeds, who wrote this in 1857 for a new Baptist hymnal put out in 1858. He published books of verse of his own, but this is his greatest piece, and it will live as long as the truths of which it speaks in such compelling words are believed, and that means as long as the New Testament is believed. It is founded on the words of Paul: "As often as ye eat this bread, and drink the cup, ye proclaim the Lord's death till he come" (1 Cor. 11. 26). And these last words are the echo of John 21. 22, which seemed to sink into the consciousness of the primitive Church and were repeated ever and anon to revive drooping hearts: "Jesus saith unto him, If I will that he tarry till I come—what *is that* to thee? Follow thou me." Paul refers to the same goal of expectation in 1 Cor. 4. 5: "Wherefore judge nothing before the time, until the Lord come" (compare Rom. 2. 16, "in the day when God shall judge," etc.), "who will both bring to light the hidden things of darkness," etc. "Till He come": it was a password whispered from one to another, it closed their letters, it was like the refrain of a song, it was their challenge to Antichrist and to their persecutors, it leaped from their lips in dying agonies, it was their immortal hope, and it was certainly one of the reasons of their endurance until their religion conquered the empire. It was as much taken for granted as death itself. Perhaps a classic expression of its inevitableness is Heb. 9. 27, 28: "Inasmuch as it is appointed unto men once to die, and after this *cometh* judgment, so Christ also, having been once offered to bear the sins of many, shall appear a second time apart from sin, to them that wait for him, unto salvation." Their own salvation could not be more certain to ancient Christians than the second coming.

"Until He come." Yes, it was a living hope once. Except with a small band of devout spirits, it is so no longer. Many have spiritualized away the whole conception, and even those of us who still believe that the heart of that early hope was sound— for us the evolutions of history and the long, long vista which

MODERNISM AND THE CHRISTIAN FAITH

that history, as well as all present prospects, open for the future have sent glimmering into dim haze the tremendous conviction which was the master light of all the seeing of the first Christians. Even so advanced and liberal a thinker as Schleiermacher saw and acknowledged that the second coming was the center of the entire thought of the last things in the early church. "Everything which has to do with the perfection of Christ's work must be referred back to His return."[1] One of the greatest scholars of modern times, perhaps the man of the nineteenth century who was most steeped in Christian ideas and spirit, Dorner, says that the center of the spiritual ideas of Jesus would be affected if he had erred in this matter, which has to do with his person, office, and Kingdom. He says that the Old Testament put everything on the first coming, while Christ made the second as the first great act of the Messianic age and the judgment as the last. His various comings in the course of history are only a preparation for the second. "All the apostles and ancient Christendom maintain this [second coming] with all the energy of love and hope as their dearest faith. Their longing anticipated it earlier than the event showed. It is in keeping with this fact that so little is found in the New Testament respecting the state of individuals between death and the resurrection."[2] The acute and thoroughly Christian rationalism (if it might be called) of the cultured Dane Martensen, who was an expert on Shakespeare, saw that the coming and the judgment that was associated with it were a part of the divine order of the universe, as Christ saw it, a denial of which would be a "denial of all rational ends, a denial of the final triumph of goodness and truth." The truth, in Schiller's pregnant word, the history of the world is the judgment of the world, Martensen says, is recognized in our religion, but to take it as fully equivalent to Christianity's last day "transmutes God's righteousness itself into a Tantalus, in continual unreality, pursuing a good which it can never reach." The judgment (and the coming which it presupposes) "is so certain that even if revelation did not foretell it, the thought of it must be postulated in order to give earnestness and reality to any true idea of a moral teleology [doctrine of ends or purpose] of the world."[3]

---

[1] *Der Christliche Glaube,* § 159, 3.
[2] *System of Christian Doctrine,* iv. 385–7.
[3] *Christian Dogmatics,* pp. 465–6.

APPENDIX

But, you say, the early Christians were mistaken as to the nearness of the coming, and if they were they might have been mistaken as to the thing itself. Yes, they did expect it soon.[4] This was due to their longing, to their natural foreshortening of the time, to their confusion of different prophecies, to not taking full account of Christ's deliberate warnings as to His own ignorance of the time, how much more as to theirs. But it had no bearing whatever on the doctrine, on the reality of the hope, and was discounted beforehand by Christ Himself. And when with the delay expectancy of an immediate return was given up, the fact of the return was held as a part of the immemorial possession of the Church, taken for granted by every Christian for eighteen hundred years.

In 1873 a young professor in the theological department of the University of Giessen came out with a new construction.[5] He said that Christ expected His return very soon, everything to take place in that generation, that that return was His resurrection, that anything else in the Gospels connected with it, such as judgment in Jerusalem by the Roman armies, the world judgment, etc.—that all this was an apocalyptic invented by His disciples. The Jewish Christians invented His glorious Messiah reign on the earth a thousand years, and the Gentile His coming at the end of the world. These were interesting discoveries by the young Giessen doctor, but as they were all subjective hypotheses we need not stop. Long before the Gospels were written we have Paul speaking of the coming for judgment at the end, and distinguishing that coming from Christ's resurrection and from our own.

In 1879 an able Congregational divine in Portland, Maine, Dr. Israel P. Warren, editor of The Christian Mirror, appeared with an interesting view,[6] which has become quite popular, as it fits in with our modern naturalism. (*Parousia* is literally "presence," but it also means "coming," as can be seen from 1 Thess. 4. 13–18 and James 5. 8.) The coming is not an event, but a dispensation. It began when Christ was upon earth, and it is to last as long as the history of time. The resurrection and judgment take place in

---

[4] 1 Thess. 4. 13–18; Heb. 10. 37; 2 Pet. 1. 8–13; James 5. 8.

[5] Wiffenbach, *Der Wiederkunfts Gedanke Jesu*, Leipzig, 1873 (see Langen in Reusch's *Theologisches Literaturblatt*, 1873, 339–41).

[6] *The Parousia: A Critical Study of Christ's Second Coming, Reign, Resurrection of the Dead, and Judgment*, second edition, Portland, 1885.

MODERNISM AND THE CHRISTIAN FAITH

the invisible world. There is truth in the theory of Warren. Much of Christ's and the apostles' language did refer to things which took place within that century. There were comings and judgments then, but there were also vaster outlooks. I might say that Professor Briggs, in a notice of Warren, says that the terms "near" and "at hand" in the prophecies from Joel to Revelation indicate the certainty of the event, but the uncertainty of the time.[7] The prophet's day is to be followed by the to-morrow of the day of Jehovah. The interval is a night of uncertain duration. Near and at hand the day of Jehovah is and ever must continue to be to the prophet, however long the interval may subsequently be to the historian.

A brother Congregationalist of London, the Rev. J. Stuart Russell, M.A., confirmed Warren as to there being no second coming, but differed from him that the destruction of Jerusalem in the year 70 was the alleged coming and not the gospel dispensation.[8] It is true that that destruction was much in the thought of Jesus, but it is not true that that was the only thing in his thought; nor does the author do justice to Old Testament background, to the Jewish Messianic ideas and apocalypses of New Testament times, which have a world significance. He is too literal and limited in his interpretation of certain words, fails to understand the cosmic sweep of some of Jesus's prophecies (as, for instance, those of the universal preaching of the gospel to the nations and the universal judgment of the nations), fails to distinguish between the setting up of the Kingdom and the judgment, and postulates startling historical events which have left no trace. It is fantastic to assume that the resurrection of the dead took place at the destruction of Jerusalem in the invisible world, that Christ then came visibly on the clouds, that Peter and John were the two witnesses of Rev. 11, and that they arose from the dead and ascended to heaven in the sight of the inhabitants of Jerusalem.[9] Israel Warren and Stuart Russell are the fathers of the recent view of the no coming. It can be true only on the theory of the deception of apostolic and early Christianity so colossal that its views on anything else are as worthless as on this.

[7] Briggs in *Presbyterian Review,*, 1885, p. 175.
[8] *The Parousia: A Critical Inquiry into the New Testament Doctrine of Our Lord's Second Coming.* London, new edition, 1887. I have not date of first edition, which was anonymous.
[9] See Briggs in *Presbyterian Review*, New York, 1887, 750–753.

APPENDIX

So much being said in criticism, it is necessary to add that the second coming is not physical or bodily, it is not literal in the sense of Allenby's entrance into Jerusalem, it is not spectacular, and it is not (so to say) geographical. It is not a going from one place to another, it is not a shooting across the heavens like a falling star, and it is not an apparition. It is a cosmic new departure, it is the entry of Christ into a new stage in the evolution of his plans, it is his coming for the perfection of his justice and his love, and for the final adjustment of the relations of his kingdom of grace and glory to all intelligences.

As indispensable conditions or preliminaries of the coming there must take place, as we are taught both by revelation and reason, the following events: the preaching of the gospel to the whole world; the conversion of that world as to majority or mass (the fullness of the Gentiles must be brought in, Rom. 11. 25); the conversion of the Jews (Rom. 11. 26); and the union of believers in Christ from all nations into one flock. A coming before these things are secured would be without sense, a premature breaking in on the orderly development of Christ's plans, and a stultification of his redeeming work and of the administration of that work by the Spirit.

In the New Testament the second coming is associated with two events:

(1) The end of the world. It is a strain on faith to think of this world as ever passing away, and the descriptions in Paul and Peter and Revelation are looked upon as mythical, or the overwrought imagining of Jewish apocalypses. But it is no strain on science. I remember reading in one of John Fiske's essays that the end of the world is inevitable, according to physical science, and Professor Rice once wrote me to the same effect.[10] Of course we must not press Oriental language, but so far as the end of the world is concerned, it is the revelation of science no less than of the Bible.

(2) The Last Judgment. Christ had two sides to his teaching here: the ever-present judgment by which men are always passing to the right or to the left, and the final Judgment of the nations as such according to their fulfillment of the law of love.

The second coming is woven into the warp of the New Testa-

---

[10] See Joseph McCabe, *The End of the World*, London, 1921.

MODERNISM AND THE CHRISTIAN FAITH

ment, deliberately taught, incidentally alluded to, now a strong organ peal, now an undertone, a hope, a vision, a faith, a program, a philosophy of history—"Even so, come, Lord Jesus." It is imbedded in the Lord's Supper:

> "And show the death of our dear Lord
>   Until He come. . . .
>
> "Until the trump of God be heard,
>   Until the ancient graves be stirred,
>   And with the great commanding word,
>   The Lord shall come.
>
> "O blessed hope! with this elate,
>   Let not your hearts be desolate,
>   But strong in faith, in patience wait
>   Until He come."

Note N

The Legend of the Apostle John's Early Martyrdom

It does not fall within the scope of this book to discuss questions in New Testament literary criticism. But I have had recently to give attention to one objection to the apostle John's authorship of the Gospel, and it occurred to me that the results are important enough to lay before my readers.

In recent years radical critics like Wellhausen, Schmiedel, Moffatt, and Bacon, in order to discredit John's authorship of the fourth Gospel, have seized upon a story that goes back to ancient times that he was martyred, and presumably early. What are the reasons for this, and are they valid over against the unanimous tradition of the second century that he lived to old age and wrote the Gospel? It will be convenient to take Charles's exhaustive summary of the evidence in the introduction to his great Commentary of Revelation (1920), pp. xlv-l. For clearness, as we come to each piece in Charles let us estimate it before we pass to the next.

1. Christ prophesied that James and John would drink of his cup and be baptized with his baptism (Mark 10. 38, 39). This means that they were to be put to death as he was—"the same

APPENDIX

destiny that awaits himself," says Charles. This came true of James (Acts 12. 2); it must also of John. Well, if we must take Christ's prophecies *au pied de la lettre*, it did not become true of even James. Christ was put to death with lingering agonies and with immeasurable disgrace, James with the instantaneous and comparatively honorable dispatch with the sword. But is it necessary to interpret Christ so very literally? The radicals themselves would do it in no other case. No apostle could live in the first century without undergoing a baptism which in the imagery of the East could be compared to Christ's, whether actually put to death or not. Much more John, on account of his long life, whether or not it was he who suffered on Patmos. Exile and work in the mines was a punishment so horrible in antiquity that it was not much to be preferred to death itself. Mark 10. 39 does not require the slaying of John, except on a hard Western literalism.

2. (a) A monk of the ninth century, Georgios Hamartolos (George the Sinner) is thought (since 1859, when Muralt published an edition of his works in Petrograd, and especially since 1862, when Nolte discussed the matter in *Theologische Quartalschrift*) to have said that John survived the rest of the twelve and then suffered as a martyr, "for Papias [first half of second century], the bishop of Hierapolis, having been an eyewitness of him, says in the second book of his Oracles of the Lord that he was slain by the Jews, having, as is clear, with his brother James, fulfilled the prediction of Christ. . . . 'Ye shall drink my cup.'" Now, inasmuch as Eusebius the historian (about 324) was thoroughly acquainted with Papias, and was especially anxious to get information about the lives and deaths of the apostles, and knows nothing of any such statement, the very careful Lightfoot in 1875 says downright that George "cannot be quoting directly from Papias, for Papias cannot have reported the martyrdom of John.[11] Lightfoot assumes that in a copy of an intermediate writer which George followed words had dropped out, and what the writer really said is probably this: Papias says that John witnessing was condemned by the Roman emperor to Patmos, while James was slain by the Jews. But it is now known that the above words are only in one manuscript of George, and that there they are evidently an interpolation. This manuscript is a working over of George's Chronicle with excerpts from different writers. In the Chronicle itself, and,

[11] *Essays on the Work,* "*Supernatural Religion,*" 1889, p. 212.

in fact, later in this manuscript, several patristic witnesses are quoted all of which speak of the peaceful death and burial of John the apostle in Ephesus.[12]

(b) There is a manuscript in Oxford of the seventh or eighth century which purports to give an epitome of the Chronicle of Philip of Side, of the fifth century, which says: "Papias in the second book says that John the Divine and James his brother were slain by the Jews" (published by De Boor in *Texte und Untersuchungen*, 1888, ii, 170). Here, again, we have a late interpolation into Philip's Chronicle, or Philip himself, who was a "wild historian," was quoting at second hand from worthless authorities, who could not have read Papias, or, if they did, quoted him wrongly or interpolated him.[13] For however "advanced" New Testament critics may like to avail themselves of an eighth-century manuscript against positive witnesses of the second and third centuries, when historians trained to the weighing of evidence—even so very liberal an one as Harnack—speak on these De Boor fragments they hold another language. For even Harnack says: "As little as Papias could have written that Paul died a natural death, so little could he have written that John was murdered by the Jews, unless it might be that he meant another John, the presbyter [which he could not, for the excerpt says John the Divine and his brother James]. But this is not even probable; for as his (Papias's) readers, Irenæus first, held the presbyter John as the apostle, then the violent death of the presbyter (elder) must have been indicated in the older literature. This, however, is not only not the case, but the very old Mestase of John—probably second century—relates something altogether different."[14] On evidence as flimsy as this you could support any superstition of the Roman Church, say perhaps the removal through the air of the Holy House of Loretto.

3. Clement of Alexandria quotes in his *Stromata* 4. 9 (about 200), Heracleon, a Valentinian Gnostic of about 145, as saying that "Matthew, Philip, Thomas, Levi, and many others confessed with

---

[12] See Zahn, *Die Apostelschüler in der Provinz Asien*, in his *Forschungen zur Geschichte*, u.s.w., vol. vi, pp. 147–48 (1900).

[13] This is shown at length by Chapman, *John the Presbyter and the Fourth Gospel*, Oxford University Press, 1911, pp. 95–99.

[14] *Die Chronologie der altchristlichen Litteratur*, vol. i, p. 666 (Leipz., 1897).

APPENDIX

the confession made with the voice, and departed." The inference is that they were not martyred by death, and as he does not mention John, the further inference is that he was martyred by death. This is a very risky inference. For (1) Heracleon does not say they were not put to death, and old legends have it that some were put to death; (2) he is not giving an exhaustive, much less exact, account of what became of each of the apostles (he makes Matthew and Levi different persons), but a general statement that some gave their witness for Christ by word of mouth. He says nothing about John one way or the other. Why should he, when John fought the Gnostic beginnings?

4. In the ungenuine and late *Martyrium Andreæ* the worthless story is given that the apostles cast lots to see to which land or people they should go. As a result Peter "was allotted to the circumcision, James and John to the east, Philip to the cities of Samaria and Asia," etc. Since there is no mention of any residence of John in Asia, why, he never lived there! But there is no mention in the Martyrium that Peter resided in Rome and was martyred there, in spite of his being assigned to the circumcision. And I suppose the lot could have indicated the east for John, and Providence later Asia Minor.

5. Clement of Alexandria, in *Stromata* 7. 17, says that the teaching "of the apostles, embracing the ministry of Paul, ends with Nero." "These words presuppose," says Charles, "the death of all the apostles before 70." Do they? They neither say it, nor imply it. Clement is arguing for the lateness of the heretics as compared with the church teaching—"their human assemblies were posterior to the Catholic Church." For Christ finished his teaching, he says, in the middle of the times of Tiberius, and the ministry of the apostles was completed by the end of Nero, the heresies coming later. But Clement, with the disregard common to all antiquity for close historic accuracy, is speaking only generally, for we know that the teaching of Christ did not begin with Augustus, that some apostles in all likelihood survived the year 68, and God knows there were enough heresies before Hadrian! While John's ministry was full and perfected ($\tau\epsilon\lambda\epsilon\iota o\hat{\upsilon}\tau\alpha\iota$) by the time of the death of Nero, Clement does not say that his life might not have extended beyond.

6. Charles says that a "tradition of John's martyrdom is attested in Chrysostom's Homily 66 on Matthew" (20. 23, about

MODERNISM AND THE CHRISTIAN FAITH

A. D. 389). Chrysostom speaks of no tradition whatever, but is giving in the most general homiletic style the meaning of Christ, that "Ye shall be counted worthy of martyrdom, shall suffer these things which I suffer, and shall close your life by a violent death" (p. 399 of P. N. F.). On a point of historical minuteness as to the relative difference between the later fates of James and John Chrysostom says nothing. But when in this same series of Homilies he comes to speak definitely of John's later life, he says that he "lived a long time after the taking of the city" (*Hom.*, 76. 2, p. 458, col. 1), that is, a long time after 70.

7. There seems to be a reference in Gregory of Nyssa (about 385) to Peter, James, and John as martyrs; but even Charles rejects this passage as proving what it is brought forward to prove, and therefore we might dismiss it were it not that it gives us welcome light here, as Gregory explains why in the third, fourth, and following centuries John also could be entered upon the list of martyrs. I follow Harnack, who reproduces Gregory's words mostly in Greek, partly in German. Harnack says: "In the address on Basil (year 379) Gregory relates that it is customary in the church to celebrate the festival of Stephen, Peter, James, John, and Paul after the Christmas festival (Migne, Vol. xlvi, col. 789). In an earlier address upon Stephen (col. 725), however, he explains why these heroes are celebrated together. Gregory says that the apostles must follow upon the protomartyr (Stephen), 'for neither martyrs without apostles nor again apostles without these. All the dear stones struck together this Stephen—the divinest heralds of the Gospels, after which the martyrs and after these again those shining through with saving virtue—chiefly those at present remembering much and lighting the lamp, the beauty of piety—I speak of Peter and James and John, those leaders of the apostolic chorus and crowns of the ecclesiastical glory.' Moreover, these 'majestic ones had to-day attested themselves by their witnessings for Christ, though in different ways of witnessing,' viz., Peter crucified, James beheaded, and John first accomplished an oil martyrdom, and further attested his martyrdom by his constant will to die for the name of Christ."[15]

The legend of John's immersion in boiling oil in Rome during the persecution of Domitian (reigned 81-96), from which he emerged unscathed, goes back to about 200, namely, Tertullian,

---

[15] *Theologische Literaturzeitung*, 1909, col. 11.

APPENDIX

De Praescr. Haer., 36, and was widely believed in following times. This martyrdom in effect gave the honor the church wished for him, and thus enabled her writers and calendar compilers to class him with the apostles who had really given up their lives.[16]

8. Charles brings in the Muratorian Canon, and though it really has no bearing on the alleged early martyrdom of John, a word must be given to it. He thinks it makes Revelation earlier than Paul's epistles because it says: "The blessed apostle Paul, following the rule of his predecessor John, writes to no more than seven churches by name, in this order: the first to the Corinthians," etc. The Canon belongs to about 180, and is a fragment and anonymous. We know that Paul did not follow the rule of John or of anyone else. Knowing that John was an apostle before Paul, and that John wrote to seven churches, the author of the Canon, without giving any critical judgment as to priority of Revelation over Paul's epistles, on which he probably knew nothing, says in passing, "Following the ordinem of his predecessor John." All we can build on this is that the author believed that John wrote Revelation. These radical critics build a pyramid on a very acute apex. Charles makes two other large inferences without sufficient foundation, namely, that the Muratorian Canon represents composition of John's Gospel prior to the dispersion of the apostles, and plainly states the revision of that Gospel. And this is the apex-foundation: "The fourth Gospel is that of John, one of the disciples. When his fellow disciples and bishops intreated him [here the author of the Canon assumes only that there were fellow workers around, and even bishops, which last would seem to point to a late time], he said: 'Fast ye now with me for the space of three days, and let us recount to each other whatever may be revealed to each of us.' On the same night it was revealed to Andrew, one of the apostles, that John should narrate all things in his own name, all recalling." Of course the whole story is a legend, the only true kernel being the fact that the author believed that John wrote the Gospel, and that at about 180 there apparently was no other belief known. The context seems to require the ordinary meaning of *recognoscentibus* as recalling; but even if it means "certifying" or "reviewing," it does not mean that after John wrote his Gospel it was revised.

9. The anonymous *De Rebaptismate* against Cyprian in favor of

[16] Ibid.

the Roman practice of not rebaptizing those baptized by schismatics or heretics, written between 250 and 300, says: "He said to the sons of Zebedee: Are ye able? For he knew the men had to be baptized, not only in water, but also in their own blood." Here also we have one of those general statements which prove nothing unless we knew (1) that the writer intended to deliberately include John with James in the latter's fate, and (2) that "on their own blood" he meant not simply sufferings and bloodshed, but actual death by bloodshed.

10. The same lack of definiteness in uncritical general statements is that of Aphraates (344)—"James and John walked in the footsteps of their Master Christ." Would Aphraates be satisfied if John suffered but was not slain, or did he think he was slain in his old age?

11. Lastly, one of the flimsiest of all the reasons for the early martyrdom of John is the fact that he is entered with James opposite the date in fifth century calendars or martyrologies. For instance, "Dec. 27 John and James the apostles in Jerusalem." But men who are known not to have been martyred at all were enrolled in lists. They were drawn up in haphazard way, their compilers had to put some one opposite each date, and since James and John were associated together they naturally were written together in the calendars, which are without any critical value. Everyone knows that John was not killed when James was, and that he was killed before 70, as Charles thinks, is a pure hypothesis for which there is no evidence. Says Harnack in reviewing these calendar entries: "The usual ancient celebration of Peter, John, and Paul immediately after Stephen was originally no martyr-celebration, but the choir of the leading apostles who witnessed for Christ was to be celebrated after the Protomartyr. Perhaps this order in the church is older than the emergence of the Christmas festival in the East on the 25th December [last part of fourth century]; but one need not settle this now. It is very easy to understand, however, the persons to be celebrated according to the calendars were almost all martyrs, and the days dedicated to them were, therefore, martyrs' memorial days—that soon the original motive vanished, and the celebration was understood as a martyr celebration, especially as Stephen the Protomartyr stood first. Perhaps Aphraates so conceived it when he wrote in Hom. 21 (see above). To reckon John among the martyrs was not diffi-

APPENDIX

cult, as the legend of his oil-martyrdom was widely spread in the church."[17] In the same review he says of these very late quoted alleged Papias sentences: "The alleged Papias-witness is so recent and in its terms so confused that it is an entirely uncritical caprice to prefer that to the choir of opposing witnesses."

A word in closing on these opposing witnesses: They are early, they are clear, they are undisputed. From the standpoint of historical evidence they have all the notes of authenticity lacking in the late testimonies recently brought in for the new view of the early martyrdom of John. Polycarp was the disciple of John, later bishop of Smyrna, martyred at the age of eighty-six in about 155. Irenæus was the pupil of Polycarp, lived in Asia Minor, later in Rome, later bishop of Lyon in Gaul, who wrote about 180. As to Polycarp's relation to the apostles see Irenæus 3. 3, 4. In his letter to Florinus, his brother-pupil of Polycarp, Irenæus says: "These are not the teachings which the elders who preceded us and who lived after the apostles handed down to thee; for I saw thee when I was still a child in lower Asia with Polycarp.... And I could still show the place where he sat when he taught and gave an account of his relations with John and with the others who saw the Lord, and how he spoke of what he had heard from them respecting the Lord, his miracles and his doctrine, and how he recounted, in full accord with the Scriptures, all that which he had received from eyewitnesses of the Word of life" (in Eusebius, *Hist. Eccl.* 5. 20). Irenæus says again: "All the Elders who met with John, the disciple of the Lord, in Asia, give testimony that he conveyed to them these things; for he lived with them, even to time of Trajan (began to reign 98). And some among them saw not only John, but also other apostles" (2. 22, 5). The context shows that Irenæus uses the word "disciple" as equivalent to "apostle," just as the Gospels frequently do. "Afterward John, the disciple of the Lord, he who leaned on his breast, published the Gospel while he dwelt in Ephesus in Asia" (3. 1, 1). "The church of Ephesus which was founded by Paul and in which John lived until the time of Trajan, is also a truthful witness of the tradition of the apostles" (3. 3, 4). In his letter to Victor, bishop of Rome, Irenæus says that Polycarp had observed the 14th of Nisan as Paschal day "with John the disciple of the Lord and the other apostles with whom he had lived" (in Eus., *Hist. Eccl.* 5. 24).

---

[17] *Theologische Literaturzeitung*, 1909, cols. 11, 12.

MODERNISM AND THE CHRISTIAN FAITH

There are other testimonies of the second century which connect John with Ephesus. Charles seeks to break the force of Irenæus's testimony by saying that he was occasionally inaccurate, but the points alleged to prove this are trivial, and some do not prove it. We cannot say from 3. 12, 15 that he confused the two Jameses. Irenæus was not a Plato, but one does not have to be an Augustine to testify to what he has seen and heard and known.

If the reader wants more light, see Ramsay, *The First Christian Century*, 1911; J. Armitage Robinson, *Historical Character of St. John's Gospel*, 1908; Chapman, *John the Presbyter and the Fourth Gospel*, 1911; and the still very important books by Stanton, *The Gospels as Historical Documents*, 1903; and Drummond, *Character and Authorship of the Fourth Gospel*, 1904. See also Iverach, in *International Standard Bible Encyclopedia*, vol. iii, pp. 1707, 1708 (1915); and Bernard, *Studia Sacra*, 1917.

NOTE O

MIRACLE AND SADHU SUNDAR SINGH

In the chapter on "Miracle" the question is asked (p. 67) whether modern heathen lands have not the same need for miracle as in the days of primitive Christianity. Since that chapter was written my attention has been called to the wonderful faith, experience, and life of Sadhu Sundar Singh, and the mighty works connected with his mission activity. I do not feel competent to give an opinion, though intelligent, rational, well-poised yet earnest missionaries have no doubt of the genuineness of these miraculous and providential dealings. See Zahir, *A Lover of the Cross*, revised edition, 1918; Mrs. Parker, *Sadhu Sundar Singh*, 1918; Streeter and Appasamy, *The Sadhu*, 1921, and (from critical though friendly point of view) Emmet, in *Hibbert Journal*, 1921, pp. 308–18.

NOTE P

THE SO-CALLED VIRGIN BIRTH

There was no man in evangelical churches who represented the "modern" point of view in theology more aggressively than the eminent philosopher, Professor Bowne. In reading his *Studies in*

APPENDIX

Christianity (1909) one has to smile over the crack of the whip on the quivering hides of the "conservatives." He was himself, however, conservative in some essentials, as the Coryphæus of orthodoxy, the Rev. Dr. James M. Buckley, convinced himself before he would consent to act as his advocate in the famous trial for heresy before the New York East Conference in 1904, where the standards for judgment were allowed on both sides to be the Articles of Religion and Wesley's Sermons and Notes. It was with deep interest therefore that I read Bowne's remarks on the miraculous birth of Jesus, and that I found that he accepted it, though not deeming it important.

"In all probability those who accept Christianity as a revelation of God will generally accept this doctrine; and it will be held because of its beauty and æsthetic fitness as inaugurating a new era in the great order of divine revelation" (p. 385). But it is not important. "The divinity of Christ and his incarnation are absolutely independent of it" (p. 386). This is the common modernist view, with the exception that, unlike Bowne, most liberals reject the miraculous birth itself. It is certainly a matter of gratification that an assailant of "orthodoxy" so violent as our learned philosopher should yet have believed in the miraculous birth. But I cannot go with him that it is unimportant or independent of divinity of Christ and incarnation.

(a) Is it unimportant? The veracity of the Gospels is not unimportant. Two of the Gospels directly bear witness to it, the other two imply it. Their falsity as to the question whether Jesus was from man or from God, whether his origin was from below as with the rest of us, or from above, as with him, was not unimportant. In fact, it was so important that if they are not to be believed as to whence Jesus came, the question is inevitable, In what else are they to be believed? This logical inference is borne out by the historical: for those who deny this part of the Gospels generally sit loose to the other parts. Besides, Jesus is a person of such commanding importance in Christianity, so much so that salvation itself is said to depend on one's attitude toward him, that the matter of his coming into the world directly from God or only mediately from God, like Wesley, is a weighty matter.

(b) Is the miraculous birth independent of divinity and incarnation of Christ? The Gospels and the whole New Testament either teach or imply the preexistence of Christ. Now, how could a pre-

MODERNISM AND THE CHRISTIAN FAITH

existent One be incarnated? By floating in, so to speak, on the semen of the male? No. The male can give only what he has. He has not God, and he cannot give God. The product of the paternal impregnation of the ovum is exactly as human or as divine as the pater, no more, no less. This is so obvious that I venture to say that those who deny the Gospel story of the birth also either deny Christ's preexistence or ignore it, either openly or tacitly let it go. Or if any of them yet have not gone so far, they are bound to do so when the logic of their premises has full effect. How, then, can the preexistent One be really incarnated? Only by a divine quickening of the womb, so that the product is divine in its origin, but human in its secondary origin from the mother, and therefore in its nature and characteristics. This seems the only way of a real incarnation of the divine, either biologically or philosophically. This is the way of Scripture, and it is—so far as I can see—the way of reason.

Of course, if you throw out an actual incarnation and a proper divinity you need no miraculous birth. God could easily endow the son of a couple of Galilæan peasants of noble lineage with remarkable powers and fine insights, and make him a unique revealer of himself, just as he did Saint Francis and Jonathan Edwards, only more. That requires no miracle, except as you and I are miracles. But that does not satisfy the Gospel facts as to Jesus, or his own consciousness, or the history of the Gospel or of the church, or Christian experience.

"Jesus himself never refers to it [his miraculous birth], neither does John nor Paul" (p. 386). This is disputed, but what of it? Did they have occasion to mention it? No. Did it fall within the scope of their argument? No. Was not their reticence fitting? Yes. Did anyone deny it, so that their affirmation was demanded? No. And the Gospels that mention it do so not from an apologetic or polemic interest, but simply because they are giving as historians a more or less full account of the birth. There were chroniclers in 1492 and after who did not mention the discovery of America. But did anyone mention it? Did enough speak of it to bring it on the field of history? A fact does not depend on the number of its witnesses, but on its being witnessed, on its fitness, reasonableness, etc. Some of the mighty deeds of Christ have only one witness. Shall we therefore deny them?

INDEX

Admiration, 66
Andover theology, 28
Annihilation of wicked, 258
Anselm, his Cur Deus Homo, 26
Aquinas, Thomas, on miracle, 75
Arius, his Christ, 79, 84, 193
Athanasius, on the Trinity, 196
Atonement, 137; Horton on, 274; Smith on, 274
Augustine on miracle, 74
Augustine on the Trinity, 195
Authority, natural, 10. See Chap. I

Barnabas, epistle of, view of Old Testament, 33
Benediction, Apostolic, 187
Bible, as authority, 20; inspiration, 20, 21, 40, 55; miracles in, 62, 65; on hell, 245. See New Testament. See Old Testament
Briggs, Dr. C. A., case of, 28
Buddhism, doctrine of inspiration, 54. See note on p. 14
Bunyan, as miracle, 73; on Christ as Saviour in his conversion, 124

Canon of Scripture, relation of to inspiration, 50
Channing, his Sparks ordination sermon against Trinity, 184
Church, relation of to inspiration, 49
Coleridge, S. T., on Bible, 46
Coming, Second, 286
Congregational Creed of 1883, 29

Conscience, as authority, 25; fuel of hell, 247
Conversion, as miracle, 61; in revivals due to Christ or faith in Christ, 128
Councils, church, as authority, 14
Creeds, on Christ, McConnell on, 272

De Lagarde on Paul, 167
Depravity, "total," 279
Devotion, Christ as center of, 128-129

Farrar, F. W., views on future punishment, 238, 239
Father, Christ's knowledge of, 130; mediated by Christ, 130
Fatherhood of God, not special message of New Testament, 276
Freedom makes hell, 251
Fourth Gospel. See John

Governmental theory of atonement, 162
Gregory of Nazianzus, views on future punishment, 241
Gregory of Nyssa on future punishment, 243

Harnack on first Christians on Christ, 111; on Christ and God, 114
Healings as miracles, 63
Hebrews, epistle of, on Christ, 101
Hegel, theology of, 209

Heine on Bible, 41
Hinduism, doctrine of inspiration, 54
Holy Spirit, his function, 82, 202, 282, 285, 286

Immortality, is it only in Christ? 258
Incarnation as help to faith, 126, 132; Dean Church on its determining position, 281
Infallibility, relation of to inspiration, 53
Interpolations, alleged of Christ passages in Gospels, 89
Irenæus, on John, 299

James, opinion on Christ, 99
Jesus Christ, the "metaphysical," 79, 191; on judgments of being, 80; was he part of his Gospel? 81; humanity of, 84; his divinity in synoptic Gospels, 86; indwelling of God theory, 90; testimony of Acts on, 93; source of faith of Christians, 113; Two-natures doctrine, 117; basis of his personality, 119; as Saviour, 122; knowledge of the Father, 130; his Presence, 134; his divinity as involved in his work, 159; not simply a revelation of the Father or endowed by Father, 189; the inspiration of Bible, 47; freedom of, 57; miracles of, 62; miraculous birth, 76; resurrection, 77
John, Epistle of, on Christ, 100
John, Gospel of, as miracle, 60; on Jesus, 105; was its supposed author John martyred early? 292
Jülicher, criticism of Wrede on Paul, 171

Justice and righteousness foundation of hell, 247

Kaftan, J., on whether Paul misrepresented Jesus, 170
Kant, theology of, 208
Kenosis, 120
Kingsley, possibility of eternal hell, 256

Ladd, Doctrine of Sacred Scripture, 30
Law, civil, authority of, 12
Law, moral, authority of, 13
Lipsius, his discussion of Trinity, 191
Lobstein on the Trinity, 203
Logos, of Fourth Gospel, 107; Philo's, 107; relation of Christ to, 119
Love, does it need atonement? 154; made hell, 251
Luther on Bible, 22; as a miracle, 73; on miracle, 76; on Christ as Saviour, 123; his significance, 216

Martyrs and Presence of Christ, 134
Maurice, F. D., on hell, 256
Mendenhall, Dr. J. W., his attacks on "rationalists," 29
Miracle, definition of, 56, 59; Dr. Gordon on, 56; Bowne on, 68; J. M. Thompson on, 58, 63; analogy in history, 72; Luther on, 76; supposed miracles in India under Sadhu Sundar Singh, 300
Mohammedanism, doctrine of inspiration, 55
Monarchianism, Patripassian, 188; Dynamistic, 189

INDEX

Moral influence, theory of atonement, 162
Muratorian Fragment on Gospels, 39

Nature and miracle, 68; Two Natures doctrine, 117
New Testament, attitude of its own writers to, 33; inspiration of, 36; Apostolic Fathers on 37; Irenæus on, 39; its testimony as to Jesus (conclusion), 109; on atonement, 138, 152; on Trinity, 187
Nitzsch, F. A. B., on Christ, 115

Old Testament, Jewish attitude to, 30; early Christian attitude to, 31; inspiration of, 36; Paul's and Christ's attitude to, 179
Origen, views on future life, 240

Parker, Theodore, on Christ as teaching eternal hell, 257
Paul, divinely illuminated, 34; testimony to Christ, 90, 95; did he supplant Jesus? 167; sources of his knowledge of Christ and Christianity, 178; Paul and the cult of Jesus, 183; suffering for his sins, 249; Alfred Seeberg on his relation to Jesus, 271
Paulus, Professor, theology of, 211
Person, meaning of in Trinity, 193
Peter, view of Christ, 100
Pfleiderer, on Paul's thought of Christ, 195
Pope, infallible, as authority, 18
Psalms, Book of, 42; imprecatory, 43
Psychical powers, 60
Punishment, future, 237

Punishment, supposed of Christ in atonement, 160, 161

Restoration, universal, 253
Resurrection of Christ, 77, 98
Retribution, principle of future, 248
Revelation, Book of, on Christ, 103
Revelation, relation to inspiration, 48
Revivals of religion, revivals of Christ, 127
Ritschl, on atonement, 149; on Trinity, 205; discussion of, 208; chief need of man is independence, 221; sin, 221, 225; forgiveness and justification, 222; Christ, 222; redemption, 226; faith, 227; on Scripture, 229; on Christian life, 230; Holy Spirit, 231; as to evangel and conversion, 232; salvation, 233; Christ not working now, 233; distrust of religious experience, 234; on Christian perfection, 234; estimate, 235
Robertson, F. W., on hell, 256
Röhr, theology of, 210
Rule of Faith, relation of inspiration to, 52

Sabatier, A., his mistake on authority, 9; on Bible, 10, 44
Sabellian Trinity, 188
Satan, ransom to theory of atonement, 144, 161, 275
Saviour, 122
Schaeder, on Christ's dependence on the Father, 271, 284
Schultz on Trinity and Deity of Christ, 282
Schleiermacher on atonement, 147; on Trinity, 204; his theol-

ogy, 211; on future punishment, 243
Science, authority of, 11
Scripture. See Bible.
Seeberg, Alfred, on Paul's relation to Jesus, 271
Sin, 152, 157; Paul's and Christ's view of, 181; Horton on, 273; "original sin," 279
Social amelioration and Bible, 47
Socinus, teaching on atonement, 146
Sonship of Christ, 190
Spirit. See Holy

Trinity, condition of when Son on earth, 117; discussion on, 184; Lipsius on Church view versus Christian view, 191; analogies in individuals, 198; a truth of and for salvation, 201; Garvie on, 203; Rothe, Sartorius, Schultz, J. Kaftan on, 205; Kirn on, 206; Gordon, Lidgett, and Kahnis on, 281; Edward White on, 283; Schaeder on, 284

Unitarians, acknowledging Christ as virtual God, 132, 135; on Trinity, 184; unity with Trinitarians advocated by Channing, 185; Unitarian J. Drummond on Trinity, 207

Virgin Birth (so called), 76, 300

Weiss, J., confession that primitive Christians started with worship of Christ, 111
Wernle, on Paul's misrepresentations of Jesus, 167
Wesley, Charles, his conversion ascribed to Christ, 124
Wesley, John, conversion ascribed to Christ, 125; his mission, theology, etc., 215; critical views, 220
Wrede, on Paul as creator of Christianity, 169